American Women Composers
before 1870

Studies in Musicology, No. 57

George Buelow, Series Editor

Professor of Musicology
Indiana University

Other Titles in This Series

No. 36   *The Early French Parody Noël*   Adrienne F. Block

No. 60   *Louis Pécour's 1700* Recueil de dances   Anne L. Witherell

No. 61   *The American Opera to 1790*   Patricia H. Virga

No. 62   *Dr. Burney as Critic and Historian of Music*   Kerry S. Grant

No. 63   *The Fertilizing Seed: Wagner's
Concept of the Poetic Intent*   Frank W. Glass

No. 64   *The Secular Madrigals of Filippo di Monte,
1521-1603*   Brian Mann

No. 65   *The Rise of Instrumental Music and
Concert Series in Paris, 1828-1871*   Jeffrey Cooper

No. 66   *The Crumhorn: Its History, Design,
Repertory, and Technique*   Kenton Terry Meyer

American Women Composers
before 1870

by
Judith Tick

Research
Press

Ann Arbor, Michigan

Produced and distributed by
UMI Research Press
an imprint of
University Microfilms Inc.
Ann Arbor, Michigan 48106

Library of Congress Cataloging in Publication Data

Tick, Judith.
American women composers before 1870.

(Studies in musicology ; no. 57)
Revision of thesis (Ph.D.)–City University of New
York, 1979.
Bibliography: p.
Includes index.
1. Women composers–United States. I. Title.
II. Series.

ML390.T53   1983   780'.92'2   82-2694
ISBN 0-8357-1326-1   AACR2

To My Mother and Father

Contents

List of Tables   *ix*

List of Figures   *xi*

List of Musical Examples   *xiii*

Preface   *xv*

Acknowledgments   *xvii*

1 Introduction   *1*

2 The Tradition of Music as a Feminine Accomplishment,
   1770 to 1830   *13*

3 Accomplishment Becomes Middle-Class   *21*

4 Music in Female Seminaries   *33*

5 Humble Beginnings, 1790 to 1825   *57*

6 A Woman Composer's Place is in the Parlor:
   New Trends in Mid-Century   *73*

7 Five Mid-Nineteenth-Century Composers   *145*

8 The Emergence of a Professional Ethos for Women Composers   *217*

Appendix. Selected Compositions Published by Women in the U.S.
            before 1870   *235*

Notes   *241*

Bibliography   *273*

Index   *281*

List of Tables

1. Curriculum Changes in Female Seminaries between 1749 and 1871, as Measured by Percentages Offering Certain Subjects   *35*

2. Studies Offered in 162 Female Seminaries, 1742 to 1871   *36*

3. Textbooks Mentioned in Seminary Catalogues, 1780 to 1870   *36*

4. Keyboard Music by Women Composers before 1830   *65*

5. The Increase of Women in Music and Music Teaching between 1870 and 1910, According to the U.S. Census   *220*

6. Distinctions between "Feminine" and "Masculine" Music around 1900   *228*

List of Figures

1. Title Page and Index of Jane Sloman's *The Melodist*   38

2. Program of the Cherry Valley Female Academy Commencement Concert, as listed in *The Musical World and Times*   44

3. Program of a Musical Entertainment at Cherry Valley, 1851   46

4. Program of a Cherry Valley concert, undated   48

5. Excerpts from the Commencement Concert, Madison Female College, 1853, as listed in *Dwight's Journal of Music*   50

6. The "Select Catalogue of Mrs. E.A. Parkhurst's Compositions" published by Horace Waters, 1864   200

List of Musical Examples

1. Mary Ann Pownall, *Jemmy of the Glen*   60

2. Mary Ann Pownall, *Lavinia*   62

3. Grace Richards, *Orphan Nosegay Girl*   64

4. A Lady, *Oft in the Stilly Night with Variations for the Piano Forte*   67

5. Harriet Mary Browne, *The Messenger Bird*   79

6. Caroline Norton, *Juanita*   85

7. Caroline Norton, *Fairy Bells*   88

8. Mrs. Townshend Stith, *Our Friendship*   96

9. Julliet Bellchambers, *The Spell is Broken*   100

10. Miss M.B. Scott, *Bird of Beauty*   104

11. Miss Smith, *A Place in Thy Memory, Dearest*   107

12. A Lady, *Thou Hast Wounded the Spirit that Loved Thee*   109

13. Abby Hutchinson, *Kind Words Can Never Die*   113

14. Miss M.T. Durham, *The Promised Land*   117

15. Miss M.T. Durham, *Star of Columbia*   118

16. Mrs. J.F. Knapp, *Jesus' Jewels*   120

17. Mrs. M.S.B. Dana, *Flee as a Bird*   *122*

18. Adele Hohnstock, *Concert Polka*   *127*

19. Mary, *Rosebud Quickstep*   *140*

20. Marion Dix Sullivan, *The Blue Juniata*   *148*

21. Augusta Browne, *The Warlike Dead in Mexico*   *154*

22. Faustina Hodges, *Dreams*   *164*

23. Faustina Hodges, *The Rose Bush*   *172*

24. Faustina Hodges, *The Indignant Spinster*   *178*

25. Jane Sloman, *I'll Make Him Speak Out*   *192*

26. Jane Sloman, *Roll On, Silver Moon*   *196*

27. Mrs. E.A. Parkhurst, *Father's a Drunkard and Mother is Dead*   *202*

28. Mrs. E.A. Parkhurst, *There are Voices, Spirit Voices*   *208*

29. Mrs. E.A. Parkhurst, *Weep No More for Lily*   *211*

30. Mrs. E.A. Parkhurst, *Don't Marry a Man if He Drinks* (excerpt)   *214*

Preface

This book is the first study of American women composers and attitudes towards female musicians before 1870. It is an attempt to map out a large and hitherto unknown history by defining issues and establishing some criteria for dealing with the large repertory of sheet music published in the mid-nineteenth century. The study traces attitudes in etiquette books, discusses education in female seminaries, and locates the most important popular composers and some outstanding works.

The study does not attempt to be an exhaustive bibliography of music written by women before 1870. Such a goal would be unusually difficult, if not impossible, at this time given the lack of bibliographical control in American music of this period. Even some basic biographical information about leading figures is lacking at present, partially because of incomplete composer attributions and also because of surname changes through marriage. Hopefully, archival research in the history of musical life of individual states or regions will bring such information to light.

The repertory that is the basis for the study are the collections of sheet music at the New York Public Library, Yale University, the Boston Public Library, and the New York Historical Society, supplemented by occasional pieces from other libraries. Most of the examples refer to pieces that were demonstrably popular according to criteria outlined in the introduction.

Acknowledgments

I would like to acknowledge with gratitude the aid and advice of a number of people. H. Wiley Hitchcock read this work with great care and offered countless suggestions for improving it. Barry Brook, Joel Sachs, and Gaye Tuckman also gave many excellent criticisms. Richard Jackson, Lester Levy, Nancy Reich, Nicholas Tawa were generous with their expertise. Irving Lowens and Jan LaRue made known the whereabouts of an unpublished index of magazine articles that proved extremely important. Walter Gerboth made many helpful suggestions concerning bibliographical matters. Many librarians answered my queries and duplicated pieces from their collections for my use: Jean Geil, University of Illinois; Jean Bonin, University of Virginia; Sam Dennison, Free Library of Philadelphia; James W. Pruett, University of North Carolina; Lenore Coral, University of Wisconsin; Dena Epstein, University of Chicago; and Georgia Bumgardner, American Antiquarian Society.

I also would like to thank a number of colleagues and friends for their enthusiasm and interest in this project. Lucille Goodman, Phyllis Bruce, Janet Sullivan, Jane Bernstein, Jennifer Lane, and Sam Dennison have performed or programmed music located from this book. Williams Brooks shared his curiosity about an obscure "Miss Browne." Carol Neuls-Bates and Adrienne Fried Block provided a forum for this research in the Symposium on Sources and Resources on Women in American Music, held at the Graduate Center, C.U.N.Y., spring 1976.

To Gilbert Chase, Gertrude Jaeger Selznick, and Mignon Garland, a special thank you for their inspiration and encouragement.

Has America no Hemans, who will awaken a sleeping lyre in behalf of her young sisters, to give them songs which instead of soiling the purity of their yet unpolluted hearts, may enlist their associations and affections in the cause of virtue?

Almira Phelps, *The Female Student.* New York, 1836.

1

Introduction

If cultural history can be equated with architectural space, then the parlor is one of the richest metaphors for early American musical life. It was no ordinary room, but both a state of mind and an economic institution, furnished by music teachers, piano manufactuers, sheet music publishers, and, if the testimony of contemporary writers is to be trusted, willing young lady amateurs.

What rich descriptions writers lavished upon the musical lady in her parlor domain! Susanna Rowson named her "Miss Tasty" in her poem "Women As They Are":

> Behold Miss Tasty every nymph excel.
> A Fine, accomplished fashionable belle.
> Plac'd at the harpsichord, see with what ease
> Her snowy fingers run along the keys... [1]

Mark Twain in *Life on the Mississippi* describes in detail a Southern parlor with a "guitar leaning against Mamma, ribbons fluttering from its neck."[2] In *Little Women,* Jo comforts her family with simple domestic hymns, and Charles Dickens's hero, Martin Chuzzlewit, confronts American "culture" through two sisters who in their parlor present a "bravura concert... sung in all languages except their own. German, French, Italian, Spanish, Portuguese, Swiss; but nothing native, nothing so low as native."[3] As for music educators, a favorite pastime was to complain about wasting musical training on frivolous girls who only wanted to get married. What "patient and laborious instruction to be so uselessly expended on those who have not sufficient capacity to comprehend the elementary principles of the art!"[4] Saturated with notions of femininity, whether romanticized or moralistic ones, the image of the musical lady amateur was a powerful symbol for the nineteenth-century imagination.

It may seem strange to begin this history of early American women composers by conjuring up the ghost of the lady amateur, but in many ways she is central to it. For one thing the image of the lady amateur was grounded in social practice in that it was formed through the conventions of musical "accomplishment." The "accomplishments" were the nonacademic subjects in "female education," such as dancing, embroidery, and painting. They were called "ornamental" as opposed to "solid" subjects, and by the mid-nineteenth century, music was the most popular of them all.[5]

To the extent that music education was rationalized as an especially desirable skill for women, the symbol of the lady amateur merges musical achievement with ideals of "femininity," as it was conceived then. If Arthur Loesser is correct in claiming that "the history of the piano and that of the social status of Woman could be read in terms of one another,"[6] then for our culture, the ideology of music as a feminine accomplishment is the reason why. Obviously this study cannot afford to ignore such a powerful complex of attitudes. The ideal of the accomplished amateur is the foil against which the reality of achievements by women musicians during this period can and should be counterpoised.

Another reason to begin with the musically accomplished lady is that she is the stereotype that dominates women's history in early American music in our own time—in fact the most typical image of the musical woman before 1900. With the exception of a few individuals, such as Marion Dix Sullivan, Mary Ann Pownall, and Susan Parkhurst, women composers in the United States before the 1890s are virtually unknown.[7] On the one hand, this is not surprising since neither aspect of this topic—the history of nineteenth-century American music nor that of American women—had received much attention from professional historians until the last few years.[8]

On the other hand, this non-history is especially peculiar in light of the role that women allegedly played after 1870. The assessment made by the historians Charles and Mary Beard deserves to be quoted in full for the questions it raises about the period before 1870:

> Indeed, women played a dominant role in American musical history during the gilded age. Millions of daughters thrummed and strummed in parlors while pinched mothers washed dishes and hard-pressed fathers toiled at trade, happy to purchase at any price the signs of good breeding and "accomplishment" or to carry the training forward to flower on the concert stage or in operatic performance. Women constituted the major portion of the audiences at concerts and the opera, furnished most of the students who in turn sustained the teachers, bought the printed music and the literature on the subject, subscribed to the trade journals, themselves became teachers of music, and talked the art in season and out. And some of the women won high honors as musicians as well as patrons. For instance, Mrs. H.H.A. Beach received an open and generous recognition at home and enjoyed the distinction of having her work rendered by important artists in London, Berlin and Paris. "I do not think," said Walter Damrosch out of his wide experience, "that there has ever been a country whose musical development has been fostered so exclusively by women as America."[9]

If indeed America was a country whose musical development was fostered exclusively by women, why is it that so little is known of women composers? The Beards mention Amy Beach, the leading figure of a pioneer generation of women composers that included the first American women to write for orchestra—Margaret Ruthven Lang, Clara Rogers, and Helen Hopekirk. Were they the first American women to write any music at all? Who were their predecessors? If there were none, then what kind of tradition encouraged women to be "fosterers" but not creators? What are the roots of this artificial division of cultural labor and how does it affect the history of women composers in this country? The Beards' analysis, which remains one of the most positive historical assessments of women's contributions to American musical life to date,[10] projects an unknown past.

This book locates a few landmarks in this seemingly barren terrain. The repertory begins with the first sheet music published by a woman in this country in the 1790s and surveys music by mid-nineteenth century composers, including brief biographies of five prominent women active in the 1850s and '60s. During this period women moved from their initial rather tentative efforts at musical composition, when they published most of their music anonymously, to becoming competitors in the flourishing sheet music market of the mid-1800s, when they wrote parlor songs and keyboard pieces that were popular commercial successes. The succeeding generation of women composers active in the 1880s and '90s was the first to write serious works (as opposed to parlor music) in the "higher forms" of symphony and opera.

The Question of the "Woman Composer"

Why study women as a special group of composers? This can be answered in many different ways. One obvious reason is to compensate for historical neglect. Feminist historians speak of "liberating women's history" and "writing women back into history," and certainly this study would have been unthinkable without the development of women's studies in the last ten years.

Another reason is methodological in that it argues for the validity and usefulness of the women's studies perspective as a historical tool. Perhaps its possibilities will be clarified through another question, namely the one formulated by Richard Crawford in his essay "American Studies and American Musicology." Crawford suggests that "a major task in both ethnomusicology and American music studies is to answer this question: according to what terms is this piece or genre comprehensible or meaningful?"[11] Our hypothesis is that the historical appreciation and evaluation of music by early American composers must take the sex of the composer into account.[12] The issues, put most simply, are: In what ways does music written by women composers during this period differ from that written by men? In what ways does the work of a woman composer reflect her experience of herself as a woman? Or, to put this in terms of the group rather than the individual, what kinds of choices do women composers make that differ from those of men?

These questions have most potential when we deal with thematic content. Most of the music written by women before 1870 is for voice, and in many cases the texts were written by the composer herself. At the very least, the composer's choice of text reflects conscious decision regarding subject matter. Subject matter, point of view, treatment of theme—these are issues that can be illuminated by considering the sex of the composer responsible for the musical choices. Obviously, there is no feminine music in the same sense that there is an Afro-American music; but we can be aware of a female sensibility insofar as it affects our apprehension of a piece. Music composed by women grew out of its own distinctive social and aesthetic context, not opposed to the mainstream, but not entirely congruent with it either. In practical terms, I have tried to point out what Patricia Meyer Spacks in *The Female Imagination* so gracefully calls "delicate divergences."[13]

How are we to judge the achievements of American women composers during this period? The enormous differences in the history of composition as a profession for men and as one for women again suggest that the categories of achievements are not identical. To make but a few comparisons: before 1830 publishing music was an extraordinary act for a woman, and her activity as a composer was not taken as a matter of course. We need only compare the confidence with which Francis Hopkinson proclaimed his collection of songs in 1788 to be the first secular music published by an American composer[14] with the reticence of his female counterparts. Most of them chose anonymity and identified themselves only as "ladies," a practice that continued throughout the century. Billings, Read, Swan, Law—these names have no female counterparts because women did not publish singing school or church music until the mid-decades of the nineteenth century. The most important indigenous music of the eighteenth century passed them by. Not until the 1840s and '50s do we find women composers in this country that are acknowledged as such by their contemporaries. Perhaps the most startling difference is the exclusivity of the genres in which most women worked: they wrote parlor music almost exclusively, songs and dances for the social circle; not opera or chamber music, and only rarely church music, comic songs, or minstrel tunes.

In short, there was a female "sphere" in music for nineteenth-century women that reflected their more restricted role in society. When we evaluate the compositional achievements of American women, this must be taken into account, not necessarily to demonstrate the effects of overpowering discrimination, so that women become noteworthy when they do anything at all outside the home, but rather to acknowledge that women's history is shaped by internal factors that are not applicable to the lives of men, and that women are not "noteworthy" only when their achievements fall exactly into those categories set up for men.[15] As with style, scholars in other fields help point the way.[16] Elaine Showalter and Ann Douglas have both analyzed the interplay between role and achievement for nineteenth-century writers. Showalter, for example, talks of a "double standard" for English women writers, who were "measured against a feminine rather than artistic ideal."[17] Douglas writes of American women writers that "there was clearly a set of conventional preconceptions as to why women should write and what kind of literature they could write."[18] All of this is true for music as well as for literature.

Douglas's research on nineteenth-century women writers is the touchstone for a comprehensive investigation of nineteenth-century popular culture. Her book *The Feminization of American Culture*[19] extends the applicability of women's studies to social history, demonstrating how the issue of sex roles and male versus female "spheres" had powerful consequences for both men and women. She links "feminization" to the "cult of sentimentality," a cult which she does not trace in mid-nineteenth-century song texts, but could have done so quite easily. Douglas sees the sentimental aesthetic as a kind of commercialization or consumer exploitation of female identity as it was defined in Victorian America, and she explores its implications not only for the female audience that supported popular culture but also for women writers who contributed to it. She sees their artistic creations as translations of the values of "true womanhood"[20] and their literary fidelity to these values as one way in which their roles as women versus professionals were reconciled. All of this was of great value to the present study, partially because her raw materials—domestic novels and poetry, consolation literature, and advice books—have their parallels in domestic music, sacred songs, and discussions of music as a feminine accomplishment. Whether or not a music historian wishes to subscribe to her theory of feminization, no student of nineteenth-century popular music can afford to ignore her analysis of the common themes and preoccupations of the culture.

Douglas's methodological perspective is significant for this study because it demonstrates that sex role can be as important to cultural history as any of the more conventional variables like class, race, or ethnicity. This perspective is not as alien to American music history as one might think. For example, Frank Rossiter's biography of Charles Ives[21] is based on Ives's division of musical style into masculine and feminine camps. Rossiter takes as his springboard the notion that Ives's rejection of particular musical styles as "emasculated" had cultural validity. Like Douglas, Rossiter equates gentility and sentimentality with feminization, although he never uses that term. Nor is he much interested in the social sources of Ives's sexual aesthetics. Taken for granted, however, is the belief that male and female roles in American musical life were different and of supreme consequence for men.

Gilbert Chase's analysis of Stephen Foster describes Foster's artistic dilemma as the conflict between a vital vernacular "Ethiopian" music and a derivative inhibited parlor music.[22] Foster's particular tragedy, as Chase sees it, was his reluctance to accept the vernacular, partially because of its connotations as low class and black. Parlor music was respectable but fatally genteel. Beneath this explanation, based on class and race, are implications that vernacular music was masculine and that of the parlor was feminine. Chase describes Foster's cultural milieu in much the same way that Rossiter depicts that of Ives in Danbury:

> Music in the Foster family was encouraged as a form of recreation and as a polite accomplishment for young ladies. Mrs. Foster, who had been raised in Baltimore and was filled with ideas of gentility, was eager to have her daughters receive the benefits of a "polite education," including the accomplishment of playing the piano and singing sentimental ballads.
>
> ... there was no question of providing systematic music instruction for the boy: music was not a serious occupation for men or boys in the Foster household.[23]

Foster's early aspirations were to be "a writer of sentimental ballads and elegant songs rendered by sentimental and elegant young ladies in the most polite society."[24] As with Ives, the implications are of an artist thwarted by social definitions of sex roles played out in music.

Joseph Mussulman's *Music in the Cultured Generation*[25] also touches on the social meaning of music for women in the late nineteenth century. In his survey of three literary magazines, Mussulman repeatedly mentions articles about music and women. In music education women, not men, were the prime targets of reformist criticism.[26]

> Almost without exception, every Cultured critic who wrote of parlor music at all felt constrained to deplore the debasement of Cultured ideals by doting parents who forced the study of the piano upon their idle young daughters merely to satisfy a thirst for "gentility."[27]

Mussulman also cites an article on the etiquette of parlor singing for women and another on the female composer and her lack of creative potential.[28] Since Mussulman is more interested in correlations between social class and taste, he does not synthesize this material into a discussion of the tradition of music as feminine accomplishment. However, it is latent since at one point he concludes that "the practice of parlor music was dominated by women."[29]

The common denominator of these books is their reliance on cultural interpretations of musical life based on sex role distinctions. All project the same critical image of the musical woman as sentimental dilettante; Foster's sisters with their "polite educations" are the kin of Mussulman's "idle young daughters" and the spiritual ancestors of Charles Ives's music teachers, the Misses Hollisters, who "emasculated"[30] his father. In fact, this image of the nineteenth-century musical woman is an ironic testimonial to the power of the tradition of music as a feminine accomplishment that has been assumed in our histories.

Perhaps we ought to take this image not as the sum of women's history in American music for 100 years, but for what it is: the paradigm of a historical stereotype. Like many social stereotypes it contains truth, although how much truth remains to be seen. Like all stereotypes, its great evil, as sociologists remind us, is its presumed universality. We ought to regard such stereotypes the way archeologists view ruins: helpful landmarks in an unknown terrain, but only the remnants of a complex culture. Although attitudes towards music as a feminine accomplishment shifted and were refined during this period, the social meaning of music and music education was integrated with the social meaning of femininity for most of the nineteenth century.

Documenting the Tradition of Musical Accomplishment

The lady amateur could turn to any number of books on how to be musical that had not a note of music in them. Advice was generously dispensed by writers on etiquette, educators, and journalists of ladies' magazines on the proper sphere for female musicianship—within the larger framework of female education. Such advice constitutes a vast prescriptive literature for social historians on which much recent scholarship in women's studies has been based.[31] A few important guides to sources are Thomas Woody's indispensable and encyclopedic *A History of Women's Education in the United States*,[32] Arthur Schlesinger's *Learning How to Behave*,[33] and Eleanor Thompson's *Education for Ladies 1830-1860*.[34]

Special primary sources for the study of music education include catalogues for female seminaries, diaries of students taking lessons privately or at school,[35] and articles in musical periodicals reprinting concert programs or courses of curriculum. Some seminaries have also been studied as separate institutions, among them two where music education was paramount: Music Vale or Salem Normal School[36] and the Moravian Seminary in Bethlehem, Pennsylvania.[37]

Books about women in eighteenth-century America that discuss the accomplishments—music among them—include Julia Cherry Spruill's *Women's Life and Work in the Southern Colonies*,[38] the catalogue for the exhibit *Remember the Ladies: Women in America, 1750-1815*,[39] and Mary Sumner Benson's *Women in Eighteenth-Century America*.[40]

Women have not figured prominently in the work of many American music historians. One recent exception is Nicholas Tawa's book *Sweet Songs for Gentle Americans*, and article, "Secular Music in the Late-Eighteenth-Century American Home."[41] Both frequently refer to musical accomplishment for women. Oscar Sonneck lists the titles of a few advice books in *A Bibliography of Early Secular American Music*.[42]

Historians of music education neglect music in female seminaries because of their preoccupation with music in public rather than private schools. Nevertheless, information about female seminaries can be found in regional studies. Among these are Charles Kaufmann's book on music in New Jersey and Katherine Mahan's book on Columbus, Georgia, both containing frequent references to the musical activities of local girls' schools.[43]

Sources of Information About Early American Women Composers

Early American women composers are barely represented in standard reference works. The bio-bibliography *Women in Music,* which surveys the entries in a "representative selection of significant music dictionaries and encyclopedias," lists two composers—Mary Ann Pownall and Faustina Hodges.[44] In other important reference works, there is no more information. Neither Waldo Pratt's *American Supplement to Grove's*[45] nor the *Bio-bibliographical Index of Musicians from Colonial Times to the Present*[46] contain further references. However, a more recent book, the *Biographical Dictionary of American Music,*[47] incorporates many names listed in Sonneck's and Wolfe's bibliographies of early American secular music and adds a few other later composers, among them Caroline Bernard and Phoebe Palmer Knapp.

Standard guides to popular music of the period occasionally mention pieces by women. In *Variety Music Cavalcade,* a compendium of the most popular songs by year from 1620-1950, there are eight songs attributed to women composers through 1870, but the information is not always reliable.[48] Two songs are incorrectly attributed to Augusta Browne instead of Harriet Browne; Marion Dix Sullivan is mentioned only by initials (M.D. Sullivan); and Jane Sloman is mentioned only by last name with an incorrect first initial (R. Sloman). Sigmund Spaeth's *A History of Popular Music in America* is more comprehensive. Some of the entries duplicate those in *Variety Music Cavalcade,* but in addition Spaeth lists several other compositions.[49]

Nicholas Tawa's list of "The Most Popular Songs of the Extant Collections of Music," that is to say, the 200 bound collections of nineteenth-century sheet music on which his study is based, includes seven works by women, among them three by the English composer Harriet Browne, and two by Marion Dix Sullivan.[50]

Occasionally works by early American women composers turn up in the modern anthologies of sheet music from the period that have appeared in the last few years: one of Mrs. E.A. Parkhurst's temperance songs is in Michael Turner's *The Parlour Songbook*[51] and one of her Union songs, "The New Emancipation Song," in the *Civil War Songbook.*[52] Piano pieces by a composer known only as "Mary" and the English composer Caroline Lowthian are included on a recording of "Nineteenth-Century Piano Music in America."[53] Names of other early American women composers are in Otto Ebel's book, *Women Composers*[54] and Arthur Elson's, *Women's Work in Music.*[55]

Beyond a name or a piece mentioned here or there, there is very little biographical information available at present in current histories. Since coverage of the eighteenth and early nineteenth centuries is so much more extensive than for the rest of the century, for the few professional women composers active before 1825, there are some secondary sources for biographical data. Mary Ann Pownall, Harriet Abrams, and Elizabeth Van Hagen are mentioned in regional and genre studies of eighteenth-century American music as well as in works about eighteenth-century women.[56]

Biographical information about women composers after 1825 is extremely sparse. Even a composer like Marion Dix Sullivan, whom Nicholas Tawa cites along with Foster, Root, and Woodbury as a highly successful parlor song composer in the 1840s and '50s,[57] is an obscure figure. *Song in America from Early Times to About 1850,* one of the few secondary sources to discuss mid-nineteenth-century women composers, includes Augusta Browne.[58]

Primary sources are virtually the only material by which to determine who are the prominent and successful women composers of the mid-nineteenth century. We can claim national "prominence" for about ten individuals between 1825 and 1870. Five are discussed at length in chapter 7 as case studies: Marion Dix Sullivan, Augusta Browne Garrett, Jane Sloman, Faustina Hodges, and Mrs. E.A. Parkhurst. A few more are included in the other chapters, among them Mary Dana Shindler and Phoebe Palmer Knapp. Information about their lives was culled from a variety of primary sources: newspaper reviews, contemporary dictionaries of music,[59] identifications made on title pages of compositions, and in a few cases, contemporary dictionaries of notable women.[60] These women were exceptional because they had a number of successful works to their credit, rather than one or two; for the most part they were also visible as professional performers or successful teachers.

No doubt as our knowledge of musical life in nineteenth-century America accumulates, more information about individual early American women composers will come to light. The impact of women's studies on music history has been significant in this respect, and there are a few recent studies and works-in-progress that deserve special mention. The most important of these is *Women in American Music: A Bibliography* by Adrienne Fried Block and Carol Neuls-Bates.[61] It covers music and literature from colonial times to the present. The section on early American women composers is an adaptation of the material in this work. Phyllis Mackowitz Bruce's study, "A Preliminary Investigation of American Women Song Composers of the Nineteenth and Early Twentieth Centuries"[62] includes an appendix of published songs and a biographical dictionary of women composers listed in major reference works on American music.

The Collection and Location of Music

The repertory for this study is based on sheet music imprints, not on compositions found only in collections, periodicals, or in manuscript. The main source is the Americana collection at the New York Public Library. Two library shelflists list music imprints before 1870, one covering the period before 1830 and containing approximately 4,900 titles; the other, covering the period between 1830 and 1865, contains about 35,000 titles.[63] Because the nineteenth-century American imprints are separated from the general composer-title catalogue, it is possible to survey the shelflist for all pieces published by women before 1870. Two other collections, one at Yale University and the other at the New York Historical Society, are surveyed in a similar manner. In most cases, but not all, their holdings duplicate that of the New York Public Library. In addition, Lester Levy, a well-known private collector, has supplied me with a list of works from his collection. Other libraries have been consulted for copies of individual imprints, among them the Pennsylvania and Maryland Historical Societies, the Long Island Historical Society, the Universities of Virginia, North Carolina, and South Carolina, and the Library of Congress.

A number of published catalogues were helpful in locating titles and composers. The most useful without doubt is the *Complete Catalogue of Sheet Music and Musical Works, 1870,* published by the U.S. Board of Music Trade. It contains approximately 80,000 titles of pieces in the stocks of 20 American music publishers.[64] The works are divided into genre, alphabetized mainly by title, and accompanied by the composer's surname. This catalogue is extremely useful for a number of reasons. It provides an overview of the sheet music repertory of the early and mid-nineteenth centuries. It also helps determine the popularity of an individual piece, whether or not it remained in print after its initial publication, whether other publishers picked up the copyright, or whether it was arranged for other vocal or instrumental combinations.

Other catalogues of more limited repertories devoted to a region, a topic, or a particular publisher are also useful. These include Richard Harwell's *Confederate Music,*[65] Dena Epstein's *Music Publishing in Chicago Before 1871: The Firm of Root & Cady, 1858-1871,*[66] and Dichter and Shapiro's *Early American Sheet Music—Its Lure and Lore, 1768-1889.*[67]

Coverage of secular music imprints before 1825 is excellent thanks to the Sonneck-Upton and Wolfe bibliographies.[68] About 70 titles of works of American and European women composers are listed. All of the music printed before 1800 is included in the comprehensive microfilm collection of *Early American Imprints, 1639-1800.*[69]

No attempt has been made to compile a list of all music published by women during this period. There are no comprehensive bibliographies of American music after 1825 comparable to those by Sonneck or Wolfe. In addition, many libraries have not yet catalogued all their sheet music imprints nor separated them out of their general composer-title catalogues. Given the lack of bibliographical control over this vast repertory, an inclusive list would be an impossibility.

Rather, it has seemed more practical to identify those pieces composed by women that were popular works with commercial viability. What determines whether a piece was successful? The following criteria have been developed for this purpose:

1) Inclusion in the stock of more than one publisher. After 1830 this often applies to those pieces composed by foreign women not protected by copyright. A number of songs written by English women composers, for example, early in the century were not only in print in 1870, according to the *Complete Catalogue,* but also in the catalogues of 13 or 14 publishers. Such works can be presumed popular. In addition, occasionally, pieces by American composers were published by more than one firm. Even after the copyright laws went into effect, it was not unusual for two or more publishers to enter into a financial agreement, particularly in different parts of the country, to publish a work jointly and divide royalties.[70]

2) Whether or not a work remained in print for at least 15 years after its initial publication. Successful songs, for example, did not go out of style quickly, and a hit tune from the 1840s and '50s was still likely to be in print in 1870.[71] Here again the *Complete Catalogue* is invaluable.

3) Inclusion in anthologies or collections. If a song or piano piece were popular, it often found its way into collections designed for the home, school, or social circle. Among the different kinds of collections, some of which carry more weight as evidence of popularity, are the collection of current hits, pieces popular at that moment; (the comprehensive anthology the series *Home Musical Library* of the 1850s is one such example)[72] and the retrospective collections of old favorites or standards (the largest is the *Franklin Square Song Collection,* eight volumes containing 1,600 songs).[73] A variation on such collections is the series of sheet music imprints, issued by a publisher under a single title.[74] Again we might add that no attempt has been made to survey all anthologies published during the period. The collection of the New York Public Library is the main source for the 50 or so anthologies that have been located containing at least one work by a woman composer.

4) Reprinting in a magazine. Musical periodicals, for example, routinely printed popular songs or keyboard works. Some were works commissioned by the magazine, but others were sheet music first.[75] Ladies' magazines like *Godey's Lady's Book* and the *Ladies' Companion* also published parlor music, as one of their "embellishments." More than 100 different ladies' magazines were published between 1790 and 1850; at least 25 published music.[76] Occasionally a popular piece of sheet music by a woman composer was included.

5) Evidence that the work was performed by a professional musician. This information is often listed on title pages of imprints.

6) Generating arrangements in another genre. Successful parlor songs, for example, became piano transcriptions, or were solo songs which became four-part pieces. This process is the nineteenth-century counterpart to what is today called "covering" a hit.

7) Producing "answer" songs, or what we call "spinoffs." For example, Florence Vane's "Are We Almost There" (Boston: Oliver Ditson, 1845) was followed by I.B. Woodbury's "We Are Almost There" (Boston: Oliver Ditson, 1847). Only popular works would be followed by such dependent or derivative compositions.

These criteria comprise the methodology of the study—the process of sifting and weighing evidence in the absence of overall bibliographical control. To date we have located about 200 works by American women composers and 50 works by English women composers that by these standards can be said to be popular or successful commercial compositions, and we have listed them in the appendix of this work. These pieces form a core repertory for this study in that most of the musical examples we discuss belong to it. Even though we cannot statistically compute what proportion of works was composed by women, we can discriminate between a parlor song that was one of hundreds and a work that made an impression in its own time. Of course, when commercial success is not the issue at hand, then the core repertory does not matter. But if we hope to gain some sense of the presence of eary American women composers commanded, then a list of successful works is extremely useful.

2

The Tradition of Music as a Feminine Accomplishment, 1770 to 1830

When in 1730 a Miss Ball, "newly arrived from London," moved to Philadelphia and became one of the first music teachers in that city,[1] she placed an advertisement in the *Pennsylvania Gazette* seeking students for instruction in "singing, playing on the spinet, dancing, and all sorts of needlework."[2] Such a combination of music with needlework may seem odd, yet for the eighteenth century Miss Ball's advertisement was typical as both music and needlework were "accomplishments" suitable for young ladies. John Bennett, in his *Letters to a Young Lady,* summarized the branches of education that fell under that heading:

> ... the accomplishments of a woman may be comprised under some or all of the following articles: needlework, embroidery, drawing, music, dancing, dress, politeness ...[3]

Like "dress," music was part of one's presentation to the world; like needlework, it was a useful craft. Within the context of female education, its justification could not be on artistic worth alone. Bennett defined music within the area of female education that was intended as refinement and ornament, a skill to enhance a woman's place within genteel society.[4]

This functional and primarily social meaning of music has a long and complex history, one that begins in Europe many centuries before the Colonies were settled.[5] As in Europe, the American view of music as feminine accomplishment raises questions about both the status of music and the status of women as well. One of the earliest and most popular works on women to appear in the Colonies was in fact a British import, *The Ladies' Calling,* for sale here in 1673. Along with writing and needlework, music is described in it as an "ornamental improvement."[6] The main elements of "the calling" were housework and the development of uprightness; music was one of the few nondomestic activities allowed.[7] Playing cards and reading novels were frowned on, but music was compatible with the desirable virtues of modesty, meekness, and piety.[8]

Cotton Mather, the famed New England minister, was the author of another widely circulated work on the same theme some 20 years later: Called *The Ornaments for the Daughters of Zion,* it is a "manual for the female sex ... in every age and state of their life."[9] Mather was a Puritan and his work was filled with injunctions against lasciviousness. "Promiscuous dancing," for example, was a temptation of the Devil, where both men and women "leap and fling about like Bedlams." Music, on the other hand, was acceptable recreation after woman's other work was done: "If the virtuous maid have any time ... to learn music, she will not loose [*sic*] her time" by studying it. However, she must remain ever cautious about taking too much pride in her achievements."[10]

In this warning against "pride," we glimpse an insistence on self-effacement and amateurism that was a staple in later prescriptive literature. Mather approved of music only as pastime, in which one could overindulge. If treated as art, music might threaten the equilibrium of a dutiful woman's life. It had a sanctioned but secondary status in which pride in personal achievement was subordinated to the "feminine" virtue of humility.

Still, Mather was not discriminating against musical women as opposed to musical men. For one thing Puritan attitudes towards music for *both* men and women revolved around music as recreation or religious worship, not high culture.[11] If women were not encouraged to become artists, neither were men. Mather's other attitudes toward women demonstrate a practical respect for their capabilities. In addition to music and needlework, he urged them to study "arithmetic, accounting and such business matters" to help them assist their husbands in making a living.[12] Mather also attacked the "petulent penchant of some forward and morose men that have sometimes treated the Female Sex with great Indignities. ... If men are so wicked as to deny your being Rational Creatures," Mather wrote, "they can be readily refuted." Thus Mather described a Puritan woman as a capable emotional equal of men in colonial society.[13]

The New American Lady

Late eighteenth-century guidebooks for women abandoned Mather's practical view of both music and women for a concern with style and manners. They place musical accomplishments beyond the ordinary woman and instead intend them for the fashionable lady.

Many of these works published between about 1770 and 1830 come from England. They reflect the "new wave of foreign influence" in American music described by H. Wiley Hitchcock:

> In the cities along the Eastern seaboard, wealth began to accumulate, and so did a taste for European standards of culture—and cultural models as well. The tendency of more-or-less

aristocratic Americans to look to Europe for lessons in "living well" had been latent for some time; it was reinforced as Americans, at least those in the Eastern cities, sought increasingly to act "urbane."[14]

Such urbanity embraced the cultural model of the fashionable lady.[15] She was concerned with etiquette, dress, deportment, grace, and, above all, acquiring "accomplishments." Among the latter was music, and as British ideals of a fashionable education spread among the middle- and upper-middle classes, music lessons for young ladies became increasingly common in the young Republic.[16] At the turn of the century, one newspaper writer critical of this trend spoke of a "rage for music so strong that I dare not give my opinion fully on the subject."[17] Fashionable ladies' demands for music lessons must be considered in accounting for the dramatic rise of secular music in the urban home in late-eighteenth-century America.[18]

Music was seen as a medium in which the role of *lady* could be acted out— through an aristocratic femininity that was self-conscious and artificial by today's standards but then apparently accepted in prescriptive literature as the ideal. "Sweet," "delicate," "soft," and "amiable" are the recurrent adjectives.[19] Music, like everything else the lady did, was "feminized": seen as a medium through which to display not only attributes of class but those of sex as well.

One of the most common themes running through this literature is that music is a way for women to please men. "It [music] may be considered one of the most agreeable arts of pleasing practiced by the fair sex," wrote John Burton in his lectures to a female academy.[20] John Gregory, in his popular work, *A Father's Legacy to His Daughter,* was somewhat more explicit. Musical women pleased men because music enabled them to show off their delicate, amiable, and sensitive natures.[21]

Dr. Gregory had an exaggerated concern for "female delicacy" and female "sensibility," which he described respectively as "soft" and "exquisite." Softness and delicacy were the most attractive characteristics a young lady might possess; wit and a "hard masculine spirit, odious." Learning was likewise unfeminine:

> ...if you happen to have any learning, keep it a profound secret, especially from the men, who generally look with a jealous and malignant eye on a woman of great parts and cultivated understanding....[22]

Music fortunately had little to do with learning. It was an "amusement and elegant accomplishment, along with dress, dancing and drawing."[23] "Accomplishments" were recreations that complemented her role as "the companion and equal of men "designed to soften our hearts and polish our manners."[24]

Dr. Gregory was training women in the rites of courtship, as more plainspeaking observers were quick to notice. One of the clichés about the lady musician that emerged along with fashionable education was how easily marriage put an end to it. Such rapid abandonment, some critics pointed out, indicated a superficiality and exploitation of music rather than any sincere inclination.[25] One warned women not to "value themselves too highly on their skills in this art, as after their utmost pains, we can hire superior artists to play for us for a few shillings and even a highly accomplished lady generally will suffer the harpsichord to go out of tune after marriage."[26] Still, the pro-music writers kept at it, reminding women that music had its uses in marriage as well as in courtship. Elizabeth Griffiths, sounding like an eighteenth-century Helen Gurley Brown, urged married women to continue with music "in order to keep the lover in the husband":

> How often we hear a young married woman when asked to sing or play, exclaim "Sing! No—my singing days are over! I am now *married:* A wife has something else to do but mind such trifles!"[27]

Such an attitude, Mrs. Griffiths warned earnestly, only led to marital discord; wise ladies knew that music kept romance alive.

A second common theme in prescriptive literature in the late-eighteenth century is that music as an antidote to the loneliness and boredom proclaimed as the typical lady's lot. Hester Chapone, a well-known writer and a member of Richardson's circle in London,[28] explained:

> . . . it is of great consequence to have the power of filling up agreeably those intervals of time, which too often hang heavily on the hands of a woman, if her lot be cast in a retired situation. Besides this, it is certain that even a small share of knowledge in these arts will heighten your pleasures in the performances of others.[29]

Chapone's rationale is echoed in a later work by John Bennett:

> Music will enable you to entertain your friends; to confer pleasure upon *others* must increase your own happiness, and it will inspire tranquility, and harmonize your mind and spirits, in many of those *ruffled* and *lonely* hours which in almost every situation, will be your lot.[30]

Not a very sanguine portrait of a lady's lot! In contrast to the busy Puritan homemaker, who had been warned by Mather not to spend her precious time with music, the late-eighteenth-century lady was urged to learn to occupy herself in her excessive leisure. Music was a palliative that was believed to promote mental health and a calm disposition. Whether or not there were that many ladies around with time to waste, Bennett evidently knew his public, for his *Letters to a Young Lady* went through seven editions in six years.[31]

A third major theme in late-eighteenth century prescriptive literature is the distinction between the private and the public performer. Chapone counselled her accomplished women to use their talents for their own amusements and forswear any public performances.

> As to music and drawing, I would only wish you to follow as Genius leads ... I think the use of both these arts is more for yourself than for others; it is but seldom that a private person has leisure or application enough to gain any high degree of excellence in them.[32]

For some writers, a lady amateur should not aspire to artistry or professionalism that might subvert her education as a lady. In *The Polite Lady,* the author, speaking as mother to daughter, praises music as an antidote to loneliness and a "genteel qualification" but emphasizes its limits:

> My dear Sophy, I do not mean that you should apply to your music as to neglect the other parts of your education; nor do I expect that you should arrive at the highest degree of perfection in this or in any other accomplishment. It is no shame for a young lady to be outdone in voice or judgment by an opera singer.... Perhaps on the contrary, it would be a shame for her to be equal... because in that case she must be supposed to have employed more time in it than is consistent with her learning all the other parts of a *complete* education.
>
> ... She who is a mere singer, a mere dancer, a mere drawer or indeed a mere anything has no title to the character of an accomplished woman.[33]

In sum, music occupied a special but highly circumscribed place in fashionable female education of the late-eighteenth century. On the one hand it was expected that every woman, even one of little talent, have some knowledge of music.[34] On the other hand even women with a great deal of talent were not encouraged to develop it to any extent. In the ornamental accomplishments it was "not expected that women should arrive at the skill of the adepts."[35] The French traveler Brissot de Warville around 1800, when he heard lady musicians in Boston, warned against such an outcome:

> Music, which their teachers formerly proscribed as a diabolic art, begins to make part of their education. In some houses you hear the forte-piano. This art, it is true, is still in its infancy; but the young novices who exercise it are so gentle, so complaisant, and so modest, that the proud perfection of art gives no pleasure to what they afford. God grant that the Bostonian women, may never, like those of France, acquire the malady of perfection in this art! It is never attained, but at the expense of the domestic virtues.[36]

The conventions of the lady musician can be distinguished from that of the gentleman amateur. Not that there weren't significant similarities. Music was an accepted recreation for gentlemen, described as an "elegant accomplishment" at which one must not be too proficient. The novelist Hugh Henry

Brackenridge, for example, satirized a gentleman's education in *Modern Chivalry* as follows:

> The most liberal studies may be pursued to an illiberal excess; as for instance in music, where it must be considered an elegant accomplishment to have some talents, yet not have made such proficiency in the execution, on the part of him who is not a musician by profession, as to induce a suspicion of attention to this art, to the neglect of others.[37]

A more serious statement of the same view was made by John Aikin in *Letters from a Father to His Son*. Aikin's ideal education included the natural sciences, moral philosophy, and classic literaure. Music is discussed in the letter on "cheap pleasures," which also embrace books, conversation, the study of nature, and the love of poetry. Later Aikin retracted the adjective "cheap," citing the high cost of instrumental lessons, and advocated the study of music only when a taste for it was a natural inclination:

> Musical pleasures may be enjoyed in moderation, and so as to make an agreeable variety without occupying the place of anything preferable, my objections are at an end.[38]

Thus, American gentlemen were not encouraged to become professional musicians any more than American ladies.

Still, there were important differences between musical accomplishments for men and those for women. One was the relative place music held in their respective educations. It was one of the few nondomestic activities for a young lady,[39] while for the gentleman it was subordinate to academic considerations. Another difference was in the rationales offered for the pursuit of accomplishments in general: his interests were explained mainly in terms of class; hers were also described in terms of sex—the expectations that centered around her role as a young woman. As Timothy Dwight, the prominent educator, observed in his travel diaries from the turn of the century, women were taught to be "sentimentalists" and use music "to gain admiration."[40]

The Reaction Against the Accomplishments

Reactions to fashionable education emerged in both England and America around 1800 wherein both the superficiality of female education and the abuses inherent in the slavish worship of accomplishments were criticized.[41] Many of the critics were liberal writers, who in advocating broader, more rational educations for women, used music to symbolize the old order.

The first major American theorist of female education, Benjamin Rush, illustrates this new trend. Rush advocated instruction in vocal music, as singing was an outlet for women to "soothe the cares of domestic life." He also believed that singing strengthened the lungs and therefore counteracted female infirmities. But his advocacy did not extend to instrumental music, which he regarded as a waste of time, and he chastized music teachers for their "extravagant fees."[42] Rush also challenged the worshiping of the accomplishments as so much British folly:

> It should not surprise us that British customs with respect to female education have been transplanted into our American schools and families. . . . It is high time to awake from this servility—to study our own character—to examine the age of our country—and to adopt manners in every thing, that shall be accommodated to our state of society, and to the forming of our government. In particular, it is incumbant upon us to make ornamental accomplishments yield to principles and knowledge in the education of our women.[43]

Yet Rush was soon to have a powerful ally across the ocean in England itself. In her *Strictures on Female Education* (1799),[44] Hannah More sounded a note that was to affect the basis of women's education for the next 60 years:

> Music, drawing, accomplishments, dissipation and intrigue—everything but solid knowledge—everything but humility—everything but piety—everything but virtue![45]

More condemned fashionable women who used music to be pleasing to men. Through music, More asserted, women learned to seek flattery and shirk their religious and domestic duties. Since music was not morally didactic, it had little use in her ideal education. It subverted women from their proper concerns:

> I look upon the great predominance of music in female education as the source of more mischief than is suspected; not from any evil in the thing itself, but from its being such a gulf of time as rarely to leave room for solid acquisitions. I love music, and were it only cultivated as an amusement, should commend it. But the monstrous proportion, or rather disproportion of life which it swallows up, even in many religious families—and this is the chief subject of my regret—has converted an innocent diversion into a positive sin.[46]

This denunciation was part of her overall scheme to reform female education by basing it on ethical rather than fashionable considerations. More managed to convert academic subjects such as mathematics and science into ethical disciplines to justify the inclusion in female education, while she rejected the accomplishments such as music as a "positive sin."[47]

Although most other writers avoided More's extremism, the spirit of her remarks can be found in a number of American works.[48] The accomplishments, according to the *American Lady's Preceptor* of 1821, "were attended with no durable advantages."[49] Hannah Foster, for example, in a tract on the ideal boarding school,[50] concentrated her comments on music around this issue; the lady amateur's primary concern was to avoid attracting undue attention through music; pride and egotism were associated with too much public performance.

The reaction against fashionable education can also be seen in the works of Susanna Rowson, who because of her associations both with music and female education, is a particularly important source. Rowson is known as the author of the best selling novel *Charlotte Temple.*[51] But she also ran a female boarding school in Medford and Boston in the 1790s, at which such prominent musicians as Gottlieb Graupner and Peter Van Hagen were employed.[52] She was also active as a librettist and song writer.[53] For Rowson, music was not the fount of evil. In her book *Mentoria* she stated that music could form a part of the training of a "well-informed cultivated mind."[54] Her objections to accomplishments came from their misapplication and the superficiality with which they were taught. Her poem on fashionable education merits full quotation:

"Women As They Are"

Behold Miss Tasty every nymph excel,
A fine, accomplished, fashionable belle.
Plac'd at the harpsichord, see with what ease
Her snowy fingers run along the keys;
Now quite in alt, 'to the highest notes she'll go;
Now running down the bass, she falls as low;
Flats, sharps, and naturals, together jumbled,
She laughs to think how little folks are humbled
While some pretending coxcomb sighing, says,
So loud that she may hear, "Heavens, how she plays."
Then she speaks French. Comment vous portez vous?
Ma chere amie! ma vie! of ciel!, mon dieu!
And dances—sink, chasse and rigadoon,
Or hops along, unheeding time or tune,
As fashion may direct....[55]

This poem is particularly interesting because it is an early satire based on a stereotype of the superficial female musician that survived well into the nineteenth century.

Miss Tasty incarnates the sins of music as defined by Hannah More. Her accomplishments have given her an inflated sense of herself, and she, who should be guided by humility, "laughs to think how little folks are humbled."

This poem, written by a woman who ran a female seminary, illustrates the degree to which American reaction against pretentiousness could focus on the stereotype of the lady amateur musician at the turn of the century. But what can replace the fashionable lady as the model of the ideal woman? How ought an educated female behave? Answers to these questions occupy numbers of music educators, writers, and moralists in the decades to come.

3

Accomplishment Becomes Middle-Class

Between 1830 and 1870 the major ideological change in the tradition of music as an accomplishment for women was the replacement of the ideal lady with that of the "true woman." The locale of accomplishment shifts from the social to the home circle, from elegance to domesticity; the rationale for teaching music to women centers about the musical mother as much as the musical belle.

Yet many of the themes present in the late-eighteenth-century literature on music as a female accomplishment can be found in mid-nineteenth-century sources as well. Despite changes in emphasis and even new attitudes towards music, a continuity of language and thought reaffirmed the tradition of music as a female accomplishment.

The notion that music was a cure for both emotional and physical ailments of women can be found in a variety of guises right through the 1860s. Benjamin Rush's advocacy of singing based on its promotion of domestic harmony and lung-strengthening powers, for example, was frequently reprinted in periodicals.[1] Editors of music journals, of course, excised his disapproval of instrumental instruction. Many writers believed in music's ability to tranquilize and soothe the unhappy female, keeping her amiable—preserving her mind in that state of "placid cheerfulness" thought so essential to womanliness.[2] Musical harmony was a metaphor for domestic harmony, and the writer Lydia Sigourney recounted the following anecdote as a serious rationale:

> An excellent clergyman, possessing much knowledge of human nature, instructed his large family of daughters, in the theory and practice of music. They were all observed to be exceedingly amiable and happy. A friend inquired if there was any secret in his mode of education. He replied: "When any thing disturbs their temper, I say to them *sing*. And ... so they have sung away all causes of discontent ... Such a use of this accomplishment might serve to fit a family for the company of angels, and the climate of praise.[3]

After a bit, such testimonials begin to sound somewhat like recipes for the taming of the shrew. Indeed, one short-story writer based a lurid description (surely as satire) on this ideology of musically tranquilized women. His women were latent psychopaths, sublimating through the outlet of piano playing and singing:

> Beware of the woman who cannot find utterance for all her stormy inner life in either words or song! If she has not musical utterance, vocal or instrumental, then—if, she is of the real woman sort, and has heartfuls of wild blood in her, and you have done her a wrong—look twice before you taste of any cup whose draught the shadow of her hand may have darkened! ... So if she can sing, or play any musical instrument, all of her wickedness will run off through her throat or through her fingers![4]

So much for placid cheerfulness and the soothing of domestic cares.

Another late-eighteenth-century theme that was elaborated by mid-nineteenth-century writers was that of the bond between music and romance. We may recall Mrs. Griffith's phrase about music "keeping the lover in the husband"; while nineteenth-century writers generally avoided such explicitness, the romanticization of the lady musician no doubt increased the popularity of music as a female accomplishment. Female musicians were idealized as "angels" or as pure and virtuous paragons of womanhood. Caroline Gilman, novelist, lyricist, and amateur composer, provides us with an exemplary description in her book *Recollections of a Southern Matron*. The hero, Lewis, is gazing at his sweetheart:

> The eyes of Lewis never wandered from Anna as she stood at her harp, or played the guitar, or gave to a few simple chords on the pianoforte a charm and tenderness peculiar to her touch, and well might he gaze, for she realized the dreams of poesy; well might he listen as a mortal would listen to the tones of a tuneful cherub.[5]

A satire of this stereotype can be found in an article entitled "Fashionable Music":

> Scientific remarks by the distinguished Sam Slick—What's that? It's music. Well, that is artificial too; it's scientific; they say it's done by rule. Just look at that gal to the piany! first comes a little German thunder, Good airth and seas what a crash! It seems as if she'd bang'd the instrument all to a thousand pieces. I guess she's vex'd at somebody, and is peggin it into the piany out of spite. Now comes singin': see what faces she makes; how she stretches her mouth open, like a barn door, and turns up the white of her eyes, like a duck in thunder. She's in a musical ecstasy, is that gal; she feels good all over; her soul is a goin out along with that ere music. Oh, it's divine! and she's an angel, ain't she? Yes, I guess she is! and when I'm an angel, I'll fall in love with her; but as I'm a man, at least, what's left of me, I'd just as soon fall in love with one that was a leetle, just a leetle more of a woman, and a leetle just a leetle less of an angel.[6]

This writer is poking fun at the ideology of music as an upper-class accomplishment as well as a distinctively female one. Along with his resentments against foreign scientific music is his rejection of the romanticization of the cultivated lady amateur.

The sexual innuendo in Sam Slick's account of the lady amateur in music ecstacy, who "feels good all over," emerges more seriously in other portraits of female musicians in fiction. In a story published in the *New York Mirror* in 1839, the idealized portrait of a lady parlor musician is not even necessary for the plot, but the writer describes her to create a scene of musical seduction.

> There was a piano and musick-books, and after having partaken of the refreshment, the young girl was requested to try the piano, of which it appeared my father had just made her a present. There was a little air of mystery about all this which I could not fathom. Our beautiful companion complied without hesitation. Her voice was full of musick; she had been well taught, and moreover possessed taste and feeling. She sang some melodies then recently published by [Thomas] Moore, with a simplicity that charmed me. Her air had in it something pensive that awakened sympathy. Her smile was soft and sweet and left her features sad; and in the melancholy passages of the musick, I thought I detected in her manner a feeling as if she were applying the sentiment to herself. I was strongly interested in her, and on our return, was vehement in expressions of delight.[7]

This kind of romanticization helped insure the popularity of musical accomplishment in the mid-nineteenth century.

Another inheritance from the late-eighteenth century was the distinction between the professional and the amateur. Mid-nineteenth-century writers continued to assert that musical accomplishment might corrupt. Charles Butler *(The American Lady)* asks whether women cultivate music excessively. Butler prophesies a dire fate for the woman who misused musical accomplishment:

> If she was taught throughout the whole course of her education that music is for display...can it be a matter of astonishment that during the rest of her life she should be incessantly on the watch to shine and be admired, that she should live and die a woman of the world?[8]

A musical "woman of the world" might even choose a career over homelife. Fanny Forrester, a popular journalist of the mid-1800s, wrote one such story of a singer named "Dora."[9] Dora is an accomplished woman gone bad. She begins her career as a naturally gifted amateur, flourishing within her home and small community, but when she leaves this world to go on stage and sing, unhappiness and misery follow.

The Fashionable Lady Becomes the "True Woman"

Only if the female musician could retain humility and a sense of obligation to please others was she fulfilling her role as a "true woman." This phrase, used by mid-nineteenth-century writers,[10] defines the feminine model that absorbed the values of music as accomplishment. In her *Letters to Young Ladies* Lydia Sigourney catechized the essence of "true womanhood" through the virtues of patience, sobriety, unselfishness, and submissiveness.[11]

Compare John Bennett's simple dictum that "music was one of the most agreeable arts of pleasing practiced by the fair sex" to Sigourney's moralistic opinions in her chapter on "Manners and Accomplishments":

> The desire of pleasing is natural and strong in youth. If guided to correct channels, it is an incentive to improvement and happiness. When it rejects the motive of selfishness and seeks only to please others for their education, it becomes a Christian virtue. This may easily be distinguished from that restless pursuit of popularity, which being the offspring of ambition and pride, ever involves some elements of disappointment and envy.[12]

Music education is justified for those with a decided taste, but:

> Instrumental musick, being more expressive in its attainment, both of money and time,... seems scarcely desirable to be cultivated, unless the impulse of native taste prompts or justifies the labour.... Even where a tolerable performance of instrumental musick might probably be attained without the prompting of decided taste, there may be danger of absorbing too much of time and attention from those employments which a female ought to understand, and will be expected to discharge.[13]

The important point is proportion. Music is not solid knowledge therefore:

> ... the value of brilliance, grace and accomplishments, must be laid in the balance, with that solid knowledge, pure principle and domestick virtue, whose aggregate is but another name for happiness.[14]

Even more elaborate injunctions against accomplished performance are expressed by a leading educator of the mid-1800s, Almira Hart Phelps.[15] In *The Female Student,* Phelps places music not in her section on the ornaments but rather under the subtitle of "affectation." The greatest evil of musical accomplishment is a by product of public performance. To Phelps, such seeking after admiration and acclaim beyond the appropriate sphere of women caused "vanity and affectation."

> ... the anticipated power of dazzling by the display of an elegant accomplishment, the hope of being the centre of a fashionable circle.... It is too painful to anticipate the evils which result from those hopes and expectations, so often the ruin of females, or of all that is truly estimable in the female character.[16]

Phelps's priorities subordinate any claims of artistic potential to feminine propriety. Accordingly, the inferior performer who was nonetheless amiable and obliging outranked the accomplished amateur musician who was vain and self-satisfied.

> If a young lady who is known to have some skill in music, after modestly stating her own deficiencies, performs but indifferently, she has at least shown an amiable, obliging

disposition in complying with the wishes of others. . . . If another young lady shows herself off with an air of vanity and self-satisfaction, however fine or scientific her performance, she has left no pleasant remembrances of herself in the minds of the beholders. And really, of what use are the greatest acquirements in music, as respects the great business of life, or as the foundation of a character?[17]

The same point of view was expressed by another writer, Margaret Coxe. Coxe reiterated the excessive condemnation of music from Hannah More's *Strictures on Female Education* before citing her own conservative views. Music was an amusement, but the lady performer must

. . . take heed that you do not allow such amusements ever to clash with duty, but make them rather subservient to it, by letting your aim be, to play and sing in such a manner, as may please those whose gratification you are bound to consult, whose comfort it is your privilege as well as your duty to promote.[18]

The taste of the lady performer was supposed to be determined by her sensitivity to her audience. If she moved beyond parlor standards, she could be accused of neglecting her duty. The true woman submitted her will to the legislation of others in musical matters as in everything else. She was advised to be less concerned about music as an elegant accomplishment for the social circle and more interested in the family circle.

It has ever been a sweet sight to me to behold a family circle gathered round a cheerful fire during a long winter's evening, while one member would touch the piano, or simply raise her sweetest notes for the amusement of that happy circle. How much more grateful should it be to an affectionate heart thus to soothe a father's, husband's or brother's cares, and increase a mother's and sister's joys, than to perform, in a crowded circle, for the gratification of strangers, whose admiration may be more loudly expressed, but whose affections do not respond with the feelings of sympathy.[19]

The musically accomplished lady was frequently derided as an inept housewife. One article in *Godey's Lady's Book* satirizes her through the complaints of her hapless husband:

Let none but the rich man aspire to the possession of a musical wife, for he must expect to pay in proportion to its annoyance; a computation which renders it extravagent indeed.[20]

A rather shy song on the same subject ("The Musical Wife") was written by T. Haynes Bayley:

My wife is very musical
She tunes it over much
And teases me with what they call
Her fingering and touch.

> She's instrumental to my pain,
> Her very Broadwood quakes,
> Her vocal efforts split my brain
> I shiver when she shakes![21]

The alleged conflict between musical accomplishments and domesticity was such a cliché that a writer in the 1860s issued the following retort:

> One hears much complaint of the direction and character of female education. It is dolefully affirmed that young ladies know how to sing operas, but not how to keep house—Doubtless there is foundation for this remark, or it never would have been made. But I have been in the East and the West, and the North and the South; I know that I have seen the best society, and I am sure that I have seen very bad if not the worst; and I never met a woman whose superior education, whose piano, whose pencil, whose German or French or any school accomplishments, or even whose novels clashed with her domestic duties. I have read of them in books: I did hear of one once, but I never met one—not one.[22]

This rebuttal demonstrates a major difference between early- as opposed to mid-nineteenth-century attitudes towards music. Susanna Rowson's "Miss Tasty" was not upbraided for her inability to keep house; she was satirized as a slavish follower of fashion. But in the 1840s and '50s the rationale for female education was not fashion but domestic duty. In short, the aristocratic lady had been replaced by the "true woman" of the middle class as the object of musical training. The locale of "accomplishment" shifts from the social circle to the home, from elegance to domesticity.

With the increasing emphasis on the family circle as the ideal audience for the accomplished female musician came a corresponding interest in "home music" and the influence of woman within it. The "true woman" promoted music within the home and chose her selections with simplicity and unaffection in mind. Articles on these themes appeared in musical periodicals as well as literary or ladies' magazine during the 1850s and '60s.[23]

Sarah J. Hale, for example, advised that musical accomplishment be reoriented towards domestic purposes in her advice book *Happy Homes and Good Society All the Year Round:*

> Girls are taught music almost as a matter of course, and too often consider it as bait to lure a lover. The lover being lured, the bait is detached from the hook and looked upon as useless for the rest of existence.... This is oftener the fault of the trainer rather than the trained. Let the mother or the teacher instill into the young girl's mind that she is learning not merely a showy accomplishment useful in society as a means to an end, but what may and should be used to the end of her life, as a means of brightening and enlivening her home; let her be taught this, and we shall cease to find music and matrimony so fatally opposed as they appear to be at present.[24]

Similar sentiments are found in the essay "Home Music" from the *Western Musical World:*

> Every woman who has an appetite for music or for singing should bless God for the gifts and cultivate it with diligence—not that she may dazzle strangers or win applause from a crowd, but that she may bring gladness to her own fireside.[25]

One corollary to this interest in home music was an attempt by music educators to redefine the purposes of musical accomplishment for women. Considering the conflicting views on musical accomplishment in female education, the efforts to extend her sphere to that of cultural and musical *teacher* within the home are quite understandable. Writers in musical periodicals were extremely critical of the poor musical educations women received. However, improvement in musical education was not a goal universally shared by ladies' magazine writers or seminary educators. They were more concerned with adding solid academic subjects to the curriculum, or proclaiming the necessity for domestic training. "Home music-making" and its teaching were seized upon as the basis for improved musical education of women and for the redefinition of music as "solid" rather than "ornamental" in the mid-nineteenth century. An article entitled "Woman's Influence" in the *Western Musical World* begins with an attack on fashionable education but ends with a plea for the upgrading of music's educational status:

> Musical education seems to be considered among American women merely as a species of fashionable accomplishment—of no real value, further than as it may serve to gratify personal vanity occasionally, or contribute by some train of accidents to a matrimonial alliance.
> ... Few American homes afford any irresistible attraction to the force of music—and few American children of either sex are submitted to its softening, humanizing, and refining influences.
> ... How different would be the result did American mothers place a deeper estimate on the objects of a musical education; ... Then would they anxiously submit their offspring as early as practicable to the most critical, thorough and comprehensive musical discipline.
> ... every wife ... whose own musical education has been thorough and comprehensive ... can materially aid in expanding in her offspring that love for the divine art.
> ... Parents of the present day should awaken to this sober truth on this subject, and instead of squandering time and money in converting their daughters into something little better than mechanical puppets—instead of resting the sum total of their musical abilities upon a few *tunes* ... let them render them accessible to whatever is or may be conceived in music ... let them lay as broad a foundation for this as for any other branch of education.[26]

Etiquette for the Accomplished Performer

In prescriptive literature the values of "true womanhood" extended beyond specific musical matters, such as choice of instruments, song texts, and the style of keyboard music.

Instruments prescribed for women performers were the piano, guitar, or harp. Recall Caroline Gilman's Anna, who played all three.[27] Even Almira Phelps allowed that "...a young lady may perform upon the piano or harp with skill and execution."[28] Ladies' magazines were "embellished with engravings, fashions and music arranged for the piano-forte, harp or guitar."[29]

In these preferences, as in so many other aspects of musical etiquette, the United States emulated England, where there was a rigid sexual distinction among various instruments. Piano, guitar, and harp were to be played by women; violin, cello, and flute by men. In a review in the *London Times* of 1817, critics objected to a concert where a young girl played a violin concerto on the ground that the instrument was "unsuitable to the prescriptive habits and accomplishments of a female."[30]

The issue was one of attractiveness and class. The flute transgressed female musical propriety because it required some physical distortion of the performer's features. In a review of a flute concert as late as on October 16, 1880, the *American Art Journal* conceded that if facial contortions could be controlled, the flute might be considered a suitable feminine instrument:

> The unusual sight of a lady playing such an instrument did not strike people as strange as we thought it would. She...avoids the ugly contortions of the lips.... Thus managed, the flute is decidedly not an unfeminine instrument.[31]

The violin was also perceived as a lower-class instrument, (a "fiddle"), and thereby unsuitable for a lady musician in the parlor.[32]

The image of femininity was paramount. Wilson Flagg, a critic for the *Atlantic Monthly,* thus encouraged men to participate in parlor music-making because they had greater latitude:

> Nobody would say that the voices of men are intrinsically as musical and agreeable as those of women. But we listen to a woman's voice as we look upon her face and observe her manners: a defect in either is more easily perceived, and is more disagreeable, than in the rougher sex.[33]

Female singers also had to consider the appropriateness of song texts from a moral point of view. Both Almira Phelps and Margaret Coxe criticized popular music texts of the 1830s as compromising and indelicate. Wrote Phelps:

> While speaking on the subject of vocal music I cannot but deprecate the improper character of most of the popular songs of the day. Young ladies are often heard to express in singing, sentiments, that they would blush to utter in conversation; if there is nothing wrong with the thought, the words set to fashionable music are usually without sentiment or moral. The beautiful and chaste songs of Mrs. Hemans are a noble exception; every thing that comes from her pen is pure, and bears the image and superscription of an elevated and chastened mind.... Has America no Hemans, who will awaken a sleeping lyre on behalf of her young

sisters, to give them songs which, instead of soiling the purity of their yet unpolluted hearts may enlist their associations and affections in the cause of virtue? ... Let not fashion, not let the popular taste seduce you from the straight and narrow path of female delicacy and propriety. ... [34]

Coxe echoed these sentiments, if a bit less melodramatically:

I must not omit one caution to you, my dear niece, in the selection of your music. I cannot but decidedly reprehend the tone of feeling and morality which pervades many of the most admired songs of the present day. ...

I have not unfrequently heard modest young females express in singing, sentiments so impassioned, and utter words so Anacreontic, that the reading of them aloud would have called the mantling blush to their cheeks. Surely, if the daughters of fashion are bound so closely by their fetters, as to be unable to make an attempt to break them, the daughters of Christian parents, more especially if they are themselves the professors of religion should dare to be singular. [35]

Phelps praised Mrs. Hemans's song "The Captive Knight" as pure and chaste, [36] but its subject matter, for another critic, was too "masculine" for the lady amateur.

Frequently a young lady is heard to sing stanzas from which she would revolt if put into simple prose ... Mrs. Hemans' popular ballad "The captive Knight," which in celebrating the events of the chivalrous ages, is certainly not the worthiest theme of our fair countrywomen. Songs of the sea and of the chase are also equally unfitted for ladies. Who can tolerate to hear a lady sing the masculine song of "The Sea"? ... Surely there is a range of subjects sufficiently broad to be found in friendship, and rational love, and innocent joys and home and its social and domestic blessings. [37]

The ideal home music, whether vocal or instrumental, was simple. Women singers and instrumentalists accordingly were frequently chastized for turning the parlor into a showcase for their accomplishments. The parlor singer was enjoined from singing operatic airs rather than ballads. John Dwight touched on this issue in one article:

We confess we do not like musical amateurs. ... We quite approve of amateur singers singing together for their own entertainment, if it really entertains them. What we object to is their inviting friends to come and listen to them. ...

... Partiality to the sex may have something to do with it, but we certainly prefer lady amateurs to their male friends and associates in the same line. In the second place they are more up to their work. The number of ladies who can play and sing tolerably well is infinitely greater than that of the gentlemen possessing the same talent and skill. The great fault of the ladies is that they are too ambitious. A girl who has a good voice which is really effective in a small room, thinks that it will be equally affective in a large concert-room or theatre. She sings ballads admirably, as well perhaps as they need be sung.

Therefore she attempts bravura airs, and does not sing them nearly as well as they would be sung by a fourth-rate seconda donna on the Italian stage. [38]

With respect to keyboard music also, the "great fault of the ladies" was that they were too ambitious—too scientific and learned in their taste. Musical accomplishment should aim at pleasing, not astonishing:

> A lady who plays well on the piano-forte and desires to make this accomplishment a source of pleasure and not of annoyance to her friends, should be careful to adapt the style of her performance to the circumstances in which it is called for, and should remember that a gay mixed company, would be tired to death with one of those elaborate pieces which would delight the learned ears of a party of cognoscenti. It is from neglect of this consideration that many a really excellent performer makes her music a social grievance. Many a sonata or fantasia to which at another time we could have listened with pleasure, has been thrown away on company who either drowned it by their conversation or sat during its continuance in constrained and weary silence. We would never advise a performer to make any sacrifice to vulgarity or bad taste, but there is no want of pieces that combine brevity with excellence, and afford room for the display of brilliancy, taste and expression on the part of the performer. A piece of this kind will not weary by its length...and with such every musical lady ought to be provided.[39]

Thus, sonatas and fantasias, played in the parlor, were "social grievances." Short and sweet was to be preferred to long and serious music. If any lady did desire to practice unfeminine socially unsuitable music, she should do so in private.

> Practice in private music far more difficult than that you play in general society, and aim more at pleasing than astonishing. Never bore people with ugly music merely because it is the work of some famous composer, and do not let the pieces you perform before people not professedly scientific be too long.[40]

Arthur Loesser cites this passage as an "underlining of music as a bland decorous parlor pleasure and a corresponding antagonism to it as a fine art."[41] It certainly does seem likely that had music been regarded as a solid rather than ornamental branch of education it would have been less likely to have been regarded as "essentially the province of females, foreigners or effeminates."[42] One reason perhaps that a view of fine-art music as "effeminate" crystalized in America was that musical accomplishment was feminized: cluttered up with the values of the fashionable "lady" and the "true woman." Loesser's observation thereby might be inverted and extended to the lady amateur herself. The very role that she played within musical accomplishment underlined *her* status as a bland and decorous parlor pleasure as well.

Perhaps then the overall significance of the tradition of musical accomplishment for women is the degree to which it generated a contradictory double standard by which their musical achievements were judged. Tradition simultaneously encouraged them to take up music, yet discouraged them from aspiring to any meaningful standards and repressed artistic ambition. The natural pride and assertiveness of the performer was decried as egotism. A musically learned woman was viewed like a literary bluestocking—an exceptional creature whose emergence from the parlor had to be accounted for and never taken simply as a matter of course. The female amateur musician was also the target for two opposing camps, criticized on one side by domestic idealogues for too much musical enthusiasm, and on the other side by professional musicians for too little. She was the scapegoat for the ambiguities inherent in the tradition itself.

Only those articles after 1830 that criticize female musicians for latent professionalism suggest any shift in the musical training of women and a general upgrading of the standards of accomplishment in the nineteenth century. The reader may recall the French traveler Brissot de Warville, who approvingly cited American girls in the late-eighteenth century as free from "the malady of perfection" in music; they did not go beyond their spheres and learn concert music. Criticism of overambitious lady amateurs indirectly suggests that by the 1850s American women were becoming far more accomplished, so much more that they needed to be reminded of the true sphere of the female amateur. One of their new faults, one which could hardly have been claimed in the early 1800s, was that they were *too* learned, *too* ambitious—too musical for the parlor.

One can only speculate on the distance between prescriptive literature and actual social behavior. Do these articles reminding musical women to stay in their place represent a response to changing conditions in female musical education? How did women who sang operatic airs or played sonatas and fantasias receive their training? Did any of them transcend the limits of female accomplishment to become professional? We know what musically accomplished women were *supposed* to do with their talent and training, but what in fact *did* they do?

4

Music in Female Seminaries

Training young women to be musically accomplished was big business in the nineteenth century. It supported private music teachers, the publication of music textbooks, and was an integral part of the curriculum in private girls' schools. Music was the "most popular of all accomplishments" in the 1840s[1] and that judgment was still confirmed 20 years later.[2] The musical education of girls was accepted as routine, while that of boys seems to have started later and have been more haphazard.[3] As one writer observed:

> During the past few years there has been considerable attention paid in this country to the musical education of boys. In the case of girls, the necessity of musical accomplishments has long been acknowledged; but until lately, boys have been ruled out of the same catalogue. What does a boy want of music? is the indignant query.[4]

Most institutionalized music education in the United States before the Civil War was located in private girls' schools, known as "female seminaries," "institutes," or "academies." These schools provided the most important base for music education in the first half of the nineteenth century, although they are usually ignored in histories of American music education today.[5] When in 1838 the Boston School Committee authorized Lowell Mason to teach music in the elementary schools, it was an historic moment. On the other hand, Mason taught only the rudiments of vocal music,[6] while female seminaries offered instrumental instruction, music appreciation, and even occasionally theory. To be sure, the quality of education varied dramatically with the institution, but in general it surpassed the level offered in elementary and secondary schools, of which there were comparatively few.[7]

Between 1830 and 1865, seminaries were a major employer of professional musicians. When Charles Grobe came to America in the 1830s, he taught piano at the Wesleyan Female Seminary in Wilmington, Delaware.[8] John Hill Hewitt was a professor of music at the Chesapeake Female College in Hampton, Virginia, in the 1850s,[9] and Abbot's Institute for Young Ladies employed George Root in 1845.[10]

In regional studies of nineteenth-century American musical life, female academies are usually prominent. One example is the history of an eastern Tennessee city, Knoxville.[11] The earliest reference to music teaching is associated with the Maryville Female Academy, which in 1813 announced that it would offer instruction in piano playing. In 1827 the Knoxville Academy for Females advertised piano lessons in its curriculum. These were planned for alternate days of the week and lasted one hour. By the 1850s there was a third female academy in the area that used music as a means of attracting students, offering piano, harp, and guitar, and stating in its catalogue that

> music has become so essentially a part of female education that no school is complete or satisfactory to the public, that does not provide for accomplishing its pupils in this branch thoroughly and elegantly.[12]

In contrast, the East Tennessee College for Men, established in 1792, did not mention music in its curriculum or in social activities until 1850, when there is a reference to a concert at commencement exercises.[13]

Music designed especially for seminaries emerged by 1840 as a new category in publishers' catalogues and included both "vocal classbooks" or textbooks and secular cantatas for women's voices. Bristow, Webb, Root, Mason, Grobe, and Septimus Winner are among those composers writing or assembling vocal music for this audience. Root's first cantata, "The Flower Queen," was written for young girls and designated for seminaries in its advertisements.[14] Piano music was similarly categorized, with A.P. Wyman's salon piece "Silvery Waves," for example, dedicated to the "ladies of the Washington Female Seminary." Other schools had pieces written for them such as the "Music Vale Quickstep" by O. Whittlesey and the "Norfolk Female Institute Polka" by Masi.[15] If sheet music experienced such enormous growth as an industry in the decades of the 1840s and '50s, one reason was the public formed from generations of young women that had passed through the halls of seminaries all over the country.

Music in the Seminary Curriculum, 1830 to 1860

Female seminaries educated girls between the ages of 14 and 17. They differed from their forerunners in the late-eighteenth century in their incorporated status, and more importantly, in the breadth of their curriculum. Earlier schools for women concentrated on the accomplishments (music, needlework, drawing, and dancing) and French, as the language of high society. Nineteenth-century education introduced academic (or "solid" as they were termed) subjects. To the extent that they offered women an education that could match that of the men's schools, female seminaries represented a major step forward for women. They helped prepare the way for the emergence of women's colleges after the Civil War.[16]

The incorporated seminary movement rose to its greatest height between 1830 and 1860, with outstanding institutions all over the country: Troy, New York; Salem, North Carolina; Elizabeth, Mississippi; Mount Holyoke, Massachusetts; Hartford, Connecticut; and Milwaukee, Wisconsin. These schools were the progressive models for organization and curriculum. Their leaders (such as Emma Willard and Catherine Beecher) set the tone of women's education throughout most of the nineteenth century.[17]

Although music as one of the ornamental branches was overshadowed by such "solid" subjects as chemistry, geology, mathematics, and the natural sciences, it nevertheless continued to be a staple in the curriculum. The number of schools offering music did not decline, but rather increased. Even in the limited sample of 162 schools surveyed by Woody, the percentage of schools offering music increased from about one-fifth to slightly under one-third (see table 1).[18] The sheer number of schools increased far more dramatically; at least three times as many academies offered music between 1830 and 1871 as compared to the period between 1749 and 1829.

Table 1. Curriculum Changes in Female Seminaries between 1749 and 1871, as Measured by Percentages Offering Certain Subjects

	1749-1829 (55 schools)	1830-1871 (107 schools)
Music	21%	30%
Ornamental needlework	43%	12%
Latin grammar	24%	59%
Chemistry	30%	90%
Geology	2%	60%

In contrast, needlework, another ornamental subject popular in the eighteenth century, became obsolete. As academic subjects rose, music held its own.

The nineteenth-century seminary typically offered the three "women's instruments": piano, harp, and guitar. However, some schools also offered organ, and exceptional schools offered other orchestral instruments. In addition, the emphasis was on social and secular music rather than religious hymns, as indicated in table 2.[19] There is parity between vocal and instrumental music and a neglect of psalmody. Seminaries were not intended as substitutes for singing schools; they trained women to function as amateur musicians within the home and the social circle.

Table 2.   Studies Offered in 162 Females Seminaries, 1742 to 1871

Subject	Number of Schools
Vocal music	48
Instrumental music	46
General music	39
Piano	30
Guitar	16
Organ	5
Harp	3
Melodeon	1
Spinet	1
Psalmody	2

Textbooks mentioned in school catalogues between 1780 and 1860 reaffirm this curriculum. There are vocal classbooks, instrumental instructors, and collections of secular music (table 3).[20] Lowell Mason was the most heavily represented compiler, and his vocal classbooks were designed for "the use of schools, seminaries and the social circle."

Table 3.   Textbooks Mentioned in Seminary Catalogues, 1780 to 1870

I. Methods

Bertini, *Piano Method*
Carcassi, *Method for the Guitar*
Carulli, *Method for the Guitar*
Czerny, *Piano-forte Method*
Carhart, *Melodeon Instructor*
Hunten, *Piano-forte Method*
La Blache, L., *Complete Method of Singing.* Boston: O. Ditson, 1850.

II. Theory

Burrowes, *Through-bass Primer*
Peters, *Elements of Thorough-bass*

III. Collections

Bradbury, W.B. *The Jubilee.* An extensive collection of church music for the choir, the congregation, and the singing school. Boston: Oliver Ditson, 1858.
_____. *The Young Choir.* Adapted to the use of juvenile singing schools, Sabbath schools, primary classes, etc. New York, 1841.
Kingsley, G. *Juvenile Choir*
Mason, Lowell, *Cottage Glee Book*
_____. *Manual of the Boston Academy of Music.* Boston, 1839.
_____. *Vocal Class Book*
Mason and Webb, *The Juvenile Singing School.* Boston, 1837.
Webb, George. *The American Glee Book.* Boston, 1841.

Editors of such textbooks often publicized the moral correctness of the song lyrics. George Webb, in the *Young Ladies' Vocal Classbook* for example assured his audience that "the selection of the poetry in every instance has been directed by a regard to its moral character and appropriateness."[21] In his *American Glee Book,* Webb dispelled misgivings about the propriety of the glee:

> In the whole range of secular music there is probably none which possesses so intrinsically the social character of the Glee and the Madrigal. On this account it is perhaps that no species of music has suffered so much from immoral and sensual association...allied with the sentiments of the grossest sensuality, or with words at once vapid and senseless.
>
> It is one of the most gratifying signs in the efforts which are being made in this country to cultivate the art of glee composition that they are accompanied with enlightened views of its capabilities as an agent of moral culture, no less than of its being most eminently suited to elevate and refine the social affections.
>
> Great care has been taken to admit no piece, however excellent the music in itself, in which there appeared the slightest immoral taint in the sentiment. In this collection will be found words to generally possess a decidedly chaste and virtuous tendency....[22]

While some of the textbooks listed in table 3 served public as well as private schools, those designed particularly for the female seminary were distinguished by a section on "vocal culture," in which rudiments of singing were presented. George Webb's *The Young Ladies' Vocal Classbook* contains "instructions for forming and training the voice." Similar collections were assembled by Bissell, Butler, Getze, Bristow, and Root.[23] One of the few known collections assembled by a woman composer is Jane Sloman's *The Melodist* (see fig. 1).

In general, vocal classbooks contain selections from Italian operas by Rossini, Bellini, and Donizetti; part-music by German composers; and parlor songs by such English composers as Glover and Blockley. Weber and Mendelssohn appear occasionally. Some compilers such as Jane Sloman and George Root wrote new works for their collections. It was common practice to rearrange selections from the European literature, pratically the operatic works. They were often simplified, arranged in trios and quartets, and most importantly, fitted with new texts to rid them of their "sensuality."[24] Only a few composers, among them George Bristow, rebelled against the practice of simplified and rearranged excerpts from the works of European masters, asserting "that much harm has been done to the cause of music, by mutilating arrangements made by those who conceived the melodies they accompany."[25]

As the education of women was taken more seriously (because of the incorporated seminary movement), music benefitted from the improvement of standards. Although the average institution offered rudimentary vocal instruction, some treated music as a legitimate subject of study.

Fig. 1.   Title Page and Index of Jane Sloman's *The Melodist*

THE MELODIST.

SELECTED GEMS

FROM

CELEBRATED COMPOSERS,

ARRANGED

FOR THE USE OF FEMALE SEMINARIES,

In One, Two, Three, and Four Parts,

WITH AN

ACCOMPANIMENT FOR THE PIANO-FORTE.

BY JANE SLOMAN.

The Pieces contained in this Work may all be sung as Solos—the Melody being always complete in the first part, and the other parts ad lib.

NEW-YORK:

PUBLISHED BY WILLIAM HALL & SON, 239 BROADWAY, (Opposite the Park.)

NAFIS & CORNISH ; HUNTINGTON & SAVAGE ; MARK H. NEWMAN & CO.; H. LONG & BROTHER ; STRINGER & TOWNSEND ; PRATT, WOODFORD & CO.
Philadelphia—E. L. WALKER, LEE & WALKER. A. FIOT ; Boston—GEO. P. REED & CO. E H. WADE, OLIVER DITSON, ELIAS HOWE. B. B. MUSSEY & CO. ; Baltimore—W. C. PETERS ; New Orleans
W. T. MAYO, E. A TYLER ; St. Louis—BALMER & WEBER ; Cincinnati—PETERS & FIELD ; Louisville—PETERS. WEBB & CO.; Athens, Geo.—W. P. SAGE ; Augusta, Geo.—
C. CATLIN & CO. ; Albany. N. Y—MAYER & COLLIER. BOARDMAN & GRAY ; Troy—J. W. ANDREWS. J. W. KENNICUTT ; Rochester—ALEX.
GRANT, G. DUTTON, Jr. ; Cleveland. O.—S. BRAINARD, JAMES STACEY ; Chicago, Ill.—A. H. & C. BURLEY; New
Haven—SKINNER & SPERRY; Hartford—H. GOODWIN, 2d.; Bridgeport—O. F. HANKS.

Fig. 1. Continued

INDEX.

		PAGE
Morning Invocation, - - - -	Rossini, - - - - - - -	25
autiful Sea, - - - - - - -	E. Ransford, - - - - - -	82
autiful Spring, - - - - - -	———	10
ght be the Place of thy Soul, - -	S. Glover, - - - - - -	59
ne, Sister, Come, - - - - -	Linda di Chamounix, - - -	97
nsider the Lilies, - - - - -	R. Topliff, - - - - - -	46
rge for a Young Girl, - - - -	Music adapted, - - - - -	84
ening Song, - - - - - - -	Poetry by Mrs. Hemans, - -	55
rewell, my Fatherland, - - - -	———	38
rewell to the Mountain, - - -	J. Barnett, - - - - - -	56
ntle Voices, - - - - - -	C. W. Glover, - - - - -	81
od Night! Good Night! - - -	La Sonnambula, - - - - -	5
od Night! - - - - - - -	I. B. Woodbury, - - - - -	74
psies' Chorus, - - - - - -	Rooke, - - - - - - -	104
ark, Hark, a Merry Note I Hear, -	German Part Song, - - - -	72
ere, in Cool Grot, - - - - -	Lord Mornington, - - - -	62
me, Sweet Home, - - - - -	Rev. Bishop Hopkins - -	102
narked the Spring as She passed a-		
ong, - - - - - - - - -	Rossini, - - - - - - -	28
is not always May, - - - - -	Donizetti, - - - - - -	64
seph and his Brethren, - - - -	Mehul, - - - - - - -	9
rd, keep my Memory Green, - -	———	32
r Home, my happy Home, - -	Jenny Lind, - - - - - -	90
Judah, thy Dwellings are sad, - -	Rossini, - - - - - - -	53
the Banks of Guadalquiver, - -	———	99
rest in the Lord, - - - - -	Mendelssohn, - - - - -	40
r own Fireside, - - - - - -	Barnett, - - - - - -	39
nz des Vaches, - - - - - -	———	76
taplæ Tambour, - - - - -	Madam Malibran, - - - -	34
st ye, rest ye, rapid Streams, - -	Rodwell, - - - - - -	17
eping, I dreamed, Love, - - -	Wallace, - - - - - -	44
ldier, rest! no cloud of sorrow, -	Donizetti, - - - - - -	92
eet Sister Fay, - - - - -	Barnett, - - - - - -	77
e Crusaders, - - - - - -	Sir Henry Bishop, - - -	36
e Deep, Deep Sea, - - - -	C. E. Horn, - - - - - -	86
e Dream, - - - - - - -	Jenny Lind, - - - - - -	15

		PAGE
The Departed, - - - - - - -	James Hine, Esq., - - - - -	61
The Evening Hour, - - - - -	Donizetti, - - - - - -	13
The Indian Girl's Burial, - - -	Bellini, - - - - - - -	21
The Light of other Days, - - -	M. W. Balfe, - - - - - -	96
The Old House at Home, - - - -	E. J. Loder, - - - - - -	85
The Pride of Italy, - - - - -	Bellini, - - - - - - -	11
The Sister Spirits, - - - - -	James G. Barnett, - - - -	67
The Stormy Petrel, - - - - -	Mozart, - - - - - - -	42
Through the Wood, - - - - -	C. E. Horn, - - - - - -	50
'Tis the Last Rose of Summer, -	Moore, - - - - - - -	101
'Twas on a Bank of Daisies Sweet,	John Hullah, - - - - -	58
Unto the merry Greenwood, - -	Arranged by John Hullah, -	80
Watch you well by Daylight, - -	Samuel Lover, - - - - -	66

HYMNS.

		PAGE
A Christmas Carol, - - - - -	Macray, - - - - - - -	107
Ailse, - - - - - - - - -	Jane Sloman, - - - - -	112
Alla Trinita Beata, - - - - -	Ancient Hymn, - - - - -	106
Beethoven, - - - - - - -	———	110
Bohemia, - - - - - - -	———	112
Cardross, - - - - - - -	Jane Sloman, - - - - -	112
Dismission Hymn, - - - - -	Jane Sloman, - - - - -	109
Holmes, - - - - - - -	Jane Sloman, - - - - -	109
Jaghella, - - - - - - -	———	108
Meyerbeer, - - - - - - -	Chorale, - - - - - -	107
Mozart, - - - - - - -	———	111
Mutter, - - - - - - -	Jane Sloman, - - - - -	111
Parsons, - - - - - - -	Jane Sloman, - - - - -	109
Prosser, - - - - - - -	Jane Sloman, - - - - -	111
Rossini, - - - - - - -	Chorale, - - - - - -	110
Russia, - - - - - - -	———	108
The Academy Hymn, - - - -	Jane Sloman, - - - - -	107
Ujhazy, - - - - - - -	———	105
Vater, - - - - - - -	———	112
Weber, - - - - - - -	———	110
Whitaker, - - - - - - -	———	108

One of the outstanding seminaries of the period, Emma Willard's Troy Seminary, illustrates how the level of education in the accomplishments rose in coordination with general educational ideals. According to its catalogue,[26] in 1840 the school offered lessons in piano, harp, and guitar, plus singing lessons. Music was listed under the "ornamental branches" and there were three teachers. By 1848 there was a "music department" in which piano, guitar, harp, and violin were taught, along with singing. The faculty numbered four, among them Gustave and Elizabeth Blessner, German musicians. By 1852 there were seven teachers and organ had been added to the choices. By the late-nineteenth century Troy called its music department a "conservatory," and in a complete reversal described it as "suitable not only for those who wish to make music a profession, but also for amateurs"! Such a statement reflects the changing status of American women by the end of the century and would not have been made before the Civil War. Female seminaries thereby contributed to the process which transformed music from an accomplishment into a profession for women.

Instrumental Instruction or "Twenty Tunes in Six Lessons"

The quality of music education varied dramatically with the institution. Some offered private lessons as supplements to their curriculum, designed to teach their charges tunes to entertain their families and friends, but little else. A young student at the Geneva, New York, Female Seminary in 1831 and 1832 has left us a record of her music lessons that apparently proceeded according to this method. Her diary is an intimate glimpse into the sensibility of a seminary student of the period.[27]

Louisa Ackley came to the seminary in June 1831, and noticed on her third day that "there is a nice little music room and a very good Pianno Forte [*sic*]." On July 19 she made this entry in her diary:

> ... This morning Mrs. B was so good as to let me practice for some time on her instrument in the house. It practices——it was cool the instrument was in good tune and I felt like practicing I have some new music which I wish to learn very perfectly before I go home as I am well aware that it will be expected I will play pretty well by this time, I should be sorry to disappoint them.... I think B——(?) with variations is a very fine piece. I think also Auld Lang Syne and——are and Kinloch of Kinloch with variations[28] I think also very pretty. There are so many pretty pieces of music it is rather difficult to point out any one piece in the common sort of music which might be considered the prettiest.

Louisa obviously decided which tunes might impress the folks back home. Apparently she did well enough, for a few months later she wrote:

> Saturday, 1 October
>
> I received a letter from NY this morning. Father has bought me a new instrument I am *very very* glad of it.

Learning tunes was the extent of Louisa Ackley's music education. In fact, it was just the sort of training that was roundly criticized in music journals. The editors of *The Family Minstrel* used the occasion of a review of a piano method to wax angrily against the "state of things in female seminaries." The book at hand was W. Nixon's *A Guide to Instruction on the Piano Forte*. The editors praised the author because he proposed to teach seminary girls theory and harmony rather than letting them "bungle for a year or two over a few simple marches and waltzes and accompaniments to songs that exhibited nothing but diversifications of the chords of I and V." They went on to hope that "never more should we hear of 'twenty tunes in six lessons,'" obviously a reference to routine advertisements piano teachers made in order to attract pupils.[29]

Louisa's diary gives us specific information about "tunes" but not enough about her actual lessons. A more detailed account of private instruction is chronicled in the letters written by Harriet and Maria Trumbull at the turn of the century.[30] Harriet was a 17-year-old girl from Connecticut who came to New York to be "finished," that is to study music, dancing, and drawing. From December 1800, through 1801, she studied with James Hewitt, one of the most prominent musicians in New York at the time.

Certain aspects of Harriet's training were typical. Music lessons were scheduled by the "quarter," or three-month period;[31] they took place two or three times a week, and the length of instruction was one or two years. Instruction included singing as well as keyboard and the emphasis was on popular parlor music.

Harriet studied with Hewitt for the length of her visit and it was very clear to her that once she returned to Connecticut, her lessons would end. When her mother suggested an earlier return than planned, after three months, Harriet replied:

11 February 1801

I am sorry you think of having us return so soon, not but I would be glad to go, even next week, but I wish to make out two quarters in music, and drawing. Music especially I dislike to leave it as it is probably the only time I shall ever have for learning it. Mr. Hewitt comes very regularly, and says he is well satisfied with my improvement, yet I can make *but* little progress in six months and *less time* would only be throwing money away... I am most frightened sometimes with all our economy, but we must try to be very prudent that I may not lose my piano-forte.[32]

Hewitt taught Harriet to sing, accompany herself, and play popular keyboard tunes. Occasionally, he wrote pieces for her, and as she was the daughter of an influential Connecticut politician, even suggested dedicating some short works to her father. Two other letters from Harriet to her brother discuss her lessons in detail:

I am much obliged to you for what you [say] concerning my music; I think Mr. Hewitt seems to be much of your opinion. Since I have gone through the first small book which he had given me, and contained simple pieces for new beginners, he has made it a practise to give me for one lesson a piece, and the next a song; and I find all of them difficult enough, so much so that I can play none of them readily and easily, tho I find that the two or three first were the hardest, he has given me some pieces that he has composed himself I suppose purposely for his scholars, he has made me sing once or twice and began with raising my notes, but we have not advanced far, as I have had a cold.

I have a most wonderfully——music master, he composes a great deal himself and told me today he intends to publish some marches, and asking me if my Papa was not Governor of Connecticut & said in compliment to me he would have one in honour of him; so when I return I shall be able to play "Governor Trumbull's March."[33]

Music Education at the Better Seminaries

The more progressive seminaries offered much more extensive traning. Probably the most outstanding music education to be found in any seminary before 1830 was at the Moravian Seminary in Bethlehem, Pennsylvania, one of the earliest schools for girls in the country. In light of the major role accorded music in Moravian culture, music education was stressed at the seminary as well.[34] Students learned guitar, keyboard instruments, and singing. In 1792 the school owned seven keyboard instruments (pianos and clavichords) for its 41 pupils. An invoice of music imported from Holland mentions keyboard sonatas by Haydn, Hoffmeister, variations sets by Vanhal, and Haydn's sonatas arranged for four hands. Visitors to Bethlehem invariably commented upon the prominence of music in the life of the school. One visitor was Eliza Southgate Bowne (a 20-year-old woman who had been "finished" at Susanna Rowson's Academy in Medford), who noted the presence of a piano in every classroom and the amount of singing that went on in daily routines.[35]

Mid-nineteenth-century seminaries attracted attention for their curriculum and concert activities in the musical press. *The Musical World and Times,* for example, made it standard practice to comment on musical events in the more important seminaries all over the country. One item praises the superior education at the Newburgh Female Seminary in New York State, which included theory and composition:

There is no well-founded reason why young ladies should not be taught the theory and practice of musical composition, and the study of music be thus rendered a rational and useful and thoroughly philosophical pursuit, instead of being as it generally is, a blend of distasteful thumping or strumming or scraping of some poor tortured instrument.[36]

Another item reported a concert in Macon, Mississippi:

> Macon, Mississippi: A concert by the young ladies of the Macon Female Institute came off lately. The composers included were Wallace, Schulhoff, G. Root, and William Bradbury. Music which has been at a very low ebb in Macon, now begins to be better appreciated.[37]

At Cherry Valley Seminary in New York, music was one of the most important subjects in the curriculum in the 1850s. The school was famous for the quality of its elaborate commencement concerts. According to a catalogue of 1854, the school taught singing, piano, harp, guitar, and organ. The textbooks included piano methods by Hunten, Bertini, and Czerny; Rink's organ method; and A.B. Marx's *Musical Composition,* a four-volume set that covered thorough-bass, harmony, melody, and form as it was routinely taught in German conservatories.[38]

The Cherry Valley board of directors was proud of its music department and described its head, Jonathan A. Fowler, as "an artist at the head of his profession" and its music curriculum as one that "cannot be surpassed, if equalled, by any institution in the country."[39] The commencement concert, which was called by the fashionable term "soirée musicale," was described by the board of examiners who attended it on August 10, 1853, and reprinted in the catalogue as part of the institutional credentials. Their description brings the musical environment to life and evokes that peculiar blend of chivalry and education inherent in the ambience of musical "accomplishment."

> Your committee cannot forbear to notice in this report that the Fine Arts, Music and Painting, are here cultivated to a degree that has seldom been reached by other institutions. The Soirée Musicale, which closed the anniversary exercises of the evening of the 10th, was a most brilliant and delightful entertainment. The fine spacious Hall of the Institution was brilliantly illuminated. The walls were adorned with beautiful and well-executed paintings, the work of the young ladies during the past term. An audience capable of appreciating the finest exhibitions of the Musical Art losely filled the room. [Names of the distinguished followed.] The perfect ease with which some of the most difficult pieces of the best Masters were executed, was a matter of the most agreeable surprise to all present.[40]

This concert may have occasioned the article on the school in the *Musical World and Times* entitled "Musical Progress" on Fowler's influence:

> When Mr. Fowler first came to Cherry Valley about twelve years since, there were only six pianos in the place. Now there are over one hundred besides the instruments used in the institution. A large Female Institution has been built up, not by stock company, but by subscription and Mr. Fowler had during last term over sixty pupils in the musical department. So much for musical progress in a little town of only nine hundred inhabitants.[41]

The magazine then printed the program at their most recent concert in full (fig. 2). The level of the performance, they glowingly stated, was outstanding:

> Twenty-five years ago such an entertainment as the one inserted below could only have been given by the best artists in the country. Now, in a Female Seminary, remote from the great Emporium of Art, some of the most difficult and elaborate compositions are rendered in a style (judging from Fowler's formal entertainments) rarely excelled by the most skillful artists. We notice in the programme over thirty different performers, and only regret that we cannot be in their midst to witness the triumph of well-directed native talent in the most divine arts.

Fig. 2.   Program of the Cherry Valley Female Academy Commencement Concert, as listed in *The Musical World and Times*

1.	Overture-Il Pirata, 2 pianos, 8 hands	Bellini
2.	March Italiene, 2 pianos, 8 hands	Donizetti
3.	Solo, Favorite Air with variations	Grobe
4.	Polka Brilliante, 2 pianos, 8 hands and harp	Strauss
5.	Duo Concertante—Variations and Rondeau Brilliante—O Dolce Concerto, 2 pianos	Herz
6.	Solo—Le Palais d'hiver, Mazurka Caprice, piano	Goria
7.	Polka brilliante, 2 pianos, 12 hands	Jullien
8.	Solo—Variations Brilliantes— Sonambula	Beyer
9.	Review March—2 pianos, 8 hands	Glover
10.	Solo—La Fille du Regiment, Grande Fantasie, piano	Strakosch
11.	Grand Divertissement—2 pianos	Greulich
12.	Solo and Chorus—Bird of the North	Root

Part Second

1.	Overture—Egmont, 2 pianos, 8 hands	Beethoven
2.	Grand March, 2 pianos, 8 hands	Blessner
3.	Grand duo concertainte, Op. 15	Herz
4.	March from The Prophet, 2 pianos, 3 hands	Meyerbeer
5.	Solo—Comin thro' the Rye	Jaell
6.	Katy-Did polka, 2 pianos, 8 hands, flute, violincello, and harp	Jullien
7.	Solo—Variations Brilliantes— Lucia di Lammermoor	Mocker
8.	Chorus—The Comparison (German)	
9.	La Sylphide, solo	Strakosch
10.	Solo, March from Norma, harp	Bochsa
11.	Solo—Duke of Reichstadt's Waltz	Le Carpentier
12.	Prima Donna Waltz, 2 pianos, 8 hands, flute, and violincello	Jullien

The program of the "soirée musicale" (fig. 2) and two others from the same period (figs. 3, 4) that were located in the Cherry Valley Library, illustrate the repertory. Note that the "soirée musicale" (fig. 3) is described as an "entertainment," not as a "concert." Yet the level of programming was quite high and similar to the kinds of concerts that were scheduled as professional events in the cities. The most popular composers were Donizetti and Bellini. The piano virtuosi Thalberg, Herz, and Kalkbrenner were also represented. Occasionally Mozart, Beethoven, and Mendelssohn's names appear, usually in conjunction with an opera overture arranged for four or eight hands. Among the American composers included were Gottschalk, Root, and Adele Hohnstock. If Gottschalk's "The Banjo" (fig. 4) was indeed played by a pupil, then the level of accomplishment at Cherry Valley was quite high. This program is a far cry from "Kinloch of Kinloch," the tune that Louisa Ackley learned at Geneva Female Seminary in the 1830s. Thus at some outstanding seminaries the level of instruction had moved away from "tunes" towards cultivated European-oriented music.

Multiple arrangements for ensemble playing on many pianos was a tradition associated with seminaries, particularly it seems in the South. When Henri Herz traveled to New Orleans, his manager arranged a concert of what he called "financial music": music arranged for eight or ten pianos, which everywhere in America had the gift of drawing crowds.[42] Herz described the concert as follows:

> He had to give into my intelligent secretary and "financial music," arranged for eight pianos and sixteen pianists recruited among the young ladies of Louisiana society, produced in the customary results. There was a crowd to hear the harmonious squadron of fashionable ladies, all of them pretty and roundly applauded, as one would expect.[43]

Such arrangements no doubt covered the deficiencies of the young girls' training and got everyone into the act.

Although Herz does not mention a particular female seminary, evidence from another concert program reviewed by John S. Dwight does. He poked fun at a concert held at the Georgia Female College in an article called "Musical Education Down South."[44] Dwight criticized the low level of the music and the custom of arranging the works for more than one piano:

> In the Augusta Ga. Chronicle we find an enthusiastic letter, describing the "Georgia Female College Commencement," at Madison. Among other things the writer appears to have been ravished by the music of the occasion, which was interspersed at intervals between the spoken parts of the fair graduates.
>
> ...Here are a few of the musical items in the Programme.
>
> Montezuma Grand March, Duet, 3 pianos (!)
> Lee Rigg—Variations, 3 pianos
> Gone to the Forest—Song, duet

Fig. 3. Program of a Musical Entertainment at Cherry Valley, 1851

SOIREE MUSICALE.

MR. J. A. FOWLER,

AND HIS PUPILS, ASSISTED BY THE EMMINENT PIANIST,

HENRY C. TIMM. ESQ., of New-York,

Will give a Musical Entertainment

AT THE

ACADEMY HALL,

In Cherry-Valley, N. Y.

August 22d, 1851,

COMMENCING AT 7 O'CLOCK, P. M.

PROGRAMME.

PART FIRST.

1. Grand Duo Du Couronnement—God Save the Queen—2 Pianos,
   (*Herz.*)   Mr. H. C TIMM, and Miss A. M. OLCOTT.

2. Cavatina from Anna Bolena, with variations—Piano, (*Herz.*)
   Miss M. E. BURTIS.

3. DUET—Air Montagnard, with variations —Piano, (*Herz.*)
   Miss C. L. METCALF and Master G. W. METCALF.

4. Le Reve—Romance, Piano, (*Wallace.*)
   Miss J. LITTLE.

5. Fantaisie—La Straniera—Piano, (*Thalberg.*)
   Miss A. M. OLCOTT.

6. SONG—Una voce al Cor d'intorno—from Gemma Di Vergy,
   (*Donizetti.*)   Miss S. J. TRULL.

7. Fantaisie—Mose in Egitto—Piano, .(*Thalberg.*)
   Mr. H. C. TIMM.

8. Hohnstock Polka with variations—Piano, (*Hohnstock.*) arr'd with
   accts. for Harp, Violoncello, and Flute,   Miss J. LITTLE.

PART SECOND.

1. Grand Duo Concertant Sur Zanetta—Piano and Flute,
   (*Wolff & Tulou.*)   Messrs H. C. TIMM and J. A. FOWLER.

2. Fantasie Sur la Cracovienne—Piano, (*Wallace.*)
   Miss E. O. LITTLE.

3. Grand Duo Sur Norma—2 Pianos, (*Rosellen.*)
   Misses R. R. MURRAY and C. L. METCALF.

4. Favorite Polka—arr'd for 2 Pianos, Harp, Violoncello and Flute,

5. Grand Duo Concertant—Donna del Lago, 2 Pianos, (*Herz.*)
   Miss J. LITTLE and Mr. H. C. TIMM.

6. Brilliant Variations, on a favorite Swiss Air—Piano, (*Hunten.*)
   Miss I. S. KNAPP.

7. SONG—Ave Maria, (*Schubert.*)
   Miss S. J. TRULL.

8. La Sylphide—Fantaisie Romantique—Piano, (*Strakosch.*)
   Mr. H. C. TIMM.

This Programme will serve as a Ticket of admission, which the bearer will please present at the door.

Fig. 4.   Program of a Cherry Valley concert, undated.

PROGRAMME.

PART FIRST.

Wilcox, Abbott, Belle & Betts

1. OVERTURE—Il Pirata—2 Pianos, 8 hands,..........(*Bellini.*)

Bradbury & Green

2. DUETT—from Linda Di Chamounix—"Come, Sister, come,"

....Vocal,....(*Donizetti.*)

Sutherland Spraker Sanders & Marvin.

3. FANTAISIE BRILLANTE—Lucrezia Borgia—2 Pianos, 8 hands

....(*Fowler.*)

Miss Bronson

4. SOLO—Fantaisie Brillante—La Straniera—op. 9,—Piano.

....(*Thalberg.*)

McKee & Searles

5. DUO CONCERTANTE—March Triomphale—2 Pianos,

....(*Kalkbrenner.*)

Browder Searles Spraker Collins & Morse

6. POLKA BRILLANTE—Harp and 4 Guitars,..........(*Fowler.*)

Diefendorf & Shipman

7. GRAND DUO CONCERTANT—Linda Di Chamounix—2 Pianos,

....(*Czerny.*)

Bradbury Green & Thornton

8. TRIO—from Parisini,—"Soft fades the glow of Even."—Vocal,

....(*Donizetti.*)

9. WEDDING MARCH—from Midsummer Night's Dream—

..................2 Pianos, 8 hands,......(*Mendelssohn.*)

10. QUADRILLES BRILLANTES,.................

Fig. 4, continued

PROGRAMME.

◄►PART SECOND.►►

Hindrix Snow Duff & Woolford.
1. OVERTURE—Don Juan—2 Pianos, 8 hands,...........(*Mozart.*)

2. TRIO—Fantaisie Brillante—2 Flutes and Piano,.........(*Kuhlau.*)
Miss Browder.
3. SOLO—Venetian Air, with Introduction and variations—Harp,
....(*Moran.*)
Bronson & St. John
4. DUO CONCERTANTE—Grandes Variations Militaires—op. 68—
....2 Pianos,......(*Pixis.*)
Miss Parshall
5. SOLO—Variations Brillantes—Lucia Di Lammermoor,....(*Mocker.*)

6. MARCH—from the Prophet—2 Pianos, 8 hands,......(*Meyerbeer.*)
Browder & Green
7. SONG—Scotch Ballad—"Comin' thro' the Rye," with Harp acc't.

8. SOLO—Grotesque Fantaisie—the Banjo—Piano,.....(*Gottschalk.*)
The whole School.
9. WEDDING CHORUS—from La Sonnambula,..........(*Bellini.*)

Julien

☞ Tickets of Admission, 25 cts.

> Florida Grand March—Duet, 7 pianos (!!)
> Hyacinth Galop—5 pianos
> Air Swiss—Trio, 7 pianos (!!!)
> Home, Sweet, Home—Variations, Flute and Piano

And so on, a rarer selection of music, on a grander scale of performance, is scarcely to be met within the world's great musical capitals. A Trio on seven pianos, we suppose, means the three young ladies played at each piano; that is, it was a piece for six hands, multiplied by seven. This was truly magnifique, and shows that music goes ahead in those regions with a full and triumphant consciousness that "this *is* a great country." *Classical* it was certainly, inasmuch as it was given in classes; but then there was no pedantic old fogey-ism of Handel, Haydn, Mozart or Beethoven about it;...

A year later Dwight reviewed a commencement concert in Madison, which in the intervening period had swelled its ranks to include 130 performers.[45] He reproduced the program (fig. 5), which is interesting from a number of points of view. First, it locates the tradition of "monster concerts" within the seminary conventions of performance; secondly, it documents instruction on orchestral instruments, rather than piano, harp, or guitar. Finally, it shows the mixture of European and American music which is assimilated into the "seminary style": arrangements for multiple performances.

Fig. 5.   Excerpts from the Commencement Concert, Madison Female
College, as listed in *Dwight's Journal of Music*

1.	Overture—To the Caliph of Bagdad (on one, three, seven and nine pianos)	Boldieu
2.	Wild Bird-Class; with Piano and Contra Basso accompaniment	Von Weber
3.	Polka-Fire Fly, (nine pianos)	Fowler
4.	Duet—Josephine Polka, (nine pianos)	Thos. Beckett
5.	Song—Ossian Serenade, Class; with piano, harp and contra basso	Dodge
6.	Airs—Selections from "Bayadere" (five and three pianos)	Auber
7.	Duet—Tyrolienne; from "La Fille du Regiment" (three pianos)	Donizetti
8.	Song and Chorus—Gypsy-Class; with piano accompaniment	M. Dix Sullivan
9.	Duet—Polka favorite, (9 pianos)	Jullien
10.	Quintetto—composed for the entire ensemble	Geo. C. Taylor
11.	Home, Sweet Home, accompanies with the harmonicon	Paine
12.	Battle-Musical Combat, or Struggle for American Independence being a Descriptive Fantasia in which "God Save the King" and "Yankee Doodle" represent England and the United States	Geo. C. Taylor

Dwight entitled his article "A Monster Concert by Young Ladies." The excerpts that follow will give the flavor of the original:

> Seldom has it been our lot in sweeping the musical firmament with our telescope, to report a new phenomenon of such entirely strange and formidable size and aspect, as the sign which we have just read in the Southern heavens....
>
> It is the programme of an annual Concert by the pupils of the "Madison Female College," in Madison, Georgia, which came off on the evening of July 27th under the auspices of Prof. G.C. Taylor, a "musical manager and director." And if this is a specimen of the scale on which they "do up" the music in the educational seminaries down South, we would advise our German encomiast, "Hoplit" to look there rather than Boston for the "music of the future."
>
> Said programme first sets forth the names of each and every performer, to the number of 130.... These consist of 97 young lady pianists, 11 young lady guitarists, 3 young lady harpists, 13 young lady *violinists* (!), 1 young lady *violist* (!!), 4 young *violin-cellists* (!!!), and 1 young lady *contrabassist* (!!!!). The entire programme, reader, would be too much for you; we select a few of the most notable items. It seems these young pianists, fire in platoons, occasionally flanked in some of their exploits by the light artillery of fiddle and guitar strings, or the deep artillery of that Amazonian double bass....[46]

His review ridiculed not only the kind of music performed at the commencement—a somewhat understandable point of view—but also the mere occasion of young ladies performing on orchestral instruments. A few months later, the musical director George Taylor rebutted Dwight in a letter to the *Journal,* on October 15, 1853:

> ...To criticize fairly Friend Dwight, thou shouldst take into consideration the object, performers & &c.—Verily, thou wouldst not expect the same from young school girls, that thou shouldst from Jullien's troupe!
>
> Music in the Southern Female Institution, is taught as recreation and accomplishment, and *not* with a view of making *Artists*. The time given to it by the pupils is one hour a day, during one to two years, and in some cases from three to four years. A concert is usually given once a year, for the double purpose of showing the improvement of the pupils, and the gratification of their parents and friends. Those concerts have an effect upon musical taste, and those of us who direct them, are responsible in a measure for the improvement of the taste of the mass, but one cannot expect us to improve the taste, otherwise than by degrees.... Germany, the very heart and brain of music, has had composers who were not appreciated in their times. Why are they now? Because by frequent hearing of their compositions musical taste has been improved.
>
> The performers at the "Monster Concert" were school girls, some of whom had taken lessons but a few weeks.... We claim to be progressive here; and if the music of Von Weber, Jullien etc.... is not progressive and calculated to improve musical taste, then we must agree to disagree forever.
>
> Respectfully yours,
> Geo. C. Taylor
>
> P.S. If being in favor of a lady learning to play the violin, viola, violincello, or contra-basso is being a Woman's Rights man then I am one, most emphatically,   G.C.T.[47]

"Progressive" (as Taylor defensively implied) is a relative term. Looking backward, one wishes that the idea of training young women to be artists might not have been so preposterous a notion for a seminary director to entertain. Still, given the climate of the times, Taylor was a liberal educator, a virtual "Woman's Rights" supporter for including orchestral instruments (in addition to the parlor instruments) among the options for his students.

Dwight's rebuttal refused to take the issue seriously, and he claimed it was "the intrinsic humor of the thing" that guided his opinions by which he meant no harm. This is followed by a short "filler" article on "Female Orchestras" in which the memoirs of an observer of an eighteenth-century ladies' orchestra in Venice is quoted. Like Dwight, this traveler thought the sight of women playing orchestral instruments was inherently ridiculous. Dwight could not take female musicians seriously because they were inextricably linked to music as an accomplishment rather than an art. Nor could he acknowledge the seminary's claims for their contributions to the improvement of taste.

Whether or not we agree with Taylor that his arrangements of second-rate European compositions constituted progress is secondary to the significance of the school's unusual curriculum. At least here was one institution where a young girl might learn instruments other than piano, harp or guitar.

The most unusual and progressive seminary in the history of early music education was Music Vale, or Salem Normal School in Salem, Connecticut; it was in fact a conservatory, not a school of general studies. Founded by Oramel Whittlesey in 1835,[48] it was the first music school in the country. The Boston Academy of Music, founded by Lowell Mason in 1833, was limited to vocal music.[49] In a letter written to an author of an informal history of the school, Whittlesey's daughter touched on this point; her father "always said it was the first purely music school established in the United States. There were other active music schools in the country but with French or some other branch of study connected with them."[50] These other schools, from this description, were like Taylor's Madison Female College, institutions specializing in music as one of the accomplishments.

Exactly when Music Vale was authorized to give "normal" or teaching degrees is not clear. But for many years it was the only music school in the country that did confer this degree. (The first general normal school where music was offered was the institution at Lexington, Massachusetts, which added vocal music to its curriculum in 1839.)[51] By the 1850s Music Vale was known as the Salem Normal Institute.

Students came from all over the country to study. During its prime, the enrollment averaged about 80 girls, from such diverse places as the Carolinas, Kentucky, Kansas, Nova Scotia, and even the West Indies.[52] After the Civil War, Southern girls no longer patronized it to the same degree, and there were competing institutions as well, so that Music Vale closed in 1876; but during the

1850s it was well known throughout the country. An article in the *New London Star* in Connecticut in the 1850s describes the school as

> in a flourishing condition and we look upon this as the result of teaching music as a specialty. The day is rapidly passing away when pupils can study a dozen different branches at once and successfully pass the public ordeal.... His students study music alone and the consequence is that he graduates some of the most thorough and accomplished artists in the country and his institution stands in the very first rank.[53]

Whittlesey's daughter Karolyn, a music teacher in Kansas, said in 1914 that her father's school "was known all about the country. He supplied schools with teachers. To this day I never go anywhere that I do not meet some of the Music Vale girls."[54] The significance of the Music Vale training, therefore, is that it was *occupational* in intent: musical accomplishment was defined as the means towards a professional rather than recreational end and women were trained as potential artists and teachers rather than parlor amateurs.

In the circular describing the school that was reprinted in *The Musical World and Times*, Whittlesey took great care to distinguish his kind of training from what he disdained as "fashionable style." His course of instruction aimed at

> a correct *expression,* which is the soul of musical culture.... By expression do not understand us to mean the distortion of the features, or the flourishing of the arms like a bass drummer of the continental army; neither is it jerking of the hands from the keys (in all sorts of movements) as if they were blazing hot; nor yet the various other gymnastics enacted by young missus under the very ludicrous sobriquet of "Fashionable Style."
>
> By Expression we would wish to be understood as meaning the tone, grace, or modulation of the Piano or voice suited to any particular subject; that manner which gives life and reality to ideas and sentiments; now taking us back to other days, when with a happy group of joyful mates (Many of whom have long since passed away), we strolled over fields and hills together, plucking the flowers of Spring....
>
> By it we mean that part of music that soothes, consoles and ameliorates the condition of man;... that part of music that speaks to the heart, making us happier, wiser and better....[55]

Instruction at Music Vale emphasized theory and instrument lessons, as well as the conventional course in "voice culture." Students learned rudiments of singing and part songs from George Root's *Academy Vocalist.* They could take lessons on organ, harp, guitar, and piano. In addition, there were classes in notation, harmony, thorough bass, and counterpoint.[56]

The repertory was more sophisticated than that of the conventional female seminary. Whittlesey bowed to conventions of accomplishment by assuring parents of prospective students that they would learn more than classical music; the description in the catalogue avowed that:

> The pupil, however, during the yearly course, finds time as recreation from study to learn many beautiful airs, songs, marches, polkas, etc. which beguile leisure hours and charm the friends back home....[57]

and he himself composed parlor music for his pupils.[58] But such pieces were seen as recreation, set apart from the curriculum. Repertory from the commencement concerts, which were often attended by noted musicans and educators, was progressive, including works by Beethoven, Schumann, Chopin, or Mendelssohn. In the 1860s the contemporary music scene was represented by an occasional transcription from a Wagner opera; Liszt's "Hungarian March"; Thalberg's variations on "Home, Sweet Home"; Weber's "Polacca Brilliante"; Rubenstein's "Melody in F"; and William Mason's "Tarantelle."[59]

Training at Music Vale represents the highest standards of musical accomplishment before the Civil War. If we see music education as a continuum during the first half of the nineteenth century, we can place the kind of education that Louisa Ackley got at one end and the conservatory approach of Music Vale at the other. Most seminaries no doubt fell in between, with a few institutions closer to Music Vale than others. Still, progressive seminaries succeeded in expanding the boundaries of musical achievement for women. Old-fashioned tune-training was replaced by that of "high accomplishment," in which professional standards were legitimized aspirations.

High Accomplishment Becomes Fashionable

The contrast between the old (that is, the generation from 1790 to 1820) and the new (that of 1830 to 1860) can be easily seen in the portraits of women musicians sketched in both memoirs and in fiction. Susan Lyman Leslie in *Recollections of My Mother* described her mother's musicianship, implicitly contrasting her with the younger generation. For her time Anne Robbins Lyman was an accomplished woman:

> In her account of my mother's youth, my Aunt Catherine has spoken of her music, as being a great occupation and pleasure for her; but after her marriage she had little time for practising and confined herself to playing for a half hour at twilight or tea, the short time before the children went to bed.... The "old parlor" contained an upright English piano, the only one in town for many years.... Before the children went to bed, my mother always played "The Copenhagen Waltz" and "The Battle of Prague with Variations" with much vigor. She was guiltless of ever having heard "classical Music" and I fear the performance would hardly satisfy us now, though we thought it charming then. On Sunday night she played a number of psalm tunes, singing also with much feeling and fervor. "Dundee," "Federal St.," "Calmar" and "Pleyel's Hymn" were always favorites.... [60]

Another woman described her mother with similar fondness. Here the lady is singing for beaux, rather than her family, but the same emphasis on naturalness and simplicity are present. Letitia Burwell, the author of the memoir, was a Southerner, writing of antebellum Virginia:

My mother's friends combined intelligence with exquisite refinement....

Italian and German professors being rare in that day, the musical requirements did not extend beyond the simplest piano accompaniments to old English and Scotch airs, which they sang in a sweet, natural voice, and which so enchanted the beaux of their time that the latter never afterward became reconciled to any higher order of music.[61]

Although these recollections, perhaps idealized by time and affection, still stand as testimony to the uses of musical accomplishment in simpler times, they nevertheless contrast sharply with the new and more educated lady musician of the 1840s and '50s. She makes her appearance in a short story that was published in a ladies' magazine[62]—"The Philosophy of a Ball-Room." It deals with the fate of one Julia Davenport, who has been mistakenly educated in the old-fashioned way—through private teachers rather than at the modern seminary. Her mother wrongly believed that Julia's level of accomplishments far surpassed those of other young women and that her debut at the ballroom would be a triumph. The outcome is foreshadowed by a description of Julia's woefully inadequate level of achievements: "she chattered French or rattled a waltz, never suspecting there could be a fault in either."

Julia is undone by the new type of accomplished musican. As mother and daughter enter the ballroom, they encounter their first surprise and witness

a masterly execution of one of Talberg's [*sic*] most difficult compositions by a young lady of Julia's age. Mrs. Davenport listened with amazement. She had looked upon Julia as an accomplished musican, but here was a degree of science and execution that neither she nor Julia had ever dreamed of.[63]

Yet, as she learns to her chagrin, the pianist was neither professional nor unique, but one of a half dozen young women who could play as well. Mrs. Davenport is slowly informed of the new level of amateur ability.

[she] ventured to ask whether there were *many* young ladies who played in that style, when her friend answered: "oh no: not more than half-a dozen certainly. Such musical talent is a rare gift; but in these days of high accomplishment no one plays in society, and indeed few attempt the acquirement, when they have not a decided natural gift for it. It is not as it was in our time, my dear Mrs. Davenport, when everybody learned and everybody played, and that playing "well enough for one's friends" is quite exploded.

One of the young ladies laughed and said, "it was paying your friends a poor compliment to think any music good enough for them!" And then there was a hush and a stir and another piece of music, during which Mrs. Davenport digested more new ideas than she had taken in since her widowhood.

Thus, the old generation, women brought up in the late-eighteenth or early-nineteenth century, were "guiltless" of classical music and learned just enough to "play for one's friends." They sang English and Scottish airs and played popular dance tunes and hymns. The new generation studied the music of European masters and sang airs from Italian opera. Their level of accomplishment was "high," as Mrs. Davenport's friends called it. By the 1850s the old style of fashionable education no longer passed for accomplishment in the upper-middle class. Although music journals continued to run articles criticizing the superficiality of female education, the model of the "tune-rattler" had been superseded by a more sophisticated musician, who relied in turn on a more discriminating audience.

Support for "high accomplishment" depended upon superior musical training which the best seminary was supposed to offer. The progressive aspect of seminary influence was that they secured an institutional basis for instrumental education for women before the Civil War. Many of them tempered the constricting notions of "femininity" that were to be found in prescriptive literature by raising the level of musical education that could be tolerated as accomplishment without threatening the conventions of female "sphere." By teaching theory and composition, and by raising standards for performance, seminaries widened the options for musical women. Oramel Whittlesey and his colleagues did not suggest that his pupils become concert artists, but they did believe that women could be trained as practical musicians and teachers. In due course, improved music education inevitably led to the inclusion of composition as a possibility. No wonder so many women composers, as we shall see, wrote music suitable for this milieu. It was a world that they knew—and one whose taste and standards were within reach.

5

Humble Beginnings, 1790 to 1825

In the late-eighteenth and early-nineteenth centuries, women who published music in this country were exceptional. From the repertory of secular music before 1825 totalling about 6,800 works,[1] only 70 secular pieces—58 songs and 12 keyboard pieces—are attributed to women. In the sacred music repertory, estimated at about 7,200 titles before 1810,[2] there are no published works attributed to women.[3] Writing a piece of music for commercial publication was an unusual, perhaps even extraordinary act for a woman in early America.

Yet before the end of the eighteenth century, works by women (American and European) began to appear in print. The earliest known piece is the song "Graceful Move," by the Italian singer Caterina Galli. It appeared in the *Philadelphia Songster* of 1789.[4] The earliest known work attributed to a native woman are the two songs by a "Lady of Philadelphia"—"The Cheerful Spring Begins Today" and "Asteria's Fields" from 1793.[5] About 10 years later, Grace Richards, a composer about whom nothing is known, wrote "Orphan Nosegay Girl,"[6] and thus became the first American woman to identify herself as a composer in print.

Music by women composers appears at much the same time as secular music began to be published in significant quantity in the United States. Indeed, the main difference between men and women as classes of composers, apart from the numbers, is that the important indigenous style of the singing school seems to have passed women by. In sects such as the Shakers and the Pietists, based on different social ideologies than classic New England Protestantism, women composers did take their place within the artistic community.[7] But in New England, although women undoubtedly composed tunes or hymn settings that remain in manuscript, few asserted a public religious artistic identity, perhaps because their role in church life was more circumscribed.

The Puritans had questioned whether women should even sing in church—the subject of a famous sermon by the seventeeth-century minister, John Cotton.[8] The more conservative Protestant churches to which most women belonged in the colonial period did not allow them much active participation; the churches encouraged women to practice private devotions and teach religion to their children, but they could not become ministers or preach.[9] The earliest known hymn attributed to a woman appears among the repertory of Methodist church music in the South in the 1830s,[10] perhaps because Methodism was one religion in which "colonial womanhood successfully asserted itself" by taking part in the official activities of the institution.[11]

The absence of women in religious music makes their presence in secular music all the more significant, small though that was. Songs were by far their favored metier.

Vocal Music

A great proportion of songs from this repertory was written by English women, many of them actresses and singers, reflecting the dominant influence of English theatrical music during this period.[12] Among the more notable figures were Harriet Abrams ("Crazy Jane" and "A Smile and a Tear"), Georgiana Spencer Cavendish ("Sweet is the Vale"), Eliza Flower ("My Native Land Goodnight"), and Dorothea Bland Jordan. Cavendish's "Sweet is the Vale" was one of the most popular songs in American music printed before 1800, while Bland's "The Blue Bell of Scotland" has been called the "most popular Scotch song in the United States of all time."[13]

Mary Ann Pownall (1751-1796) is the outstanding presence in this group, her work alone accounting for more than half of the total. Known as Mrs. Wrighton in England, where she was famous as an actress and a singer in opera and at the pleasure gardens, Pownall came to America in 1792. She was perhaps the most accomplished female singer that American audiences had heard up to that time, at least according to some contemporary accounts. In her brief career here, ended by death from fever in Charleston, South Carolina, Pownall was extremely active in theater, opera, and concert entertainments in Boston, New York, and Philadelphia. She was a regular member of the Old American Theater Company and she often appeared in concerts arranged by James Hewitt, a well-known musican and her collaborator in the volume of *Six Songs for the Harpsichord or Piano Forte* (1794) to which Pownall contributed three. (She also wrote the text for Hewitt's popular song, "The Primrose Girl.")[14]

Pownall published eight songs during her years in America.[15] She generally composed them for her own performance either as part of her roles in comic opera or as contributions to concerts, at which she varied serious works from Handel oratorios, for example, with her own lighter material. Announcements from newspapers suggest the kinds of varied entertainments at which she sang her songs. In New York City, for example, a concert that was followed by a ball was given at the City Tavern in June 1793. Mrs. Pownall's role was described thus: "After the concert Mrs. Pownall will read the story of Old Edward taken from *The Man of Feeling.* In which will be introduced a song taken from the 'Poem of Lavinia' and composed by her." Another concert on August 29, 1794, was advertised as an "open-air concert" in the manner of Vauxhall Gardens. It was organized in part by Hewitt and she sang among other works "Advice to the Ladies" and "A Happy Rencontre."[16]

Pownall's songs display her intimate knowledge of both English popular song and classical music as well. The idioms of operatic ornamentation, the vocal assurance to sustain dramatic skips, the large ranges of her supple melodic lines are characteristic of her best work, exemplified in the "Scotch" piece "Jemmy of the Glen" (ex. 1) and in the plaintive "Lavinia" (ex. 2). In "Jemmy" the line spans a tenth within its opening two measures, and its first cadence is a flourish of sixteenth notes. Here the text is written in the first person and strikes an intimate tone even within the pastoral conventions of the poem. That is true for "Lavinia" as well, an extremely suave triple meter song. It is a strophic song with an extremely attractive and supple melody that ranges from d to a high a-flat. The verse shows Pownall's sensitivity to text, as the melody descends to the word "ground." The climb to the melodic climax of high a-flat coincides with the textual climax of "Lavinia's sweet smile." Trills, little melismas, and written-out ornaments (at "chorus") suggest the typically elegant yet controlled style of London's theatrical tradition.

Other British singer-composers from this period deserve some mention—either for their contributions to the mainstream popular repertory or to correct errors that have crept into the slight information that has been written about them. Harriet Abrams (1760-1825) ought to be acknowledged as the composer of a well-known version of "Crazy Jane." This piece, frequently listed among the most popular works of the period, was also set by the British composer John Davy. It seems likely, however, that contrary to popular opinion, the Abrams version was more successful. Her version, written in ca. 1800, can be found in later imprints in the early 1800s. The Board of Trade Catalogue, moreover, lists it in print through 1870.[17]

Eliza Flower's song "My Native Land" merits a comment because it was among the first works to be popularized by an American rather than a foreign-born singer. Mrs. French, a star pupil of Benjamin Carr, was the singer whose name graced a version of this piece in 1820. A later version of the same song, without vocal ornamentation appeared as well, geared for the amateurs at home rather than the concert stage.[18]

Although many women were active as performers, lyricists, and teachers during this period,[19] very few of them seem to have become composers. The most notable figures were usually foreign-born singers, and to much lesser extent instrumentalists. One of the earliest biographical dictionaries of music

JEMMY OF THE GLEN.

WORDS AND MUSIC BY MRS POWNALL.

too love-ly Jemmy   cou'd I behold him   once a-gain   But ah his   Mary

he'll   deceive   I ne'er shall see   the   Lad a-gain.

2

The Lasses all when I complain
Wi scornfull faunts my mis'ries shun
But ah had they beheld my Swain
Too sure, like me they'd been undone
Then do not blame an artless Maid
But pray ye ne'er my Jemmy ken
Or hear those Vows my heart betray'd
To sigh for Jemmy of the Glen.

    Bonny Jemmy &c.

3

If Fame he seek, 'mid hostile strife
Or Gayly gangs, fair Glasgows Pride
Some fatal Ball may end his life
Or City Dame become his wife
Or if on Tays green bourn he tread
Some Lord-ling's Child his heart may win
And far from me my Shepherd wed
I ne'er shall see the Lad again.

    Bonny Jemmy &c.

Ex. 2. Mary Ann Pownall, *Lavinia*

lists 10 women musicians active before 1824.[20] All but two were English (and in one case, German) singers, a few of them having an occasional song printed here by an American publisher. In studies of urban or regional musical life, women's names occasionally appear, although these were often individuals of local rather than national reputation.[21]

Of the nine women identified by full name on sheet music,[22] only three are known in any professional capacity: Angelica Martin, Sally Sully, and Mrs. Van Hagen, the latter by far the best known and a member of a prominent family of Boston musicians.[23]

We should not assume, however, that the others were all amateurs. Grace Richards, for example, known by only one song, "Orphan Nosegay Girl" (ex. 3), was a skilled composer familiar with the latest fashions in secular song. The lyric, written by Susanna Rowson (whose poems were set by many other composers, among them James Hewitt and Benjamin Carr), tells of a pathetic child, orphaned by the Revolutionary War, selling nosegays and roses, "each bud moistened by gratitude's tear." Such pathos is typical of American song at the turn of the century.[24]

Richard's suave melody is enlivened by an occasional dotted rhythm. The refrain reaches for the melodic climax at the appropriate word "pray," and relieves the otherwise syllabic setting with brief melismas. Richard's song was sufficiently forward-looking to be reprinted as sheet music 50 years later.[25]

The majority of women publishing songs in the United States were accomplished amateurs of a wide range of abilities. Certainly with the growth in secular music, the home and social circle proved a far more favorable environment for women with musical aspirations than did the singing school or the church. By 1825 there were a number of women publishing music anonymously, in keeping with the conventions of music as a feminine accomplishment. Etiquette frowned upon publicity for the individual woman and this held the potential for professional recognition in check. As a direct consequence, more than half the pieces written by women in the United States before 1830 were printed anonymously, with only an indication of class and/or locale (e.g., "A Lady from Philadelphia").

Curiously enough, there is one instance of an imprint attributed to a Lady that was in fact the work of a man. The piece in question is Benjamin Carr's popular "The Little Sailor Boy," with lyrics by Susanna Rowson. What lay behind the imprints issued as the work of a "Lady"[26] is hard to say. Anonymous publications by "gentlemen" composers were not unknown. On the other hand, they represent a far smaller proportion of the whole.[27] Perhaps this curiosity represents the greater prevalence of anonymous composition among women, the already crystalizing image of the female composer as the lady amateur, active in a private decorous world. Still, such instances (and this was not the only one) throw our assumptions about the other lady composers into

Ex. 3. Grace Richards, *Orphan Nosegay Girl*

ORPHAN NOSEGAY GIRL

The Words by

Mrs ROWSON.

composed by Grace Richards

BOSTON. Printed and sold by G Graupner, at his Musical Academy N? 6 Franklin
Street, Franklin Place; Piano Fortes for Sale, to Let, and tuned at the shortest Notice.

Andante.

Pray buy a Nosegay cry'd a sweet Child, an Orphan left wretchet and poor Here's Rosebuds &

Pinks and sweet Briar wild, and heaven will bless you thrice over   Then pray buy my roses indeed they're not

dear, each bud shall be moistened by gratitudes tear.

2

Hard hard is my Fate, my Father is dead,
He fell in the Nations Defence ;
Those friends who once courted our favour are fled,
And prov'd all their Friendship Pretence.
          Thn pray &c.

3

My Mother was by when my brave Father fell
The Bullet which robb'd him of Life,
Sunk deep in the Bosom which lov'd him so well
And murder'd the Health of his Wife.
          Then pray &c.

4

Do pray buy my Roses for hard is my Fate,
My Parents to Heaven are fled,
Bestow then a Trifle before 'tis too late,
My poor little Sisters want Bread.
          Then pray &c.

45

question. We can only take them at face value, perhaps with a bit of caution, until shown otherwise. Who can prove the identities of anonymous composers beyond doubt? One of the clichés of women's studies is that "anonymous was a woman" but in this case the "lady" turns out to be a man.

Keyboard Music

The instrumental repertory written by women before 1825 differs from song not only because there is far less of it, but also because it is indigenous rather than English-dominated (see table 4).[28] Most of the pieces were written in the 1820s, with all but three works coming from that decade, so that there is about a one-generational difference between the appearance of instrumental as opposed to vocal works by women composers. In fact, not until the 1850s does any sizeable repertory of instrumental music appear.

Table 4.   Keyboard Music by Women Composers before 1830

1. Elizabeth Van Hagen, Variations on "The Country Maid" or "L'Amour est un enfant trompeur" ca. 180-.
2. Lady of Charleston, S.C. "March, composed and dedicated to the U.S. Marine Corps," Philadelphia: G.E. Blake (1814-1815).
3. Marthesie Demillière, "Malbrook with four variations" (New York: Mr. Demillière, n.d., ca. 1812-1818).
4. Catherine Bauer, "A Favorite Waltz. With 12 variations for the pianoforte," Philadelphia: G.E. Blake (1814-1817).
5. A Lady of Baltimore, "Spanish Rondo" (Baltimore: C. Wollig, 1824).
6. _____, "The Titus March" (Baltimore: John Cole, 1824).
7. _____, "The Titus Waltz" (Baltimore: John Cole, ca. 1824).
8. A Young Lady. "LaFayette's Welcome to Philadelphia." A new march with variations. (Philadelphia: G.E. Blake, 1824).
9. A Young Lady. "Lafayette's Grand March." (Philadelphia: J.G. Klemm, [ca. 1824]).
10. Caroline Clark, "Lafayette's March" (Boston, 1824).
11. A Lady, "Colonel Wm. Stewart's March and Quickstep" (Baltimore: John Cole, 1824).
12. A Lady. "Oft in a Stilly Night with Variations" (Philadelphia, Geo. Willig, 1827).

This repertory is modest indeed. There are no sonatas or battle pieces like Kotzwara's "The Battle of Prague" or James Hewitt's "The Battle of Trenton." Short dance forms predominant. There are, for example, three marches written in honor of Lafayette's visit to America in 1824. Caroline Clark's "Lafayette's March" was written for the Boston Independent Cadets and performed by them at the review in honor of Lafayette on August 30, 1824.

The most ambitious works are sets of variations, with three of them published before 1825. The first instrumental work written by a woman is one of these sets. In the early 1800s (before 1809/10) Mrs. Van Hagen published keyboard variations on "The Country Maid" or "L'Amour est un enfant trompeur." Joanetta Catherine Elizabeth Van Hagen was a member of one of the leading musical families active in both New York and Boston. She was an organist, pianist, and teacher; frequently she participated as a harpsichordist or pianist in public concerts.

The record of her professional career begins in 1792, with an advertisement for a concert in New York City:

> Mrs. Van Hagen, lately from Amsterdam, will perform concertos, sonatas and accompaniments on the piano forte.[29]

Two months later she announced herself as a teacher of the theory and practice of music on the harpsichord and piano.

In the late 1790s we find Mrs. Van Hagen teaching music in Salem and Boston, including a stint at Mrs. Rowson's Academy, one of the leading private girls' schools of the period.[30]

Three keyboard works, all written by anonymous ladies, deserve special mention: the "United States Marine March" by a lady of Charleston, S.C.; the "Titus March," by a lady of Baltimore, and a set of variations on Thomas Moore's song "Oft in the Stilly Night" by a Lady. Unlike most of the music written by women before 1825, these works survived throughout the nineteenth century. The marches, in fact, did more than endure: they became conventional pieces that publishers routinely printed as amateur keyboard music. In the *Complete Catalogue* no less than 13 different publishers issued editions of these marches.[31] Both pieces were listed as anonymous works, the old attribution to "a lady" having been dropped. One reason so many publishers could print these works is that they were in public domain, having been published without copyright.[32] Still, many other works fell into that category, and of all the marches listed in this catalogue, these two works are in the catalogues of more publishers than any others.

Not surprisingly, the marches appeared in anthologies as well. The "United States Marine March" is in *The Welcome Guest,*[33] a collection intended "to meet the wants of the majority of piano-players as a book of Home Amusements," and in the *Instrumental Preceptor* of 1816.[34] The "Titus March" is in *The Parlor Companion* of 1850,[35] on the same page as the "College Hornpipe," an old Irish fiddle tune. These anthologies assembled popular tunes that doubled as teaching pieces as well.

The set of variations on Thomas Moore's "Oft in a Stilly Night" (ex. 4) was not quite as popular as the marches, but by 1870 it was in the catalogues of four publishers.[36] It is a charming work, and the last variation, with its play on major and minor harmonies, is especially inventive. An opening theme accompanied by nothing but octaves, variations that begin on six-four chords and a whimsical rather than bravura statement of the tune at the close of the work, are gestures that suggest a folkish rather than academic approach to composition.

Ex. 4.   A Lady, *Oft in the Stilly Night with Variations for the Piano Forte*

Ex. 4, continued

OFT IN A STILLY NIGHT VAR.

OFT IN A STILLY NIGHT VAR.

Ex. 4, continued

OFT IN A STILLY VAR.

With instrumental music, as with vocal music, the range of women's compositions is narrower than that composed by men. Women typically wrote parlor dances rather than virtuoso pieces or sonatas. Almost all of the keyboard works were written by amateurs or perhaps semiprofessional composers and none are difficult. Rather than comparing these pieces to sonatas or variation sets written by, say, Alexander Reinagle, a leading composer of the period, we might profit from a comparative perspective in which we juxtapose them to other artifacts of female "accomplishments," such as needlework samplers and painting. Indeed, the unsophisticated techniques and naive charm of some of these pieces suggest their early kinship to American popular crafts rather than to cultivated serious music.

6

A Woman Composer's Place is in the Parlor: New Trends in Mid-Century

At the beginning of the nineteenth century, composition in the United States was almost exclusively the creative monopoly of men rather than women. Most of the women publishing music before 1830 in America were anonymous "ladies." Yet by the end of the century women were composing symphonies, operas, and chamber music. The mid decades, from about 1830 to 1870, bridge these two extremes of achievement, spanning the distance between music proscribed by feminine accomplishment and music legitimized as art. Perhaps then the best way to describe the cultural climate of the period is as transition, a period in which a number of factors served as catalysts for change, and old beliefs about music as feminine accomplishment were modified to accommodate newer generations of better trained, more ambitious female musicians.

Although it is impossible to account for all pieces written by women during this period, the evidence suggests that the repertory is far richer than the few works before 1825. Quantity increased, but even more important, a fair number of works were demonstrably popular, particularly after 1840.[1] Some of these, to mention only a few titles, were Marion Dix Sullivan's "The Blue Juniata," Penelope Smith's "A Place in Thy Memory Dearest," Faustina Hodges's "Dreams," and Julliet Bellchambers's "The Spell is Broken."

In contrast to the decades before 1825, when the few notable works were composed by anonymous ladies, women composers become "visible" after 1830. However fragmented and incomplete the records of their activities may be, by the mid-nineteenth century a few women are active on the national musical scene, acknowledged as composers by their contemporaries. This is a great change. The most prominent were Marion Dix Sullivan, Mrs. E.A. (Susan) Parkhurst, Augusta Browne, Faustina Hodges, and Jane Sloman.[2] Other professional female composers include members of singing families such as Abby Hutchinson,[3] Sophia Baker,[4] and Julia Daly, an actress associated with Wood's Minstels.[5]

A few were singers active locally; they include Anne Pearman, whose "I'll Think of Thee" (1829) is inscribed as "A Ballad sung by Mrs. Pearman"; Ella Wren (later Nesbit), a Southern musician active in the 1860s;[6] Anna Ablamovicz from Louisville, Kentucky,[7] and Elizabeth Higgins from Chicago.[8]

Others were music teachers, for on the whole, teaching was one of the few occupations open to women during this period. Like their male colleagues, they wrote music for their pupils. Among them are Frances Thomas, whose "Silver Lake Quickstep" (1850) was "dedicated to the ladies of the Charleston Female Academy: Mrs. Townshend Stith, Julie Pettigrew, and a Miss Jackson."[9]

All these women were vanguard figures in that their music making extended beyond the home. It would be misleading to suggest, on the strength of these names, that professional female musician-composers were typical. They were not. They were outnumbered by countless numbers of women who took up composition as an extension of musical accomplishment; by the 1850s writing music had become a widespread and accepted activity for the accomplished female musician. Many women seem to have published one or two works and no more; whether they were professional, semiprofessional, or amateurs is difficult to determine.

Composer Attributions and the Custom of Anonymity

Publishing music was an act that brought women into the public eye. Victorian-American mores did not encourage such self-assertion and the conflict between the two roles of private lady and public composer is reflected in the variety and types of composer attributions found on music by early American women composers. Anonymous publication, for example—a pattern set earlier in the century—declines, but by no means disappears. We still find works by a Lady or, for example, a Lady from Virginia.[10] The height of such reticence may have been reached by a composer who called herself a "Veiled Lady" and wrote the "No-name Waltz" dedicated to the "Woman in White."[11] As late as 1870 the *Complete Catalogue* listed works by a Lady, though no anonymous gentlemen composers are to be found.[12]

Some of the pieces by Ladies were quite well known. Among them are "Thou Hast Wounded the Spirit that Loved Thee" (1846) and "God Will Defend the Right," a confederate ballad (1861). Another is "My Hopes Have Departed Forever" (New York: Firth, Pond & Co., 1851); it was published as composed by a Lady, but its royalties were paid to none other than Stephen Foster. This curious incident has never been satisfactorily explained. According to John Tasker Howard, it was not an original composition, but a tune Foster became familiar with in the 1830s.[13] In fact, the melody is an adaptation of "The Valley Lay Smiling Before Me" from Thomas Moore's

Irish Melodies,[14] and Foster seems to have adopted the pseudonym of a Lady to publish his arrangement of an old tune. Whether this song was originally known to be the work of a Lady in the 1830s is impossible to say. Perhaps Foster used the pseudonym of a Lady rather than a gentleman because the convention of anonymous female publication was more widely accepted by this time.

A variation on anonymous publication is the convention of publishing music under a first name only. We find pieces by Mary, Adeline, and Nita, to name a few. Mary published music over a 15-year span, yet never used a last name.[15] No male counterpart to this convention has surfaced. American women may have been following the example of British women composers who also published under single names (for example, Claribel and Dolores).[16]

As for pseudonyms, no examples of women adopting male pen names to publish music before 1870 have been located to date. In fact, a contrary practice can be documented. Members of the Winner family, among them Joseph and Septimus, adopted female pseudonyms to publish parlor music.[17]

Occasionally, initials plus a surname are encountered. Marion Dix Sullivan, for example, sometimes published music as M.D. Sullivan. Most women used Miss or Mrs., initials, and a surname, e.g., Mrs. S.R. Burtis. Rare were the women composers who used both their first and last names on a work.

The variety of composer attributions captures the ambiguities of propriety for early American women composers. Anonymity and the variations on it were designed not to foil discrimination or insure impartial judgment but to check any accusations that the individual was seeking notoriety or publicity. The appearance of modesty and humility mattered a great deal, and Victorian women were adept at glib deceptions. One is reminded of Sarah Hale's advice to the lady performer:

> If you intend to sing, accept at once. Do not hurry up to the piano, as if glad of an opportunity to show off, but go gently. If by request, you have brought your music, leave it downstairs; it can be sent for.[18]

Expectations for the lady composer conformed to the central axiom of accomplishment—that music must serve their feminine role. The women composer was described as "the fair composer," a term that was conventional in the period.[19] The stereotype of "fair composers" was one of amateurs, trained to be accomplished rather than scientific and almost always self-taught. This was occasionally the case. Marion Dix Sullivan, for example, almost always found a collaborator to harmonize the tunes she created.[20] Other examples of collaborative efforts are Adeline's "Why Ask Me Now to Share With Thee" (1845), arranged for harp by Samuel Carusi, and "Tread Lightly, Ye Comrades" (1861), its melody suggested by Miss Sadie Crane and the arrangement by Mrs. F.L. Bowen."[21]

Critics tended to treat female composers deferentially, since they judged them as amateurs. Augusta Browne's technical faults were excused as "those of a writer whose style has not been strictly cultivated nor her errors corrected by example."[22] A review of Mary Dana's *The Southern Harp* (Boston, 1841) also illustrates critical chivalry. Dana had taken great care in her introduction to justify her public authorship and in a long poem recounting the terrible deaths of her entire family, she confessed that "twas sorrow made me write these plaintive lays." The critic of *The New World* took note:

> This is an unassuming and interesting little volume. However much we might have felt inclined to cavil at...certain sins of commission against the grammar of music, the simple and pathetic Introduction by the talented authoress completely disarmed us.[23]

The tolerance for composition written according to standards of female accomplishment rather than art had a double edge. While it assured some mid-nineteenth-century women of critical generosity, it sanctioned amateurism as an expected characteristic of their work. An article by Charles Grobe illustrates a prevailing stereotype built on this double standard. His portrait of a not-so-humble student suggests that the image of the lady composer as fashionable dilletante exploiting music for social status had crystallized by the 1860s. He entitled it "Musical Miseries":

> You are giving lessons to a young lady, who as her mother informs you, has a "decided turn" for composition. You have never yet perceived any indication of this "turn" but some morning you receive a letter enclosing the melody of two ballads, which your pupil requests that you have the kindness to "look over, and arrange with symphonies and accompaniments." The first is called, "I met her at the flower show"; the second has no particular title, but is one of those peculiar fashionable effusions, which are usually illustrated with a portrait of Miss A B D as the case may be, and in which some gentleman is desperately in love with a young lady's dress and ornaments. It commences—
> "She wore a gem of dazzling light
> upon her snow-white brow;"
> and then goes on to describe sundry bracelets, wreaths and scarfs; leaving not a shadow of doubt upon the mind that the amorous youth has an eye to wardrobe and jewelry. The music of these ballads is utterly incomprehensible. In vain you sing them over and over, to endeavor something like rhythm. At length, tired of speculating upon the subject, you call upon the composer, and request her to play them to you. To your surprise, she plays them in a totally different manner; and you now find that she can imagine an air, but has not the slightest notion how to write it down. You suggest a few lessons on this important point. She declares that it would ruin her natural genius, and that she does not "profess to be a professional musician."[24]

All of this may sound like familiar grumblings of a dissatisfied teacher, but the content is not quite so innocuous. The notion that women were supposed to have a special gift for melody and that they could (or would) not learn theory and "scientific" music is part of the stereotype of the woman composer that appears in the late-nineteenth and twentieth centuries.

Catalysts for Change

Victorian Models

One important catalyst in liberalizing the creative climate was an import from abroad—the music of English women composers, who, as in the previous decades, were prolific and influential contributors to the home-song repertory.[25] Their works were perceived as examples of "female genius" and they were held up to American women as models for their own efforts. English women, moreover, gave ballad writing a special kind of social aura, with titled ladies like Lady Carew and Lady Dufferin giving the genre a sense of class.

One can gain a quick impression of this repertory from an anthology of sheet music from the end of the period, *Lyric Sparks. A Collection of Songs and Ballads* (New Orleans: A.E. Blackmar, 1869-70). It includes a number of works by the most popular English writers, among them "Juanita," by Caroline Norton; "The Brook" by Dolores (Ellen Dickson); "The Bridge" by Miss Lindsay, also known as Lady Carew; "Thy Name was Once a Magic Spell" by Augusta Cowell; "I Remember How My Childhood Fleeted By" by Mrs. E.F. Fitzgerald; and "Bye Gone Hours" by Mrs. Price Blackwood (Lady Dufferin). Other well-known composers not represented here include "Mrs. Heman's Sister" or Harriet Mary Browne, "Claribel" (Charlotte Allington Barnard), and Virginia Gabriel, to name the most important.[26]

Two composers from this group can serve as examples of style and influence. The first, Harriet Mary Browne, is a somewhat obscure figure. The fame of her sister, the poet Felicia Hemans, who has received considerable attention from American cultural historians, eclipsed her reputation in her own lifetime,[27] and the popularity of her settings has gone unacknowledged.[28] In the United States her compositions have been incorrectly attributed to Augusta Browne, because the sheet music never included her first name.[29] Yet a number of Harriet Browne's settings, written in the late 1820s and early '30s, were extremely popular throughout the nineteenth century. In her panegyric on these songs, the educator Almira Phelps explained their particular importance for women:

> While speaking on the subject of vocal music, I cannot but deprecate the improper character of most of the popular songs of the day. Young ladies are often heard to express in singing, sentiments that they would blush to utter in conversation; or if there is nothing absolutely wrong in the thought, the words set to fashionable music are usually without sentiment or moral. The beautiful and chaste songs of Mrs. Hemans are a noble exception; every thing that comes from her pen is pure, and bears the image and superscription of an elevated and

chastened mind. The plaintive and thrilling air of her "Bring Flowers," the spirit stirring "Pilgrim Fathers," and the wail of the "Captive Knight" are only equalled by some of the noble efforts of Heber.[30]

We can add to the list some additional titles: "The Messenger Bird" (1833), "The Tyrolese Evening Hymn" (1828), and "Evening Song to the Virgin" (1833), all standards of parlor music found in innumerable collections.[31]

"The Messenger Bird" by Harriet Mary Browne (ex. 5) is a good example of the Hemans-Browne style. The poet's intent was to construct a quasi-dramatic narrative of a spiritual quest for comforting; the messages the bird relays come from the afterworld, and the question that it is asked by the speakers is whether friends who have died can still love those back on earth: "Can those who have loved forget?" "Oh say do they love us yet?" "Oh say do they love us still?" The bird never answers but the implication is that love endures. Browne faithfully depicts the text by highlighting the questions in a gentle yet effective way: lengthy fermatas at the end of questions and frequent melodic repetitions substitute for a rhetorical or dramatic declamation. Each question gets asked three or four times. Nothing interrupts the placid tunefulness of the song, and even the "molto espressivo" section at "but tell us" is harmonized entirely through major chords. One nice touch is the absence of accompaniment to indicate the silence of the dead at "and they answer not again." Twenty years after its original publication, the ballad was still popular enough to produce two answer songs, both written by American women composers: Caroline Dole's "Answer to the Messenger Bird" (1848) and Augusta Browne's "Reply to the Messenger Bird" (1848). Dole's recalled the music as well as the text.

Unlike Harriet Browne, our second Victorian musician, Caroline Norton (1808-77), was known in her own right as both songwriter and composer. Her reputation did not quite equal that of Mrs. Hemans, but to Sarah Hale, the editor of *Godey's Lady's Book,* she stood

> ...at the head of the living Women of Genius who now make England distinguished as the favored country in Europe for the development of the virtues, the talents, and the true graces of womanhood.
> ...Even the most impassioned passages of her poems are characterized by a sweet feminine delicacy and purity of tone.[32]

Both Lady Norton and her sister, Lady Dufferin, who also wrote music,[33] learned to sing and play the harp and piano. Neither had any serious training in composition. Most of Norton's songs were written in the 1830s, but they remained popular for many decades, particularly in the South.[34] Her most famous works include "Fairy Bells" (1839), "The Officer's Funeral," "Bye-gone Hours," "O Take Me Back to Switzerland," and especially the lovely duet "Juanita."[35]

Ex. 5.   Harriet Mary Browne, *The Messenger Bird*

THE MESSENGER BIRD.

Espressivo.

Thou art come from the spirit's   land, thou bird! Thou art come from the spirit's   land!   Thro' the

Thou art come from the spirit's   land, thou bird! Thou art come from the spirit's   land!   Thro' the

dark pine grove let thy voice be heard, And tell   of the shadowy band!   tell   of the shadowy band!

dark pine grove let thy voice be heard, And tell   of the shadowy band!   tell   of the shadowy band!

901

Ex. 5, continued

We know that the bow'rs are green and fair In the light of that summer shore, And we

We know that the bow'rs are green and fair In the light of that summer shore, And we

know that the friends we have lost are there, They are there _ They are there _ And they weep no more!

know that the friends we have lost are there. They are there _ And they weep no more!

Ex. 5, continued

"Juanita" (ex. 6) is perhaps her best-known song. Norton's poetic virtues, as defined by Sarah Hale, have their musical parallels in this duet: "purity of tone" and "sweet feminine delicacy" easily translate into a limpid vocal line formed by two-bar phrases, separated regularly by rests. Note how even the first word "soft" is followed by a moment for a breath. Figuration reinforces the triple meter through triplets. Only at the climax of the song: "Nita, Juanita..." is the flow broken for a small change in the accompaniment pattern.

"Fairy Bells" (ex. 7) on the other hand, is somewhat more complicated and in fact more typical of the Victorian ballad that was imitated in the United States. The phrases are longer and the melody is sprinkled with ornaments. Typical also is the potential moment for a cadenza in the penultimate line. Here the figurations in the keyboard change from moment to moment and have little rhythmic continuity: one can imagine how the meter might have been distorted in performance because of this. Occasional touches to pictorialism justify some of the changes; the echo of the bells, for example, is depicted in the vocal line "Merrily, merrily, merrily it fell"; the flow of the water at "came tinkling o'er the water" is also suggested by arpeggios in the accompaniment. Note also the elaborate keyboard postlude.

Ladies' Magazines

A second catalyst for change were the new outlets for women's music that were offered by mid-century ladies' magazines. These publications multiplied in great profusion between 1830 and 1860, and they catered specifically to the market of fashionable ladies and domestic culture.[36] *Godey's Lady's Book* and the *Ladies' Companion* began the trend in the 1830s, and by 1850 more than 100 magazines aimed at women had appeared.[37] Many of these magazines routinely printed music, along with fashion plates, lithograph reproductions of popular art, and embroidery patterns. Their titles are indicators of music's status as an ornament or accomplishment, for it was described as an "embellishment." The *Ladies' Companion,* for example, described itself as a monthly magazine *Embracing Every Department of Literature, Embellished with Original Engravings and Music Arranged for the Piano Forte Harp and Guitar.* It was only one of several publications located to date that printed music as a regular feature.[38]

A brief survey from several such periodicals can suggest their scope and relevance. For one thing, some disseminated music by English female composers such as Caroline Norton.[39] Works were also commissioned: *Godey's Lady's Book,* for example, printed "The Gondola Waltz" by a "Lady of Georgia, composed expressly for the magazine."[40] A *Godey's* "Lady's Book Polka" appeared in 1852 and remained in print as sheet music in 1870.[41]

Ex. 6.   Caroline Norton, *Juanita*

JUANITA.

THE POETRY BY

THE HON. MRS NORTON.

Ask thy soul if we should part? Ni _ ta! Jua _ ni _ ta!
Let me lin _ _ ger by thy side! Ni _ ta Jua _ ni _ ta

Ask thy soul if we should part? Ni _ ta! Ni _ ta!
Let me lin _ ger by thy side! Ni _ ta Ni _ ta

p

tenderly. *slentando.*

Lean thou on my heart.
Be my own fair bride!

Lean thou on my heart.
Be my own fair bride!

mf a Tempo.

Juanita (Duet.)

Ex. 7.   Caroline Norton, *Fairy Bells*

I earth's happiest son,   And thou her love-liest daughter, While fai-ry

bells   came tink-ling o'er the   water,   Merrily, merrily, merrily it fell,

Merrily, merrily, merrily it fell, The echo of   that   fai-ry   bell.

1435

Ex. 7,   continued

Now when I'm musing sad and lone-ly.   With but my harp and thy remembrance on - - -

- -ly,   In vain as o'er those chords I bend, One joyful note I try to send, For sad, sad

sad and chang'd, Sad, sad and chang'd they seem, The fairy bells of   that dear dream.

8 va.

loco

pp

1435

Ladies' magazines provided outlets for both the professional composer and the accomplished amateur. We find works by anonymous "ladies",[42] single-name composers;[43] unknowns, with only one or two pieces to their credit;[44] and others whose works also appeared as sheet music.[45] The editorial policy was to convince women to identify with the magazine, and their practice of encouraging women writers had a smaller but nevertheless significant parallel with women composers. The editorship of at least one magazine apparently decided to favor women composers over men. This journal was the *Columbian Lady's and Gentlemen's Magazine*. Out of the 55 songs it published in its four-year run, a remarkable 47 were by women. Among the composers who contributed to the *Columbian* were Elizabeth and Anne Sloman (English singers who had come to America in the early 1840s),[46] Augusta Browne,[47] and Mrs. C.L. Hull.[48] The style of the music in the ladies' magazines concentrated on sentiment. The songs are typically set to lugubrious texts; no dialect songs are to be found. Instead, ornamental melodies and decorative gestures abound.[49]

Ladies' magazines represent the commercialization of musical accomplishment in composition within a feminine subculture.[50] Just as female seminaries provided a milieu for amateurs to perform in entertainments, ladies' magazines offered women composers the opportunity to publish music within a circumscribed female market. They did not have to compete directly with men to get their music published.

Both ladies' magazines and the popularity of music by English women composers helped create a more congenial climate for American women. As the definition of accomplishment broadened to include composition, these two factors increased the likelihood that more American female musicians would take up the craft. Still, links to past traditions were maintained through the connection of music with upper-class gentility and the connotations of music as a fashionable commodity. This mixture of old and new was an inevitable part of the transition that characterized the mid-nineteenth century. Women composers did not move directly from being lady amateurs in the early-nineteenth century to artists at its end without passing through an intermediary stage in which their identities as both woman and composer were in flux. What was shaped during these decades was a woman's place in composition—a "sphere of influence" to use a mid-nineteenth-century phrase—that remained intact until almost the close of the century.

A "Sphere of Influence" for the Woman Composer

This sphere was the parlor—as opposed to either the minstrel hall, the church, or the concert stage—and its musical counterparts were the parlor song and ballad and the keyboard dance. Opera, orchestral music, and chamber music were allegedly beyond them until the 1880s. Even within the genre of solo song there were restrictions. Dialect songs and minstrel music were considered too crude and vulgar for accomplished ladies; besides, women were excluded from the minstrel stage until the 1860s,[51] so that the natural connection between composer and performer was severed from the start. Only in the late 1850s, when sentimental songs were introduced into minstrel shows,[52] do we find women composers—but only a few. A statement made by the critic Henry Tuckerman about female poetry serves as an accurate guide to parlor song. "Men," he wrote, "do not expect extensive knowledge and active logical powers from a female poet. They do expect to feel the influence and power of the affections."[53]

The affections (or emotions) most suitable for a female composer as for a female poet were love, piety, and friendship, most often tinged with melancholy. The most typical kind of piece she composed after 1830 was a sentimental ballad or parlor song, with texts often written by the composer or taken from a contemporary domestic poet such as Lydia Sigourney, Caroline Norton, or Anne Stephens.

Of course, both men and women composed sentimental parlor songs. But again the issue is one of proportion. This genre assumes far greater importance to women because it is the first one in which they made their mark as composers and because it dominates their work for the entire century. It was an ideal medium to reconcile the ambiguities in and marginality of the woman composer's status, for no one could cast aspersions on the womanly quality of such themes as the death of a beloved, or going to the spirit land, or longing for a friend. In this respect the sentimental ballad "opened wide the doors to woman . . . as poet and composer."[54]

Love songs in particular, which after 1840 were characterized by emotional intensity,[55] attracted them. "Oh! Must We Part to Meet No More" by Laura Hewitt (1851), "I Cannot Sing Tonight" by Mrs. L.L. Deming (1854), and "The Forsaken" by Mrs. William Disbrow (1848) are titles of well-known works whose theme was unrequited love.

Perhaps the main difference in texts chosen or written by women composers is in the point of view. In contrast to the majority of texts for love songs in which the "I" is a male,[56] many women composers wrote from a female point of view suggesting the personalistic nature of their compositions. Frequently the narrator sings about her broken heart, as in Mrs. L.L. Deming's "I Cannot Sing Tonight":

> I cannot sing that song tonight
> For its words and music dwell
> While all hearts seem gay and light
> To me a sad and fearful spell.

> For this the song I used to sing
> For him when all was hope and truth
> Before I knew that time would fling
> One shadow oer my happy youth

Julliet Bellchambers's "The Spell is Broken" shared similar feelings:

> I thought he loved, I was deceived
> Oh would that we had never met!

Both of these songs were written for female singers. In contrast to the idealized heroines that are so common in the works of contemporary male composers, such as Stephen Foster, no corresponding pattern is to be found in the works of women composers. Occasionally they adopted the convention of the idealized woman but did not write or choose texts about a male counterpart. The lover appears most often as a wrong-doer and an agent of distress allowing a woman to vent a range of emotions from anger to self-pity.

Another theme shared by women composers is the celebration of friendship between two women. One example is "Mary, Dear Mary" (1852), a ballad sung by Madame Antoinette Otto, with both words and music by Mrs. A.R. Luyster. The song was dedicated to Miss Mary A. Underwood of Boston and may have been intended as a personal tribute to a friend who was perhaps moving away:

> Mary, dear Mary, in spirit I see thee
> In spirit I hear both thy song and thy voice
> But swift as a meteor the vision flies from me,
> And leaves me exclaiming, dear Mary is gone.
>
> Years may elapse ere in friendship we greet again,
> And oh! in the future what changes may be,
> But long will the days spent together remain,
> As fresh in our hearts as when gladdened by thee;
>
> Then Mary, dear Mary, mid life's varied shadows,
> Forget not the friend who would shield thee from ills,
> Who would welcome thee more in an hour of sorrow
> Than when fortune wreathed thee in sunniest smiles.

Mrs. Townshend Stith's ballad, "Our Friendship" (ex. 8) may have a similar theme, although the two parties involved are not explicitly defined. The poem concerns a friendship that has "died in beauty like the night." It is easy to assume that this song was written about the friendship between a man and a woman and is in the unrequited love tradition. But that may not have been the case. Intense friendships between nineteenth-century women were often expressed in highly emotional terms;[57] perhaps music served as one of many outlets for those friendships. Although the values of accomplishment consistently stressed the role of music in courtship and male-female relationships, girls had the experience of making music together at school. We know from diaries and letters for the period that women met in social circles to sing and dance together.[58] Composing songs about friends or to sing with friends is an extension of such social custom. Harriet Hopkins's song "Madgie to Minnie"[59] is one such example. Hopkins wrote the song as a duet for her friend Miss Thompson and herself to sing while they were both at Oxford Female College in Ohio. The song is about a young woman grieving over the death of her sister.

A Cultivated Style to Suit Musical Accomplishment

The most significant characteristic that sets music by women composers apart from the total body of concert-household repertory is the preference for the cultivated ballad. If we plot the development of American popular music between 1830 and 1870 as a movement away from English domination to an indigenous American style,[60] then the work of women composers goes against this trend. Consistently the standard songs written by women reflect the influence of English songs or Italian opera both in gesture and spirit. Accomplishment meant "vocal culture," to resonate of the European salon not the Ethiopian minstrel hall.

Most of these pieces are intended for female singers. Either the text is written from a female "I" or the vocal range is for a soprano. Probably the amateur or semiprofessional composer performed them in the parlors of friends and family. Some, however, were written by actress-singers who performed them in concert, like Julia Daly and Ella Wren.[61] Faustina Hodges's two ballads, "Dreams" and "The Rose Bush," were also sung by professional singers.

Characteristics of these cultivated ballads include a reasonably high level of vocal sophistication and elaborate piano parts that demand accompaniment by a second person instead of self-accompaniments by the singer. Melodies are often decorated with operatic gestures such as occasional ornamentation and miniature cadenzas, or climactic leaps to a sustained high note.

A number of cultivated quasi-operatic parlor songs became standards in the literature. One of the earliest is Mrs. Townshend Stith's "Our Friendship."[62] It appeared both as sheet music and in *Godey's Lady's Book* in 1830.[63] In 1868 it was included in a series called *Gems of Our Time*. It is a parlor aria in a modified *da capo* form in a loose *bel canto* style. The text, written by the composer, is built on a single conceit: the death of a friendship, referred to only as "it" in the song, without much explanation of how, why, or between which parties "its" demise has occurred. An inferior text is graced by a competent and suave melody (ex. 8).

Ex. 8.   Mrs. Townshend Stith, *Our Friendship*

Ex. 8, continued

2

It died in beauty, like a rose blown from its pa – rent stem; It died in beauty like a pearl drop'd – – from some di – – – – a – dem, It died in beauty like a lay, A – long a moon lit – lake; It died in beau – ty like the

"Our Friendship."

"Our Friendship".

"The Spell is Broken" (ex. 9) by Julliet Bellchambers was another great favorite. Published in 1842, it was in print in 1870 and sufficiently successful to warrant both an "Answer to 'Spell is Broken'" by the composer, a simplified arrangement of the original piece by L.T.H., and arrangement as a trio by James G. Maeder.[64] "The Spell is Broken" is a classic example of cultivated taste. Written in simplifed imitation of *bel canto* melody, it is a passionate and effective work, unusually intense for a popular song. One rhythmic pattern serves for all stanzas but the last; occasional appoggiaturas, a chromatic moment marked "con affeto" at "we must part," the repetition of the crucial phrase, "the spell is broken" and the obligatory cadenza ground the piece in opera.

The *bel canto* elements in "Bird of Beauty" (ex. 10) by Miss M.B. Scott are less pronounced than in the Bellchambers ballad. There is no repeated refrain and the ornamentation in the last line is minimal. Note also that the rhythmic pattern of the vocal line of the two songs is virtually identical; this pattern had become one of the clichés of ballad style by the 1850s. The one notable feature of this emotionally bland piece is the depiction of the bird, who sings in vocalize in the second stanza, and whose song is foreshadowed in the piano introduction. This unremarkable little piece fared even better than "The Spell is Broken." It was a parlor classic in 1870 listed in the catalogues of ten publishers. Compilers of vocal classbooks adopted it and arranged it for duets and trios to suit their purposes.[65]

Moving Towards the Vernacular

Since women composers were traditionally cut off from the vernacular, the parlor as a symbol of creativity, a "room" in Virginia Woolf's sense of the term, is both open and closed space. Revival hymns, songs and choruses, and songs about topical rather than domestic subjects that appear more frequently after 1850 assume greater historical significance because of their rarity.

To be sure, before 1850 occasional pieces in more popular styles had appeared. Echoes of Thomas Moore's familiar adaptations of Irish airs can be heard in two highly popular works: Penelope Smith's "A Place in the Memory, Dearest" (ex. 11)[66] and a Lady's "Thou Hast Wounded the Spirit that Loved Thee" (ex. 12).[67] Here the compound time, the dotted rhythms, and the occasional melodic leap of an upward sixth recall Thomas Moore's adaptations of Irish tunes. "Thou Hast Wounded...," a suave and attractive song, might be compared to Moore's "Believe Me If All Those Endearing Young Charms," found in his *A Selection of Irish Airs.*[68]

One of the plainest pieces in the repertory is Abby Hutchinson's "Kind Words Can Never Die" (ex. 13). The didactic homilies of the text don't require much elaboration, and they are set to a childlike melody that outlines three

Ex. 9. Julliet Bellchambers, *The Spell is Broken*

Ex. 9, continued

THE SPELL IS BROKEN.

7161

Ex. 9, continued

thus am I, all hope is o'er   That hope so cherish'd in my heart; . . I

dare not wish to see him more, The spell is broken! we must part. The spell is

broken, we must part.   thought he loved I was de-ceived, Oh! would that we had never met! . . For

7161

Ex. 9, continued

BIRD OF BEAUTY.

SONG.

Words by ELLA of Woodlawn.   **Music by MISS M.B.SCOTT.**

Ex. 10, continued

I. Bird of beau-ty whose bright plu-mage Spar-kles with a thousand dyes,
II. Com'st thou to me in the si lence Of my snowcladhometo cheer,
III. Where the southern ro ses blos som By the prairie's spreading plain
IV. Wel - come for a leaf sweet wand'-rer Thou hast pluck'dand borne to me,

Soft thy notes and gay thy ca - rol, Tho' stern win-ter rules the skies,
Dost thou bear a mes sage to me, From the friends be lov'd and dear?
I have lis-ten'd to thy warb-ling, Charm ed by the ma-gic strain.
Bear ing words of joy and glad-ness Min - gled with sweet me-lo-dy.

Soft thy notes and gay thy ca - rol, Tho' stern win-ter rules the skies.
Dost thou bear a mes sage to me, From the friends be-lov'd and dear?
I have lis tend to thy warb-ling, Charm-ed by the ma - gic strain.
Bear - ing words of joy and glad-ness Min-gled with sweet me - lo - dy.

rall:

La,   la, la,la, la,la, la,la,la,la, la,   la!   La,   la, la,la,la,la, la!

La,   la, la, la, la, la, la, la,la, la,   la,   la!   La,la, la,la,la,la, la, la.

Ex. 11.   Miss Smith, *A Place in Thy Memory, Dearest*

2

Remember me not as a lover,
  Whose hope has been crost;
Whose bosom can never recover,
  The light it has lost:
As the young bride remembers the mother,
  She loves, tho' she never may see,
As a sister remembers a brother,
  So dearest remember me.

3

Could I be thy true lover, dearest,
  Could'st thou smile on me;
I would be the fondest and nearest,
  That ever lov'd thee:
But a cloud on my pathway is glooming,
  That never must burst upon thine,
And heaven that made thee all blooming,
  Ne'er made thee to wither on mine.

4

Remember me then, oh, remember,
  My calm light, love;
Tho' bleak as the blasts of November,
  My life may prove:
That life will tho' lonely be sweet,
  If its brightest enjoyment should be,
A smile, and kind word when we meet,
  And a place in thy memory.

Ex. 12.   A Lady, *Thou Hast Wounded the Spirit that Loved Thee*

Ex. 12, continued

834

Ex. 12, continued

ear‿li‿est pin‿ions to try, 'Round the nest will still lin‿ger‿ing

hover Ere its tremb‿ling wings can fly.

2

Thus we're taught in this cold world to smother

Each feeling that once was so dear;

Like that young bird I'll seek to discover

A home of affection elsewhere .

Tho' this heart may still cling to thee fondly ,

And dream of sweet memories past ,

Yet hope, like the rainbow of summer,

Gives a promise of Lethe at last.

Ex. 13.   Abby Hutchinson, *Kind Words Can Never Die*

BRIGHT THINGS CAN NEVER DIE.

The HUTCHINSON FAMILY.

Bright things can never die, E'en tho' they fade,

Beau_ty and minstrelsy Deathless were made; What tho' the summer day

Passes at Eve a...way, Doth not the moon's soft ray Sil...ver the night.

Ex. 13, continued

Kind words can never die,

Cherish'd and blest, God knows how deep they lie Stor'd in the breast;

Like Child..hood's sim..ple rhymes Said ..o'er a thou..sand times,

Age in all years and climes Dis..tant and near.

Ex. 13, continued

Child...hood can never die, Wrecks of the past,

Float o'er the mem.o..ry Bright to the last. Ma...ny a hap.py thing,

rall: *tempo.*

Ma......ny a dai...sy spring, Float o'er times cease.less wing,

Far far a...way.

p

G. Kirk, Engraver.

chords repetitiously. In contrast to the many political and topical ballads of her brothers, who were known as composers, Abby Hutchinson's song is "more than any of the other Hutchinson compositions, still sung today."[69]

By the 1850s the secular song and chorus had become the predominant form of American popular song. Hardly any women composers, however, seem to have adopted it. The very few women who are known to date to have composed in this genre were individuals who moved beyond this convention and whose work was occasionally used by professional singers. Hattie Livingston wrote one of the few songs by a woman to be described as an Ethiopian song called "Young Folks at Home" (1852) for Wood's Minstrel Troops.[70] It has no connection to the Foster song, "Old Folks at Home." A Miss Armstrong supplied the melody for "Poor Juna at the Gate," a song and chorus that was arranged by James G. Clark, musical director of *Ossian's Bards*. Nellie Morton wrote two songs for the singer J. Cairncross, among them "Ida May" (1856) and "Silvery Moon."[71] Martha Hill's "The Ghost of Uncle Tom" was sung by the Hutchinsons.

Topical Songs

A few topical songs find their way into the commercial repertory of 1870. These include songs inspired by political reform movements (abolition and temperance) and political events, in particular the Civil War. Topical songs have a *raison de'être* beyond entertainment and reflect the involvement of women in various reform movements, a trend which produced much more music after the Civil War than before it. Women, it seems, were more likely to write temperance poetry[72] rather than temperance music before 1870. Susan Parkhurst is the one major exception.[73]

Suffrage songs by women are similarly scarce before 1870, as far as is known. An antisuffrage work, "Woman's Right" by Kate Horn (1853), mocked the platform of Women's Rights Conventions of the 1850s. One prosuffrage song was an arrangement made by Elizabeth Higgins (Mrs. E.H. Jackson) of the Hutchinson Family's song "Vote It Right Along." Published in 1869, it was dedicated to the "Universal Suffrage and Equal Rights Association of Illinois."[74]

Works associated with the Civil War are far more numerous. Many Southern women wrote patriotic pieces dedicated to their local regiments or to generals in the Army.[75] Popular hits from this period by women composers include Margaret Weir's "Dixie Doodle," Alice Lane's "The Stars of Our Banner," and "God Will Defend the Right," by a Lady of Richmond, Virginia.[76]

Religious Song

After 1830 the pattern set in the late-eighteenth century—in which women did not compose church music—seems to be modified, but only rather slowly.[77] They contributed very little music to Protestant hymnals between 1820 and 1860.[78] Nor are they represented in revival hymnody before 1840.[79] Apart from sects like the Shakers, who were led by a woman, one of the earliest repertories in which they do appear is Southern folk hymnody. A Miss M.T. Durham, for example, contributed two pieces, "The Promised Land" and "Star of Columbia" that were widely disseminated.[80]

Both pieces are worthy of a closer look. "The Promised Land" is a rousing vigorous tune in the strange key of F-sharp minor with a very appealing refrain. "Star of Columbia" is a bit more complicated. Its rhythms are much more similar to Shaker song than to singing-school hymnody and perhaps the text attributed to "Dr. Dwight" was fitted to it later.[81] (see exx. 14 and 15.)

Ex. 14.   Miss M.T. Durham, *The Promised Land*

The earliest known female gospel hymn composer, Phoebe Palmer Knapp (1839-1908), began her career in the 1860s.[82] Active through the end of the century, Knapp wrote her most famous pieces—"Blessed Assurance" and "Open the Gates of the Temple"—after 1870;[83] however, a number of her earlier works received recognition. Two hymns, the "Cleansing Wave" and "Welcome to Glory," appeared in the collection *The Revivalist*, 1868.[84]

Ex. 15.   Miss M.T. Durham, *Star of Columbia*

STAR OF COLUMBIA. 11's.   *Miss M. T. Durham.*   Words by Dr. Dwight

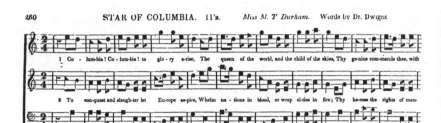

1 Co - lum-bia! Co - lum-bia! to glo - ry a-rise, The queen of the world, and the child of the skies, Thy ge-nius com-mands thee, with

2 To con-quest and slaugh-ter let Eu-rope as-pire, Whelm na - tions in blood, or wrap ci-ties in fire; Thy he-roes the rights of man-

rap-tures be-hold, While a - ges on a - ges thy splen-dours un-fold: Thy reign is the last and the no - blest of time, Most

kind shall de-fend, And tri-umph pur - sue them and glo-ry at - tend. A world is thy realm, for a world be thy laws, En-

fruit ful thy soil, most in - vi-ting thy clime; Let crimes of the east ne'er en - crim - son thy name, Be free-dom, and sci-ence, and vir-tue thy fame.

larged as thy em-pire, and just as thy cause; On free-dom's broad ba - sis that em-pire shall rise, Ex - tend with the main, and dis-solve with the skies.

3 Fair science her gate to thy sons shall unbar,
And the east see thy morn hide the beams of her star;
New bards and new sages unrivall'd shall soar
To fame unextinguish'd, when time is no more.
To the last refuge of virtue design'd,
Shall fly from all nations, the best of mankind,
There, grateful to Heaven, with transport shall bring
Their incense, more fragrant than odours of spring.

4 Nor less shall thy fair ones to glory ascend,
And genius and beauty in harmony blend;
Their graces of form shall awake pure desire,
And the charms of the soul still enliven the fire:
Their sweetness unmingled, their manners refined,
And virtue's bright image enstamp'd on the mind;
With peace and sweet rapture shall teach life to glow
And light up a smile in the aspect of wo

5 Thy fleets to all regions thy power shall display
The nations admire, and the ocean obey;
Each shore to thy glory its tribute unfold,
And the east and the south yield their spices and gold,
As the day-spring unbounded thy splendours shall flow,
And earth's little kingdoms before thee shall bow,
While the ensigns of union in triumph unfurl'd,
Hush anarchy's sway, and give peace to the world.

6 Thus down a lone valley with cedars o'erspread,
From the noise of the town I pensively stray'd,
The bloom from the face of fair heaven retired,
The wind ceas'd to murmur, the thunders expired
Perfumes, as of Eden, flow'd sweetly along,
And a voice, as of angels, enchantingly sung,
Columbia! Columbia! to glory arise,
The queen of the world, and the child of the skies.

Knapp's collections, *Notes of Joy* and *Sabbath Schools,* are both cited in Moore's "List of Modern Musical Works Published in the United States."[85] She was also well represented in the collection *Women in Sacred Song.*[86] As one of the few female composers to be represented in Ira Sankey's *Gospel Hymns,* Knapp occupies a historically significant place in revival music.[87] She represents a new type of composer that appeared in the 1860s—the woman who was not primarily interested in household music or accomplishment, but came to music through another path. Phoebe Knapp's parents were famous leaders in the Perfectionists Revivals of the 1840s and '50s, and her mother, Phoebe Palmer, was a hymnist and the author of several well-known religious treatises.[88] "Jesus' Jewels" (ex. 16) is a solo song and chorus from *Women in Sacred Song.* Its harmonic vocabulary is richer than the standard gospel hymn written by Sankey. Note, for example, the move to F-sharp minor at "Any poor and sinful wand'rer."

The literary rather than the musical impulse was a main factor in changing the pattern of male-dominated religious song. Many women were highly successful hymnists and religious poets in the mid-nineteenth century.[89] As the practice of arranging secular tunes with "sacred" or quasi-religious texts became common, women writers inevitably became arrangers and, in passing, composers.

The genre of "sacred song" is the most important example of this process. Sacred songs are a type of religious parlor song, broadly defined to include edifying ballads such as the Hemans-Browne duet "Evening Song to the Virgin"[90] or Emma Willard's "Rocked in the Cradle of the Deep." They became increasingly popular after the 1840s[91] and were commonly created by fitting secular music with new texts. Mozart and Cherubini, along with conventional parlor composers such as Stephen Lover and J.P. Knight, provided the tunes and American hymnists such as Lowell Mason and I.B. Woodbury changed the lyrics.[92]

Mary Dana Shindler (1810-1883), better known as Mrs. Dana from sheet music imprints, was one of the most successful sacred-song writers in the mid-nineteenth century.[93] Her two most popular pieces, "Flee as a Bird" and "The Ruler's Daughter," come from her collection of sacred song, *The Northern Harp,*[94] which was published in 1842; and they were later issued as sheet music by Oliver Ditson and in print in 1870. Both songs are arrangements of unidentified tunes listed only as a "Spanish air" and a "French air," respectively.[95]

"Flee as a Bird" (ex. 17) is an extremely successful piece. Its plaintive lovely melody suggests opera more than national airs, and the tune had enough integral shape to withstand its adoption into a variety of styles, running the gamut from keyboard variation to gospel hymn.[96]

Ex. 16. Mrs. J.F. Knapp, *Jesus' Jewels*

JESUS' JEWELS.

Ex. 16, continued

Je - sus, help us, Je - sus, guide us, Je - sus, ev - er walk be - side us; Tell, Oh! tell us what to say, Help us win a soul to-day.

Mary Dana typified the female sacred song composer because her allegiance to a female audience is so clear. She was concerned with defining musical accomplishment in Christian rather than social terms and attempted to place its values into a moral context. The preface to *The Northern Harp* illustrates the method:

> Female elegance and loveliness, especially, are often set off by the accomplishments of a fine voice, and of skills exquisite in bringing out the powers of an instrument. Why should not her heart—whose fingers sweep the keys of the Piano-forte,—learn to beat with emotions of love to that Saviour, who has loved her and died for her, and who invites her to the bliss of Heaven. The lovely song of one that hath a pleasant voice, and can play well on an instrument, delights moves melts us. Let her forgive us while we remind her that she may be yet without the grace of God to fit her for heaven. And we pray that she may become a Christian, and thus be prepared to touch a golden harp in Heaven.... [97]

Dana had a Victorian sensibility. If we are to believe her compatriot Sarah Hale, whose long sketch in *Women's Record* supplies more biographical information than any other source known to date,[98] Mrs. Dana was almost forced into public print.

> Her works were composed not without any view to publication, but as she herself says in one of her letters, "Burning thoughts were struggling within my breast, and I must give them utterance.... My friends... urged me to their publication, giving a reason that what has comforted me in my sore extremity, might comfort other afflicted ones...."

Mrs. Dana's trials were indeed severe, for she lost her son and husband in the same year (1835). We only suggest that the need to supply a reason at all is the issue at hand. Again, one can understand why sacred song attracted mid-nineteenth century women: like the sentimental ballad it mediated the conflict between their professional and private role in society because the respectable content placed them beyond reproach.

Ex. 17.   Mrs. M.S.B. Dana, *Flee as a Bird*

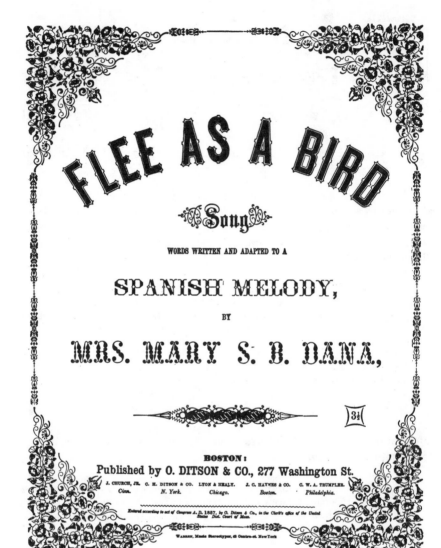

FLEE AS A BIRD.

Written and adapted by Mrs. M. S. B. DANA.

1. Flee as a bird to your moun - - tain,

Thou who art wea-ry of sin;......... Go to the clear flow-ing foun - tain,

Where you may wash and be clean; Fly, for th' aven - ger is near........ thee;

MODERATO.
ESPRESIVO.

nev - - er, Shelt - ered so ten - der - ly there; Haste, then, the hours are

fly - - - ing, Spend not the moments in sigh - - ing, Cease from your sor - row and

un poco ritenuto.

cry - - - ing, The Sa - viour will wipe ev - 'ry tear, The Sa - viour will wipe ev - 'ry

tear.

8907

Keyboard Music

Although parlor songs were a more popular genre for women than keyboard music, a number of piano pieces by women were published commercially by 1870. The evidence suggests that the 1850s were a turning point in that most keyboard works in the collections examined for this study were published after that date.

Far fewer keyboard works enjoyed the extended popularity of some songs that we have already discussed as standards of the literature. No doubt this reflects a smaller market in general for keyboard music, but it also is related to the smaller number of professional female instrumentalists. Perhaps, when more regional studies are completed, the picture may change; at this point, however, professional women pianists before 1870 seem to have been exceptional figures.[99]

The great Teresa Carreño (1853-1917) began her career as a child prodigy in 1862 and published an early work, the "Gottschalk Waltz," in 1863.[100] Before her there were a few other professional musicians who also compared keyboard works.[101]

The most difficult keyboard piece published by a woman composer before 1870, and indeed the outstanding concert work, was written by Adele Hohnstock, a native of Germany, who came to the United States in the 1840s.[102] She composed a virtuoso work "Concert Polka with Variations" that she played at her own concerts. The piece (ex. 18), a series of elaborate and ambitious variations in a lovely polka tune, is written in the style of French salon composers of the 1820s and '30s, such as Thalberg or Herz. It successfully exploits the resources of the newer, larger, more resonating piano of the period. Variation 1, for example, has repeated notes that extend beyond the conventional keyboard range and oblige the composer to provide an alternate passage for the "piano ordinaire." In variation 2, every melodic note is trilled and accompanied by quickly moving chords in the left hand. The third and most difficult variation has tremolos in the right hand and arpeggios in the left.

Because the piece was for virtuoso performance, publishers issued the work in a second format which detached the polka themes so that it could be used as dance music. This became widely known as the "Hohnstock Polka."[103] Stephen Foster published the polka tune (melody only) in the *Social Orchestra;*[104] we also find the concert version "arranged with accompaniments for harp, violoncello, and flute" on a program given by one of the better female seminaries (Cherry Valley in New York) on August 21, 1851.[105]

Hohnstock's variations on a polka theme are extraordinary, not only because of their virtuosity but also because they are one of the few piano variation sets by women composers located before 1870. Although this form was the most popular kind of keyboard piece before the Civil War,[106] it was

Ex. 18.   Adele Hohnstock, *Concert Polka*

2

ADÈLE HOHNSTOCK'S CONCERT POLKA.

Hohns, C. Polka.

Ex. 18, continued

4

Holms. C. Polka.

Hohns. C. Polka.

Hohns.C.Polka.

Ex. 18, continued

Hohns. C. Polka.

Hahns.C.Polka.

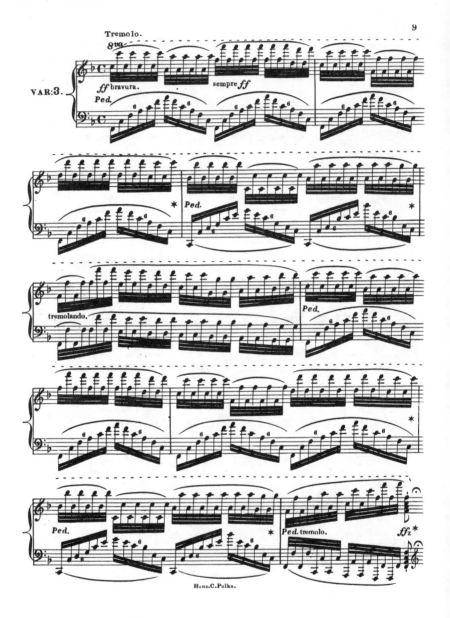

Hons. C. Polka.

10

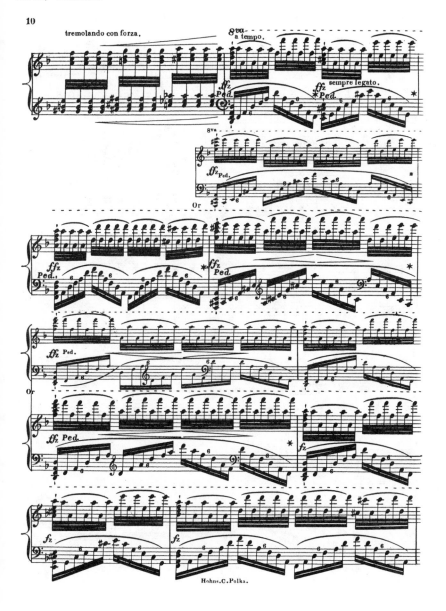

Hohns.C.Polka.

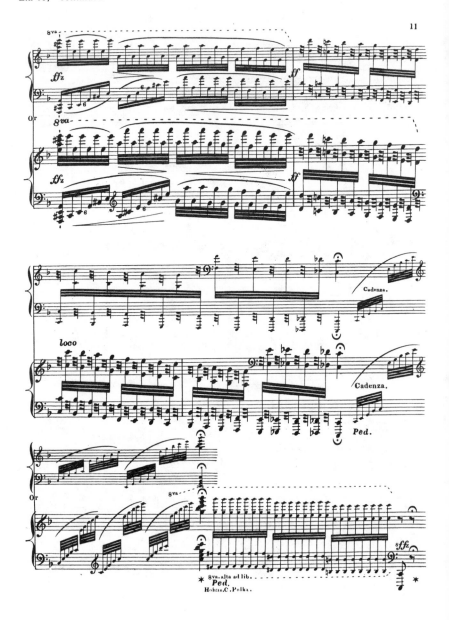

11

12

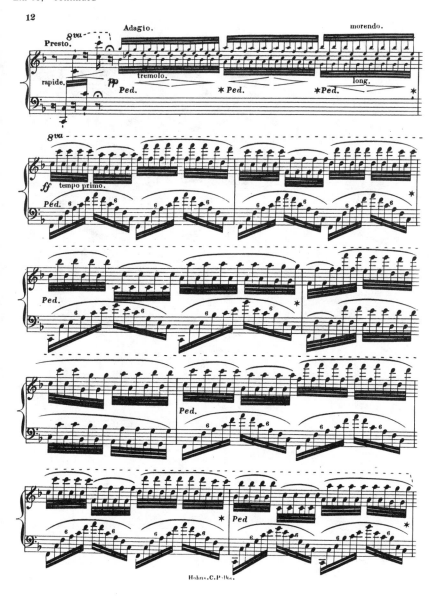

Hohns.C.P-lka.

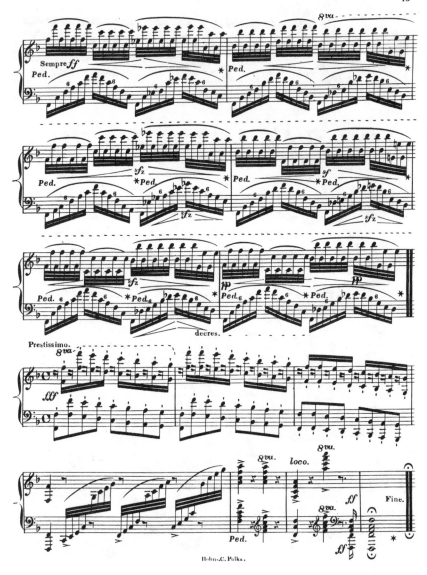

Hohn.C. Polka.

associated most closely with virtuoso performance. Since so few women were professional pianists, it is not surprising that keyboard sets are rare. The few others known to date include a set based on "The Wild Ashe Deer" by a "Lady of Virginia" (1854); a set based on "Annie Laurie" by Miss M.L. Schindler; and Eliza Pattiani's "May Breeze," variations brilliante for the piano (Chicago: Root & Cady, 1865).[107] Only the first of these has been located, perhaps because it alone of the three remained in print in 1870.[108]

Occasionally some virtuoso gestures appear in a dance, especially those with French titles. Marie Siegling's "La Capricieuse" is a "valse originale" that begins with an extended introduction and later introduces Chopinesque figurations into the waltz itself. This piece remained in print in 1870.[109]

Most women composers wrote pieces either for teaching purposes, for amateurs of only moderate skill, or for parlor dancing. Consequently, the most frequently found genres are compositions based on dance forms, such as waltzes, polkas, quicksteps, and marches. These pieces conform to prevailing trends in conventional dance music: two-bar phrases organized in eight-bar strains; middle section in a contrasting key, often IV or VI, and "oom-pah" basses in the left hand.

The majority of the pieces are more typically light-hearted entertainment for the amateur, and their casual titles suggest an informal milieu: Mrs. E. Sanderson's "The California Quiver Polka," Hattie Calder's "Arch St. Polka" (1856), or Estelle De Lisle's "Cape Cottage Waltz," and Miss Clarkson's "The Fairmount Quadrilles," dedicated respectfully to the "Ladies of Philadelphia" (1849), are representative.

Many of these pieces were written primarily as functional dance music for the parlor. Miss Gerrard, the composer of "The Fire Bell Polka" (1854), left a note to the player that her imitation of fire bells (octaves clanging away for two measures in the middle of the piece) are to be omitted "if the piece is played for dancing."

The functional dancing pieces are all organized around the eight-bar phrase. One charming example is "The Rosebud Quickstep" by Mary (1848) (ex. 19), later included in *The Folio of Music No. 2* (Philadelphia, 1888).[110] It is an unpretentious little piece that uses dynamics to achieve some whimsical effects. Note the *pp* marking followed by one measure of *forte* in the third strain.

A few exceptional works were intended to be performed by dance bands, and the keyboard versions were, in fact, arrangements made for home use. The two sets of "Keowee Waltzes," composed and arranged for the piano-forte by a "Lady of South Carolina" are examples.[111] Although there is no indication on the title page that this music was ever played by a band, the third waltz of the second set, called "Eastatoia," has an indication for "corni" over the first measure. Other examples include: Mrs. Charlotte Peterson's "Parade March,"

Ex. 19. Mary, *Rosebud Quickstep*

NEW YORK *Publ by* FIRTH, POND & C°. *1 Franklin Square.*
Brooklyn THOMAS D. SMITH *202 Fulton S*

Ex. 19, continued

219

dedicated to the Honesdale Parade Band (Boston: Oliver Ditson & Co., n.d.); Mrs. William Garrett's "The Emily Polka" (1857), "played with great success by the Germania Serenada Band"; "The Celebrated Italian Polka," arranged by a Lady in Baltimore and performed by the band in Newport (1847); and two polkas by Mrs. S.R. Burtis. Her "Morning and Evening Polkas" were played by Beck's Celebrated Silver Band in Philadelphia.

Conclusions

The mid-decades of the nineteenth century were a period of transition for the American woman composer. A number of changes occurred. One was the extension of musical accomplishment to include the composition of parlor songs and dances. Another was the growth of a female subculture for the accomplishments, symbolized by the ladies' magazine market. A third was the prominence of English women composers, who provided models for their American counterparts. Thus, in comparison with the earlier period, more women composed songs and keyboard music, and if they themselves did not become notable figures, many of their individual pieces became famous.

The reconciliation of the two roles of woman as opposed to composer can be seen in this period as well. As a proportional minority within the profession, women had a separate "sphere of influence" that blunted their direct competition with men. This sphere, located at home in the parlor, was shaped through the adaptation of beliefs about music as a feminine accomplishment. The distinctions between professional and amateur and between art and entertainment that we found with respect to performance carried over into composition so that the stereotype of the lady composer was that of the amateur or natural songwriter. Parlor music, especially sentimental ballads, was perceived as the ideal medium for fledgling efforts. Indeed, only a few women wrote for the concert stage as opposed to the social circle.

The music written by early American women composers differs from that written by men in subtle yet distinguishable ways, that parallel some of the differences in their professional development. As the role of the lady was above the vernacular and below that of artist, women composers seem shut off from some native traditions, such as minstrel show music, fiddle, or dance tunes, and from authentic European tradition. They were most likely to write cultivated ballads that display the "vocal culture" of the female seminary and a genteel Victorian sensibility than comic songs, dialect numbers, or concert arias. Thus, the dominant musical style of middle-ground cultivation between art and entertainment corresponds to their social status as marginal composer between the concert hall and the popular stage.

On the other hand, the lack of professional expectations for women composers and the interplay between music and femininity had certain compensations. They freed women from constrictions about their own abilities and sanctioned the expression of emotions that would have been inhibited in ordinary social intercourse. So many songs written by women during the 1840s and 1850s (texts as well as music) were subjective: first-person poems that convey the world of intimacy and private emotional experiences. "Young ladies are often heard to express in singing, sentiments that they would blush to utter in conversation," wrote Almira Phelps in 1833. In the mid-decades of the nineteenth century women learned to write these songs as well as sing them. The "wounds" and "broken spells" of love were translated into an acceptable medium through the expressive genre of parlor song.

Five Mid-Nineteenth-Century Composers

For women composers the polarities of the nineteenth century can be reduced to the opposing images of the lady amateur at the beginning of the century and the professional artist at the end. The lives and work of the outstanding mid-nineteenth-century composers suggest some of the choices available to women who were among the first to bridge the distance between these two extremes. They are, in this sense, case studies in a much larger historical process of transforming music from a feminine accomplishment to a profession—from functional domestic education to art.

The nineteenth century was three-quarters gone before an acknowledgement of American women composers appeared in the contemporary literature. The earliest known sources are two reference works published by John W. Moore in the 1870s—*Appendix to the Encyclopedia of Music*[1] and *A Dictionary of Musical Information.*[2] The *Appendix* named Augusta Browne, who, by virtue of this entry, is probably the first American women to be acknowledged in the literature as a composer in her own lifetime.[3] Moore added other names in his *Dictionary,* and we quote these rare entries in full.[4]

Shindler, Mary S.B. born at Beaufort, S.C. author of "Southern Harp"; "Northern Harp": many songs for piano and guitar. Some works written under name of Mary S.B. Dana. Also "Western Harp."

Marion Dix Sullivan. Published at Boston, Mass. 1856 a collection of well-harmonized "Bible Songs," the melodies suitable for children to sing. Also "Juniata Ballads."

Miss Jane Slowman. *Melodist,* N.Y. 1850. Also seen as Sloman: work written for use in female seminaries; contains a number of her compositions.

Mrs. J.F. Knapp. *Notes of Joy; Sabbath Schools.*

Mrs. J.B. Paige. *Paige's New and Inductive Method for Piano.*

Miss M.E. Bailey. *Parlour Melodies.*

Mrs. M.F.H. Smith published music N.Y. 1867; also "Sparkling Stream," "Temperance Melodies."

Of this group, Sullivan, Sloman, Knapp, and Dana can be proven to have been composers. Mrs. M.F.H. Smith has not been identified nor her collections located. Miss Bailey *(Parlour Melodies)* was the editor and arranger, not the composer of the collection.[5]

None of these women are included in W.S.B. Matthew's *A Hundred Years of Music in America* (1889)[6] or in Frederick Louis Ritter's *Music in America* (1883).[7] In fact, the only other known nineteenth-century source to refer to a mid-nineteenth-century American woman composer in the United States is an article by Rupert Hughes in *Godey's Lady's Book*.[8] Hughes's survey was devoted to living composers, but Faustina Hodges had died only one year earlier and was posthumously included.

Nineteenth-century sources indicate that Marion Dix Sullivan, Augusta Browne, Jane Sloman, and Faustina Hodges were notable composers of the mid-nineteenth century. We can add to this list Mrs. E.A. Parkhurst, a prolific composer of the 1860s, who although not in reference works, is well represented in sheet music collections.

In effect, these women represent the two midpoint generations of each half of the century: the earliest, Marion Dix Sullivan, was most active in the 1840s; the latest, Mrs. E.A. Parkhurst, was most active in the 1860s and lived into the twentieth century. In order to appreciate their achievements, we ought to view them as a transitional generation. Looking ahead to the 1890s, they are hardly a match for the one that followed them, which included Amy Beach and Margaret Lang. Their work, moreover, is uneven; Hodges and Parkhurst were by far the most talented. For Sullivan, the term "professional" might overstate the case, for so little is known of her life. In comparison to the proceeding generations and in relation to their own contemporaries, they represent the emergence of women in a professional world of music. They are the first group of women to establish themselves as composers among their own contemporaries and to achieve national prominence.

Marion Dix Sullivan

Marion Dix Sullivan was a songwriter active in the 1840s and '50s. Very little is known of her life. She came from New England and was married in 1825 to a J.W. Sullivan of Boston.[9] Ten songs and two collections, *Bible Songs* and *Juniata Ballads,* have been located to date, all from the 1840s and '50s. Her reputation as a composer rests largely on a few songs written in the 1840s, in particular the ballad "The Blue Juniata" (1844). One of the most popular parlor songs of the nineteenth century, "The Blue Juniata" is the first composition by an American woman to become a commercial hit song.[10] It was anthologized in countless collections[11] and used for variation sets by the composer-pianist Charles Grobe and an unknown composer named Gould.[12] In his

Autobiography, Mark Twain mentioned this song in his recollections of minstrel shows:

> The minstrel troupes had good voices and both their solos and their choruses were a delight to me as long as the Negro show continued in existence. In the beginning the songs were rudely comic ... but a little later on sentimental songs were introduced, such as "The Blue Juniata," "Sweet Ellen Bayne," "Nelly Bly," "A Life on the Ocean Wave".... [13]

Other famous works by Sullivan date from the 1840s as well: "The Field of Monterey," a ballad written for the Mexican-American Campaigns, and a sacred song, "Oh! Boatman, Row Me O'er the Stream."[14] In addition, Sullivan composed a ladies' magazine song, "The Bridal,"[15] "Jessie Cook," "Marion Day" (both 1844), "Mary Lindsay" (1848), "We Cross the Prairie as of Old" (1854), "When the Bright Waves are Dashing" (1958), and "Gypsy." This last work is unlocated but is listed on the program of a concert at Madison Female College, July 27, 1853, as a song and chorus.[16]

Marion Dix Sullivan probably received little formal training in music. Some of her songs were in fact published in collaboration with a musician who completed the harmonizations: in 1856, for example, her *Bible Songs* appeared with harmonizations by B.J. Lang, organist in Salem, Massachusetts.[17]

By her own description her creativity was spontaneous, often "unsought and undesired," and she viewed herself as a people's composer, describing the public for one of her collections, the *Juniata Ballads,* in the broadest, most democratic terms:

> To my friends of the forest and the mountain, the river, the lake and the sea-shore,—of the poor—of the laboring—and to EVERY child, the "Juniata Ballads" are affectionately and respectfully dedicated. They are to be sung to the oar, the loom and the plough,—through the forest, over the prairie, and in the small log cabin by the light of a pine knot.
>
> They are written as they came to the mind of the composer, often unsought and undesired; the melody and the words together. The latter may not be poetical, but they at least harmonize with the former. Most of them comemorate in the mind of the writer some event, or place, or circumstance.[18]

The collection contains 50 unaccompanied songs, with words and music by the composer. The settings are almost entirely syllabic, either in 4/4 or 6/8, intended as folk-song rather than parlor song. The *Juniata Ballads* were in print in 1870 and categorized as school songs.[19]

Sullivan's musical style is modest, perhaps deceptively simple. Her best song, "The Blue Juniata" (ex. 20), integrates a number of skips into a seemingly artless melody without disturbing the placidity of the vocal line. Its absence of dynamics, rare among parlor songs of the period, is another feature of its folk-like style and deliberate aesthetic plainness.

Ex. 20. Marion Dix Sullivan, *The Blue Juniata*

Gay was the mountain song Of bright Alfarata,

Where sweep the waters Of the blue Juni-a-ta. Strong and true my arrows are

In my painted quiver, Swift goes my light canoe A - down the rapid river.

3

Bold is my warrior good
   The love of Alfarata,
Proud waves his snowy plume
   Along the Juniata.
Soft and low he speaks to me,
And then his war cry sounding,
Rings his voice in thunder loud
From height to height resounding.

4

So sang the Indian girl,
   Bright Alfarata,
Where sweep the waters
   Of the blue Juniata.
Fleeting years have borne away
The voice of Alfarata,
Still sweeps the river on
   Blue Juniata.

Sullivan wrote the texts as well as the melodies for most of her pieces. In many, the central figure is a woman, whether or not the song is about love or war. In "The Blue Juniata," for example, the main character is an Indian girl, with the convenient name of "Alfarata." In "The Field of Monterey" the depiction of the battle is written from the point of view of a woman grieving over the death of a soldier.

Augusta Browne

Augusta Browne was one of the most prominent women composers in the 1840s and '50s. The entry in John Moore's *Appendix* describes her as:

> Browne, Augusta or Mrs. Augusta Browne Garrett, late of New York, now residing in Washington, D.C. A composer of note. Her productions, which are in all styles—fantasies, airs variés, waltzes, songs sacred and secular—number about 200; and many of them, such as the brilliant romance "La Brise dans les Feuillage," "Airs a la Russe," "National Bouquets," and various songs have gained great popularity.
>
> Besides occupations in music, Mrs. Garrett has long had literary pursuits. She has written *Hamilton, The Young Artist* and *The Precious Stones of the Heavenly Foundation.*[20]

Moore's figure of 200 works establishes Browne as the most prolific woman composer in America before 1870. Her compositions were widely disseminated and are to be found in a number of different libraries, including the Bodleian Library at Oxford.[21] She also published extensively in musical periodicals and ladies' magazines. About a quarter of her total output has been located to date; it was written between 1840 and 1855, with at least 20 pieces remaining in print in 1870.[22]

From the beginning of her career Augusta Browne published her work under her full name. In no sense did she present herself as a lady amateur, and as we shall presently see, title pages of her music frequently cite her other professional activities. Despite this, in her own lifetime, she was confused with another woman who published music as "Miss Browne." This "Miss Browne"—one Harriet Mary—was English and the sister of the popular poet Felicia Browne Hemans. Since Mrs. Heman's fame was international, Harriet Mary was frequently identified only as "Mrs. Heman's sister"; other times "Miss Browne" was used—but without a first name. One setting, "Pilgrim Fathers" ("The breaking waves dash high"), had an American theme and was mistakenly attributed to Augusta. Simeon Cheney, for example, in *The American Singing Books,* described Augusta as the composer of this ballad in an otherwise accurate entry:

> Miss Augusta Browne of New York (now Mrs. Garrett) of Washington is an American composer of note. She is of English descent, many years ago becoming famous on piano and organ. She is best known for *The Pilgrim Fathers.* The age of Mrs. Garrett is not known.[23]

A death certificate for Augusta Browne Garrett, located in the Vital Records Division of the District of Columbia, establishes her country of origin as Ireland and her dates of birth and death as 1821 and 1882. Apparently, by her fifties she had lost the prominence of her early career and her occupation on the death certificate is listed as "none."

Browne's family emigrated from Ireland to America by 1830, living in various cities in the East—New York, Philadelphia, Boston.[24] Of her education and musical training we know nothing, but her family by her own account was fairly well to do.[25]

Augusta Browne did not marry until she was around 35, and she was widowed within a few years.[26] Consequently, she was largely self-supporting, and she put together a livelihood in a variety of ways—teaching, performing, composing, and writing journalism.

Her career as a composer began in the popular ladies' periodicals. *Godey's Lady's Book* printed her sentimental ballad "The Stranger's Heart" in January 1841.[27] That same year another song, "I Wish I Were a Fairy," appeared in the *New York Mirror*.[28] She attracted attention quickly, for on January 8, 1842, *The New World* published this criticism of her work:

> Bonnie Bessie Green.—A Ballad, dedicated to Mrs. J.L. Motley of Boston, by Miss Augusta Browne. A very pretty poem, set to a beautiful old melody, with new symphonies and accompaniments by Miss Browne. This young lady is fast improving, and her faults are those of a writer whose style has not been strictly cultivated, nor her errors corrected by example. We shall take an opportunity of speaking of this young lady at more length in a short time.[29]

Information about her other professional activities comes from the title pages of her published sheet music. Between 1842 and 1844 Augusta Browne was described as "professor of music and theory, Brooklyn, Long Island," and "professor of the Logerian System of Music."[30] Between 1842 and 1844 she was also the organist at the First Presbyterian Church in Brooklyn,[31] for which presumably she composed two anthems for four-part chorus, a rare genre for a woman composer at the time: the "Grand Vesper Chorus"[32] and "Hear Therefore O Israel" (the latter was revived for the centenial celebration of the church in 1922).[33] She also performed in some public concerts during 1842 and 1843.[34] The most important of these was on April 15, 1842, when she appeared with the celebrated English singers, John and Charles Braham.[35] One of her works, "The Family Meeting," was dedicated to John Braham and sung by him as well.

By 1846 Browne's works had reached opus 73, with her "De Meyer Grand Waltz." In 1847 she wrote "The Volunteer's War Song," which was rearranged as "The Mexican Volunteer's Quickstep" and played by the well-known Dodworth's band. The next year she wrote one of her better known compositions, "The War-Like Dead in Mexico" (1848). The title page is embellished with a brilliant lithograph of the battles of the Mexican compaign, and the song is dedicated ("by special permission") to Henry Clay.

Browne's career was considerably aided by the increase of popular magazines that occurred in the 1840s and '50s.[36] She was a journalist as well as a composer, and in addition to songs, she published short stories and music criticism in leading magazines. She was a steady contributor to the *Columbian Lady's and Gentleman's Magazine,* in particular; in its ten volumes between 1844 and 1848 she published several compositions and articles.[37] Browne was one of the important contributors to the *New York Musical Times and Musical World,* the *Boston Musical Gazette,* and the *Monthly Musical Review.*[38] She wrote light essays on a variety of musical topics (Musical Echoes,"[39] "Rockets from an Organ-Loft"[40]), short stories ("Five Shillings Worth of Talent"[41]), and even excerpts of her book on her brother, *Hamilton, the Young Artist,* found their way into musical magazines.[42]

Throughout her life Browne ordered her work and regulated her musical taste by two standards—her religious convictions and her sense of class. Music was sanctified by its "divine origins," and many of her articles were erudite compilations of references to music in Biblical literature.[43] She was a strict moralist. Opera was "an unGodly pasttime and like the theater, ever a deadly foe of religion."[44] She described the class to which she belonged as "refined intellectual society"—the urban audience that appreciated scientific European music. Minstrel show music was lower class and corrupted the ignorant masses. In a review of some compositions by the French pianist Henri Herz, she condemned popular music:

> Polkas, negro songs and such like, those pernicious banes of musicians, have, we blush to acknowledge, obtained a far greater dominion over the fancies of the populace, than any other—shall we call it *music*—published, Go where you will—always excepting refined intellectual society—and you are very apt to be entertained with senseless dances, or some of the Ethiopian gems. It is often more than a teacher's popularity is worth to prevent a pupil from wasting time lesson after lesson on such taste-corrupting nonentities.[45]

As a professional teacher, she attributed the "low estate of scientific music among us to the presence of common Yankee singing schools," that "corrupt taste and pervert the judgement of the rural populace."[46]

Browne's music was shaped by these attitudes to the extent that she avoided vernacular music. More central to our understanding of her music, however, is the realization that her main musical influences come from her position as a church organist, her familiarity with conventional English oratorio, and her admiration for English composers like John Braham and Charles Horn, both of whom she knew personally. Even though she composed music in the 1840s, her sense of figuration and her harmonic vocabulary is old-fashioned, more appropriate to the 1820s.

Browne's stylistic influences were English and Irish. One keyboard work, "The Hibernian Bouquet,"[47] a set of keyboard variations on Irish tunes, was a tribute to Thomas Moore's *A Selection of Irish Melodies.*[48] Three of Browne's tunes are taken from Moore, including an extensive quotation of Sir John Stevenson's keyboard arrangement of the tune "Carolan's Concerto."

Her songs, most of which were too elaborately structured to suit American popular taste, are best described as parlor arias, often in modifed ABA plans. There is no trace of Italian melody, however; rather the musical style is solidly English. The song, "The Warlike Dead in Mexico,"[49] one of her popular works, recalls John Braham's famous "The Death of Nelson" in its military dotted rhythms and marchlike melodies.

"The Warlike Dead in Mexico" (ex. 21) is Browne's song about the Mexican-American campaigns of 1848 and thus offers us a direct comparison between her and Marion Dix Sullivan, whose "The Field of Monterey" is based on the same theme. While Sullivan is all musical humility, Browne aims for passion. The "largo" introduction depicts the text "Toll, toll the knell, for the hearts laid low on the blood-stained fields of Mexico," and strains for martial intensity in the harmonic changes in measures 5 through 8. The overall plan is modified *da capo* with a middle section *("affetuoso, con molto espressione")* in relative major. One tonal peculiarity of the piece is that the key of the A section opens in *g* minor but ends in *b*-flat.

Other songs in this sober vein include "The Chieftain's Halls" (1844), "The Reply of the Messenger Bird" (1848), and "Song of the Redeemed" (185-).

Browne's keyboard compositions are included in numerous sets of variations, an atypical genre for most mid-nineteenth-century women composers. Most often these are based on national airs, and one of her more popular groups include Hibernian (Irish), American, French, English, and Caledonian (Scotch) Bouquets.

Perhaps Browne deserves to be remembered today more for her prolific output rather than for the individual merit of any single work. In addition, she was articulate about her status as a woman composer. In 1863, some years after most of her compositions had been published, she wrote a long article that acknowledged her personal feminism and her own struggles to be judged objectively; it had the contemporary title "A Woman on Women—with reflection on the other sex."[50] The article is in many ways similar to other feminist writings of the period. It is extremely critical of male attitudes towards the female mind, citing a long history of intellectual oppression. Since Browne, like many feminist organizers, was deeply religious, it also attempts to reconcile church teachings with women's rights. Women's suffrage is supported indirectly by recalling famous women rulers of the past who were politically competent. In addition, the article indicts men as vain and intemperate slanderers of women's true worth, all standard themes by the 1860s among women's rights advocates.[51]

Ex. 21.   Augusta Browne, *The Warlike Dead in Mexico*

THE WARLIKE DEAD IN MEXICO.

The Poetry by Mrs BALMANNO.

Composed by AUGUSTA BROWNE.

Ex. 21, continued

thous _ ands slain, In seige, in storm, or on bat _ tle plain. No

more for them shall the roll - ing drum, Or thrill - ing blast of the

trum - pet come; The charg - er's tramp and the can - nons roar, Shall a_

rouse their daunt - less hearts no more. Toll, toll, toll the sol - dier's

knell,   In the   thorny   chap - po - ral.

On the mountains brow, in valley dim,
In deep defile, in the war-ranks grim,
Still on they rushed like the rolling sea,
With a conqueror's shout to victory.
On, on, like a whirl-wind o'er the land;
With the speed of light, and sword in hand,
O'er plains where the chargers hoofs grew red —
With streams from a thousand bosoms shed.
*   Toll, toll the soldier's knell,*
*   On the mountains where he fell!*

3

In vain o er them the embattled tower,
From its iron crest rained a deadly shower,
Neath the sweeping fire of each booming gun,
They charged, they strove, they fought they won.
While trumpets pealed with a lively breath,
Midst the shouts of life, and groans of death,
As the stripes and stars were seen to wave
Oer the victor ranks, and fallen brave.
*   Toll, toll the soldier's knell,*
*   By the conquered citadel.*

Ex. 21,   continued

No more on the night watch's drea - ry toil, The lance shall fly or the

las - so coil; From am - bush'd brake, or the dark mo - rass, From

ra - pid ford, or the rock - y pass; Nor ev - er more to a-

smile or sigh, Shall the sol - diers si - lent heart re - ply; But the

Ex. 21, continued

maids they loved shall mur - mur low, Our heroes have fal - len in

Mex - i - co. Toll, toll, toll the sol-dier's knell, At

ves - per hour in the convent cell.

dim:

p

5th. VERSE.

CON MOLTO SPIRITO, E ENERGIA.

They have fear - less fought, and no - bly died, In noon of fame in their

f

p

Ex. 21, continued

man - hood's pride In the glo - rious light of a proud ca - reer,' Un_

_sul _ lied, stain - less, wept and dear. Their bed is made in the

scorch - ing sand, Far, far a - way from their na - - - tive land, From

homes be - loved they shall see no more, Toll, toll the knell and the

Ex. 21, continued

re - - quiem pour.   Toll,   toll,   for   sol - dier's sleep - ing

low!   For the   dead   in   Mex - - i - co.   For the

dead   in   Mex - - i - co.

S. Ackerman.

One particular resentment was toward men who exploited women as helpmates and simultaneously denied them creative or intellectual equality.

No genuine woman grudges her husband or friend the benefit of her assistance or counsel, or covets a share in his fame, even one leaf of his laurel crown; rather, on the contrary, she glories in his exultation, is proud to do him service, richly recompensed for an entire self-renunciation, by a word of esteem or a glance of love ... but it is scarcely pleasant, after devoting her best efforts to man's aggrandisement, to be treated as an animal of inferior grade. I once heard a poetling—one of the species whose productions abound in the classical rhymes of "love and dove" and "sparkling and darkling," remark with melting condescension, when advised to read a noble new poem by a lady: "Aw! Well, to please you I will read it; but really, I—I never read *female* poetry.[52]

Another source of her anger was the traditional model of male protection and female dependency, a relationship conventionally expressed through naturalistic imagery like the sturdy oak and the clinging vine, the sunflower and the violet. Such standards for "true womanly" modesty compromised the healthy assertiveness of the artist seeking recognition.

It is a nice poetic conceit to liken woman to the lowly violet, and a very significant hint too, that she is expected to comport herself with the humility of that odorous blossom; in other words, she is to "keep shady"—to keep shady, robustious reader, while man as is befitting, like the bold towering sun flower, arrogates to himself all the light and warmth and glory of the day. No matter what triumphs of art or letters a woman achieves, she for ever acts as under a cloud, the shadow of the said umbrageous vegetable. Every step of the rugged way up the hill of Parnassus is disrupted by some envious brother, who ingeniously thrusts in her path some stumbling stone, or deals to her sly shoves. If man could but warble soprano, the sum of her tribulations would be full; he would soon hustle her out to the poor specialty of singing, the least intellectual and feeblest phase of art.[53]

Browne knew that her own education made her exceptional. "A learned lady was a creature to be handled with gloves," as much as an oddity as a "learned pig who eschewed his allotted sphere."[54] Despite the hue and cry over incompatibility of the accomplishments with homemaking, she argued that women could write poetry, work out a harmonic fugue, or manipulate a magnificent symphony of Beethoven—rather remarkable standards for mid-nineteenth-century music education—and still fulfill her domestic obligations.

Why should concocting a sonnet hinder a woman from concocting a pudding: ... working out a harmonic fugue from working a pan of dough; or manipulating a magnificent symphony of Beethoven from deftly handling a broom?[55]

The article concludes with another outburst against "cavalier comments on womanly genius."

... It is really trying to hear a fopling with a glass wrinkled into his eye, and a drooping jaw, in short, a picture of imbecility, I say it is trying to hear such a thing lisp out regarding the superb production of a lady: "Oh! aw—aw—vewy well for a woman, vewy well indeed; I must weally notice her"—when the fair Minerva in question would hardly deign to honor the pigmy with the custody of her fan. A Dutch grocer's lad, on hearing a lady play the piano delightfully, anxiously inquired, "She got man?" On being answered in the negative, he rejoined with a sign of benediction: "Well, she *deserve* to have man." Could mortal approbation go further.[56]

Such sarcasm leaves little doubt that her personal frustrations as a professional musican and writer had accumulated into a powerful and bitter animus against the double standard by which women were judged.

Faustina Hasse Hodges

Faustina Hasse Hodges (1822-1895) began her long career as a composer in the 1850s and published songs (sacred and secular) and keyboard music until her death. Works by her located to date include eight keyboard pieces, a set of 10 sacred songs ("Cloister Memories of Sacred Song"), one "Te Deum," a vocal trio "The Holy Dead," and about 25 secular songs. Many of these works were written after 1870, as her style grew increasingly cultivated,[57] but her reputation was secured through the sentimental ballads composed before the Civil War, rather than the art songs of her later years. Her most famous works include "Dreams" (1859), "The Rose-Bush" (1859), and a sacred duet, "Suffer Little Children" (1860). Other works worthy of mention are "The Indignant Spinster" (1867), a comic song; the three "Reveries for Piano" (1862-63); and "L'Amicizia," a "polka duet for women's voices" (New York: Beer & Schirmer, 1863).

Faustina came from a family of professional musicans. Her father, Edward Hodges, a well-known organist and church composer (who named all his children after famous musicians), journeyed to America from England in 1838 to assume the musical directorship of Trinity Church in New York.[58] Faustina spent the last years of her life writing his biography.[59] Since it was finished by Faustina's brother after her death in 1895, it became a memorial to both father and daughter; an obituary notice from a local church magazine was reprinted in it along with her photograph.

The biography is also a fortuitous source of other information about her; details of Faustina's life creep through her own account of Edward Hodges's life: her birthdate on August 7, 1822 (probably in Bristol, England); her arrival in New York in 1841; and her associations with other English musicians such as Charles Horn.[60]

Faustina was genuinely devoted to her father. It is unclear whether he undertook her musical education, although her taste undoubtedly benefitted from "his exquisite fugue playing." She acknowledged his influence through this testimony: "What I inherited from my Father was of more value than all the acquirement I could gain; indeed it was all."[61] Still, he was less than enthusiastic about her musicianship, as his opinions about women musicians in general and her own talent in particular suggest: "He said, 'No woman could play the organ.' And in this, as in all else, he was perfectly true and right."[62] Since she became an organist, perhaps she understood this remark as an implied comparison: a woman might become an organist but she could not be as good as a man. He was equally ambivalent about her compositions, and she equally determined to interpret all constructively:

> ... he spoke from his own unapproachable summit. On my shewing him one of my earliest compositions he helped and strengthened me much by these words: "What is original is not good, and what is good is not original." Of course he alluded to its being original with *me;* as he afterwards told me that the same thought might be "original" with many people.[63]

When Hodges returned to England in 1863, Faustina remained, by that time well established as a professional musican. She taught music at Emma Willard's Troy Seminary, and their 1852 catalogue listed her as a professor of organ, piano, and singing. Anthony Philip Heinrich was her "esteemed friend," and to him she dedicated her vocal trio "The Holy Dead." By the late 1870s she had moved to Philadelphia. There she was the organist for two Philadelphia churches, and it is in this capacity that her musical reputation survived into the twentieth century.[64] An obituary read as follows:

> *The Living Church,* March 2, 1895:
> No musician of the present time will be more deeply lamented than Miss Faustina Hasse Hodges, who departed this life in the city of Philadelphia on February 4. Up to the very eve of her illness, she had devoted her life to the study and practice of her musical art with unabated vigor and enthusiasm. She composed freely and with a grace of feeling which none who ever heard her compositions could forget. Who ever heard her beautiful "Rose Bush" or "Dreams" or her "Suffer, Little Children," each one so full of sentiment and feeling, without the thought that its author was well-nigh inspired. Her interpretations of Bach's fugues and other recondite forms of classic art were a daily delight to her choice circle of friends and admirers.[65]

A year later Rupert Hughes wrote:

> She deserves praise for some of her religious music. "Blessed Are They That Mourn" is majestically solemn like the hymnal Beethoven. "The Psalm of Life," though somewhat monotonous is of real depth. Mrs. Hodges also wrote that immensely popular but rather cloying song "The Rose Bush."[66]

Hodges' familiarity with "recondite forms of classic art" is apparent in her skillful assimilation of German and Italian song styles.[67] "Dreams" (ex. 22), an

Ex. 22.   Faustina Hodges, *Dreams*

2

DREAMS.

Oh! I have had dreams, I have had sweet dreams Of child - hood's bright and sun - - ny hours, When I wan - der'd all day, by the spark - ling streams, And cull'd for my moth-er the gay wild

flow'rs. When I wove her a wreath of the green wood-bine, And twin'd in it berries and vi-o-lets gay! And I crown'd her pale fore-head and she kiss'd mine, Ah! she like the flow-ers has fa-ded a-way, She has fa-ded a-way! fa-ded a-way!

Ex. 22, continued

4

I have had   bright dreams   of the old   elm   tree,   Be - neath whose   branch - es spread - ing wide,   I have sport-ed a - way,   in   child - ish   glee,   The fleet - winged   hours   of the e - ven-tide.   I have dream'd of   the

friends once gath - er'd there, To frol-ic a - way the long summer's

day, Un - trammel'd by fear, un - wearied by care, But they like the

rest have fa - - - ded a-way, They have fa - ded a - way,

fa - ded a - way.

Ex. 22, continued

hope's de - lay, And the vis-ions I wove of my des - ti - ny then, Ah!

they like the rest have fa - - ded a-way, they have fa-ded a - way!

fa - ded a - way!

espress.

4

I have had sweet dreams of a fairy form,
    That was ever around me there,
Of her bird-like voice, with its silvery charm
    Floating away on the evening air.
But alas for the flush and the wasting breath!
    Alas for thy terrible power, decay!
An angel beckoned her home from the earth,
    Like the morning star she faded away!
    She has faded away! faded away!

enormously popular ballad she wrote in 1859, is graced by a beautiful melody that is wedded to the waltz meter of the song.[68] The initial melodic skips that underlay "childhood's bright and sunny hours," and above all, the reprise that is built entirely on rising sequences capitalize on the lilting triple meter. Another German-derived feature is the integrity of the piano parts that open and close the song with independent musical material, rarely doubling the vocal line. One bel canto touch is the cadenza and leap to the octave that differentiates the last stanza at the text "visions of hope."

This song is about various dreams of childhood, nostalgically and affectionately recalled. As the song progresses, the mood becomes increasingly melancholic, shifting to one of revery for the loved ones who have died and can only be evoked through memory. The tag ending that is repeated at the end of each stanza sums up the main affection of the text: "they have faded away."

In another commercial success, "The Rose Bush" (ex. 23),[69] the text translated from an anonymous German poem, again depicts the passage of time, here through the double image of the fading flower and the successive stages of a woman's life. A dramatic rather than melodic vehicle, it was a great favorite of the opera singer Adelaide Phillipps (1833-1882). It may have been "cloying" to Rupert Hughes, a critic of the post-Civil War generation, but a description of one of Phillipps' performances clarifies its appeal for mid-nineteenth-century audiences:

> Between the acts of "Martha," in response to the uproarious encore of "The Laughing Song," Miss Phillipps sang "The Rose Bush," (an epitome of woman's life), a ballad which must have been written to suit the wonderful pathos, passion and sensibility of her ripe and mellow voice.... She threw a world of sentiment into every line, but her power was conspicuously displayed in rendering the tender couplet "She pressed her hand to her throbbing breast, With love's first rapture blest," and the sadly suggestive refrain, "Withered and dead they fall to the ground, and silently cover a new-made mound. And the years glide by."[70]

Fading roses and fading dreams were typical conceits of parlor culture in the 1850s, and can be found in painting as well. Hodges was a gifted musical genre painter, and her work invites comparison with that of her contemporary, the artist, Lily Martin Spencer (1822-1902), whose portrait of a young woman holding a rose is titled (predictably enough), "We Both Must Fade."[71]

The key phrase in the review of "The Rose Bush" is its description as "an epitome of woman's life." Like other female composers of the period, Hodges chose material to connect her musical expression with her sense of herself as a woman. Her comic song, "The Indignant Spinster" (ex. 24), is a most extreme example of the intimate nature of her material. Having written a spinster song in her twenties entitled, "Because I'm Twenty-Five," Hodges in her forties continued the autobiographical narrative with a long parlor aria about a

Ex. 23. Faustina Hodges, *The Rose Bush*

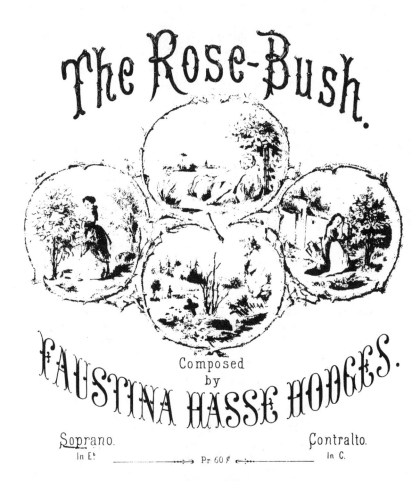

Sung by

Adelaide Phillips.

100 ᵗʰ Edition.

The Rose-Bush.

Composed
by

FAUSTINA HASSE HODGES.

Soprano.   Contralto.

In E♭   Pr 60 ¢   In C.

NEW-YORK,

PUBLISHED BY G. SCHIRMER,

701 Broadway.

The Rose-Bush.

Words Translated from the German by
W. CALDWELL.

FAUSTINA HASSE HODGES.

A child sleeps un – der a Rose-bush fair, The buds swell out in the soft May air; Sweet-ly it rests and on dream-wings flies, To play with the an – gels in Par – a – dise: And the years glide by.

273

Ex. 23, continued

Sweetly it rests and on dream wings flies, To play with the angels in Par - a - dise, To

ritard

play with the an - gels in Par - a - dise, And the years glide by.

tempo 1mo.

A maiden stands by the rose-bush fair, The dew—y blossoms perfume the air, She

presses her hand to her throbbing breast, With love's first wonderful rap—ture blest,

And the years glide by.

She presses her hand to her throbbing breast, With

Love's first wonderful rap-ture blest, With Love's first wonderful rap-ture blest,

And the years glide by.

A mother kneels by the rose-bush fair,

Soft 'sigh the leaves in the evening air, Sorrowing thoughts of the past a - rise, And

Ex. 23, continued

tears   of anguish be – dim   her   eyes,   And   the   years glide   by.

Sorrowing thoughts of the past   a rise,   And tears of anguish be–dim   her eyes,

Tears   of an–guish be–dim   her   eyes,   And   the   years glide   by.

Na–ked and lone stands the rose bush fair,   Whirled are the leaves in the autumn air,

273

Ex. 24.   Faustina Hodges, *The Indignant Spinster*

the

Indignant Spinster

BALLAD

Words and Music by

Faustina Hasse Hodges.

NEW YORK
Published by WM. HALL & SON. 543 Broadway.

| Boston | New Haven Conn | Chicago | New Orleans |
| TOLMAN & CO. | SKINNER & SPERRY. | ROOT & CADY. | A.E. BLACKMAR. |

Entered according to Act of Congress, in the year 1871, by Wm. Hall & Son in the Clerk's Office at the District Court of the Southern District of N.Y.

Ex. 24, continued

THE INDIGNANT SPINSTER

WORDS AND MUSIC BY F.H.H.

Im a liv-ing re-proach to the tastes of the times! I ap-peal to the

Pope or the men who make Rhymes I sigh for a Beau— not a scrap of one

comes— So I gaze out the window, and twirl my thumbs.

6176

Ex. 24, continued

A-las af-ter wast-ing my life all a-way, In vain ef-forts to catch them day af-ter day: I say they're sour grapes, and with an-ger and scorn, I en--joy my sad Ti-tle a Spin-ster for-lorn! A Spinster! Heigho! well that's bet-ter I own; Than the slave of a ty-rant no

6176

Ex. 24, continued

moment her own: Obliged to sew Buttons and cobble old Hose, And numberless horrors, that

no-bo-dy knows.

Tempo primo.

They say I am free with no one to

teaze, Where's the use of being free? I can't do as I please; I make up my

espress:

mind to a concert to go_ And I can't stir a peg! all for want of a Beau!

Ex. 24, continued

6

And then af-ter a par-ty if perchance I get out, When I hire a small boy to escort me a-bout; It makes me feel hor-rid to see the kind pairs, Filing off in pro-ces-sion all down the stairs. And I've stood in the shade and bit-ter-ly

Lento.

Tempo.

Gioroso.

6176

Ex. 24, continued

Ex. 24, continued

being his wife, To be jumbled along in the rumble of life.

And many such

things I could tell if I choose, But it is not a prudent nor sensible

use 'Tis not proper nor fit to be getting Bouquets, And receiving at-

Ex. 24, continued

ten-tion in such small ways.   Most sin-

-cere-ly I pi-ty those fool-ish young things, Who are bartering their hearts for

flowers and rings,   And fall-ing in love with mous-tache or a purse_ Oh

dear! but a Spins-ter is aw - - - - - - - - -ful - ly worse.

6176

tremolo. Ped.

10

And then as to Love— oh Pshaw! all,
stuff, What you hear every day is quite e-nough. What do young girls get married for, sure I can't

see, They should wait till they're forty years old like me.

Well, well! you may laugh if you choose at us now, But 'tis no laughing

6176

woman who was also about the composer's age. This song is self-parody and, of course, a musical comment on the status of single women in the 1860s:

> ...A Spinster! Heigh ho! Well that's better I own;
> Than the slave of a tyrant no moment her own....
> They say I am free with no one to tease
> Where's the use of being free—I can't do as I please;
> I make up my mind to a concert to go—
> And I can't stir a peg! All for want of a beau.
> ...Most sincerely I pity those foolish young things,
> Who are bartering their hearts for flowers and rings
> And falling in love with a moustache or a purse—
> Oh dear! But a spinster is awfully worse!

The composer suggests irony by setting the text as an operatic melodrama, with elaborate expressive indications, unprovoked tremolos on diminished chords, and sudden chromaticism, all to suggest the spinster's ambivalence and to parody an inflated sense of tragedy.

Most of Hodges's eight keyboard works located to date were composed after 1870. Two, "Reveries du Soir" and "Marigena: Three Reveries by the Waterside," date from the 1860s. In general Hodges wrote keyboard studies in the French salon style, and favored nocturnes and transcriptions of songs rather than variation sets. She did not write keyboard music for dancing, unlike most of the women composers of the period. Her music instead might be compared to that of Richard Hoffmann, a contemporary American pianist.

Jane Sloman

Jane Sloman as a composer, concert pianist, and singer, born in England in 1824 and brought to the United States in 1839.[72] The date of her death is not known, but her concert career lasted through 1850,[73] and her compositions, published as Sloman Torry after 1862, appeared in the United States through 1902.[74] Four keyboard works, 22 songs, and a vocal classbook have been located to date.

The vocal classbook *The Melodist* seems to have brought her the greatest recognition as a composer before 1870. It is a collection of "Selected Gems from Celebrated Composers arranged for the use of female seminaries in 1, 2, 3 and 4 parts." In addition to the standard excerpts from such composers as Rossini, Donizetti, Mendelssohn, Bellini, and Charles Horn, Sloman contributed nine hymns in a choir style.[75] The collection is mentioned in Moore's *Dictionary of Musical Information*,[76] and one of Sloman's hymns, "Holmes," was reprinted by Simeon Cheney in *The American Singing Book*.[77] Cheney described Sloman as "Miss Jane Sloman of New York.... As evidence that the work was one of merit, it may be mentioned that several editions were printed by William Hall and Son, New York."

Other well-known works by Sloman include "Roll On, Silver Moon," "Forget Thee," "The Maiden's Farewell," and "Ericssons's Schottish," all written in the 1840s or '50s and in print in 1870.[78] Later songs, among them "Titania," "Margery Drew," and "Queen of the Night" are mentioned in Otto Ebel's handbook, *Women Composers.*[79]

"Roll On, Silver Moon" is probably the most popular of her vocal works. Stephen Foster included the melody in *The Social Orchestra,* and Charles Grobe wrote a transcription; Mark Twain mentioned the song in his catalogue of music popular in a Southern parlor.[80] However, the only imprint located to date is an arrangement of the tune by Nathan Barker rather than the original composition. It is this arrangement that is listed under Barker's name rather than Sloman's in the *Complete Catalogue.*[81] Barker arranged the tune as a song and chorus for his singing family, and another edition of his arrangment illustrates a rival troupe, *The Alleghanians,* on its cover.[82]

Sloman was one of the first female virtuoso pianists to appear in the United States. She was presented as a young prodigy in an extremely successful concert tour in 1841. Her first concerts here were accompanied by a lengthy biographical sketch intended to publicize her career by presenting her musical and social credentials to the American public.[83] This sketch published anonymously confirms the conventions surrounding the Victorian professional woman. It establishes her first as a properly educated young lady and then explains why she had moved into the public eye beyond the protection of the home. Her education included study with the pianist to Queen Victoria, Madame Dulcken, and early appearances at the court.[84] In composition she was entirely self-taught.[85] But in keeping with the conventions:

> ... music was pursued *merely* as *one* of her numerous studies, claiming only an equal share of attention with the French, Italian and German languages, with all the accomplishments common to females expensively educated, for study of any kind was full interest to her thirsting mind.
>
> Yet no household duties were neglected, nor were the varied demands of affection disregarded. Her education was conducted exclusively within the sacred precincts of *home.*[86]

Sloman was described as a paragon of virtues that would have disarmed Hannah More, for it was necessary to explain how such a lady could have brought herself to public exposure and actually play for money in a foreign country. Between 1839 and her debut in 1841, she

> gave lessons to a limited number of pupils on the piano, loved and respected by all who knew her. In her own family, a cheerful and affectionate disposition made her an idol; and with all her hopes and wishes enclosed within its charmed circle, her fine intellect and splendid acquirements seemed likely to be forever confined to a circumscribed sphere....

But about the first of this last summer combined circumstances of a private nature, which cannot with propriety be explained, induced Miss Sloman after a painful struggle, to place herself before the public. . . . The unwilling and reluctant assent to public performance given by her father, united with her own strong repugnance to that species of celebrity, as well as exciting course of life, caused her to shrink with all the feeling of a sensitive woman from voluntarily placing herself in such a state of dependence upon popular favor.

But duty demanded the sacrifice and with her wonted energy she determined to submit, and brave, for the sake of principle, what she otherwise dreaded to encounter.[87]

So launched, Jane Sloman made her American debut at Niblo's Gardens in New York. She appeared at the Grand Saloon on July 16, 1841. An advertisement in the *Herald* described "a splendid orchestra" and a set to "represent the Temple of Apollo a la Musard, in which Jane Sloman, pianist, will perform."[88]

The notices Sloman received at her concerts in New York, Philadelphia, and Boston were uniformly excellent. The *Boston Post* (November 8, 1841), praised her

extraordinary talents. She executed the most difficult compositions of the great masters with apparent ease. . . . The audience would not be satisfied without a repetition of the brilliant variations on the prayer from "Mosé in Egito" and on the march in "Otello."

Another favorable review appeared in *The Musical Cabinet*, December 1841:

Miss Sloman played a Concerto, Grand Fantasia with Brilliant Variations on the March in Rossini's Opera of "Otello" with orchestral accompaniments by Herz. She made a decided and favorable impression. . . . She has not the physical strength of a man, and therefore may be excelled in this point of view. But for grace, sentiment, expression and pathos, she certainly ranks high among the pianists who have visited this country. . . . She also sang at this concert, and in a style which showed her accomplished in this branch of the art.

In 1842 she gave additional concerts in New York, including a testimonial concert for the singer Clara Fisher and another with the Germania Orchestra.[89] The last notice of a New York performance is on February 18, 1850, when she played at a "soirée musicale" at the Female Academy.[90] The advertisement listed her as a "pianiste, harpiste and vocaliste." (This was the year that Sloman published her collection, *The Melodist,* designed for female academies.)

Despite the simplicity of the hymns in *The Melodist,* Sloman, as one would expect from her training, wrote in a cultivated style. Her songs are most aptly described as a mixture of Italian gestures within English strophic forms. In addition, the harmonies include frequent altered chords and secondary dominants, that is to say, a full-blown Romantic language. This remains constant whether she was writing waltz songs with Italian lyrics or English ballads.[91]

The texts, many of which Sloman wrote, are typically about some aspect of courtship, depicted intensely through the melancholy eyes of a female narrator. Two songs, "The Maiden's Farewell" and "Take Back the Ring," are about women who don't want to leave their mothers. In the first of these, the maiden is a "Trembling, tearful bride," whose reluctance is depicted through chromaticism and ornamentation. Another ballad, "I'll Make Him Speak Out" (ex. 25), is described on its title page as "dedicated to the ladies."[92]

"Roll On, Silver Moon" (ex. 26) is much less cultivated than either of these pieces. The melody skips in alternate directions, outlining triads and seventh chords: a pleasing lilting quality well suited to the text. Barker's arrangement presents the song as a strophic piece with four additional stanzas. It may be that the original version by Sloman was more complex, and that lines like "I'll embrace the cold sod and bathe with my tears, the sweet flowers that bloom oer his grave" were set with ornamentation and appropriately mournful harmonics. Foster's version of the tune in the *Social Orchestra* is almost identical to Barker's, but leaves out the chromatic touch at the final cadence; that may have been added to enrich the four-part arrangement.

Perhaps more than Browne or Sullivan, Sloman seems to have tailored her musical output to the "ladies." If any style could be considered the analogue of music as a feminine accomplishment, it is her mixture of female-oriented texts, bel canto conventions, and strophic ballad forms. She found success with this style, for the "Maiden's Farewell," published in 1848, remained in print in the *Complete Catalogue of 1870*.

Mrs. E.A. Parkhurst

Susan Parkhurst, who published music solely as "Mrs. E.A. Parkhurst," was a well-known composer in the 1860s. Her name survives in this century mainly through a temperance ballad, "Father's a Drunkard and Mother Is Dead," although her music has recently begun to attract the attention of scholars in American music.[93] Very little is known of her life, but the discovery of a marriage certificate to her second husband has recovered her first name and allowed both birth and death dates to be traced.[94] She was born Susan McFarland in Leicester, Massachusetts, in 1836, and died in Brooklyn, New York, in 1918.

Although she was sufficiently well known to have her songs published by the midwest firm of Root and Cady,[95] she seems to have been best known in the northeast, and in particular, New York and Brooklyn, where she lived and worked. The *Brooklyn Eagle* called her songs "as familiar as household words."[96] Her main publisher was Horace Waters, who in 1864, issued a "Select Catalogue of Mrs. E.A. Parkhurst's Compositions" on the back of one of her works (see fig. 6). When he was bought out by Charles Tremaine, Mrs.

Ex. 25.   Jane Sloman, *I'll Make Him Speak Out*

I'LL MAKE HIM SPEAK OUT.

Ex. 25,　continued

tain that for shy men some ex-cuse may be made, Sure wo-man was never so

rallentando.

tor - tur'd with doubt, Tho' I lose him for - ev - er, I'll make him speak out, Tho' I

a tempo

lose him for - ev - er I'll make him speak out, I'll make . . . .

. . . him speak out, I'll make . . . . him speak out, I'll

Ex. 25, continued

make him speak out   I'll

make him speak out, I'll   make him speak out, I'll   make him speak out.

p

crescendo.

con leggierezza e piano.

8v.

loco.   8v.

cres.

2

On my life it's provoking to worry me so,
If he's serious or joking, how on earth shall I know!
One moment he'll say things, which the next he destroys,
Are women's hearts playthings, to be broken by boys?
No! he'll never deceive me, tho' I now and then doubt,
When he knows he'd relieve me, why can't he speak out!

Ex. 26.   Jane Sloman, *Roll On, Silver Moon*

2

ROLL   ON   SILVER   MOON.

Melody by SLOMAN.   Arranged by .   N. BARKER.

Published by Firth, Pond & Co, No 1 Franklin Square, N.Y.

VOICE.

AFFETTUOSO.   As I

PIANO

FORTE.

stray'd from my cot at the close of the day 'Mid the ravishing beauties of June........ 'Neath a

jessamine shade I es_pied a fair maid And she plaintively sigh'd to the moon.

Entered according to act of Congress AD 1848 by Firth, Pond & Co in the Clerks Office of the district Court of the Southern Dist: of New York.

125

Ex. 26,   continued

3

Roll on silver moon point the trav'ler his way While the nightingale's song is in tune.......... I

Roll on silver moon point the trav'ler his way While the nightingale's song is in tune.......... I

never, never more with my true love will stray By thy soft silver beams gentle moon.

never, never more with my true love will stray By thy soft silver beams gentle moon.

125

Ex. 26,   continued

4

2

As the Hart on the mountain, my lover was brave,
So noble, and manly and clever,
So kind and sincere, and he loved me full dear.
Oh my Edwin his equal was never.
Roll on silver moon &c.

3

But alas he is dead and gone to death's bed
Cut down like a rose in full bloom
All alone doth he sleep while I thus sadly weep
Neath thy soft silver light gentle moon.
Roll on silver moon &c.

4

His lone grave I'll seek out until morning appears
And weep o'er my lover so brave
I'll embrace the cold sod and bathe with my tears
The sweet flowers that bloom o'er his grave
Roll on silver moon &c.

5

Ah me ne'er again may my bosom rejoice
For my lost love I fain would meet soon
And fond lovers will weep o'er the grave where we sleep
Neath thy soft silver light gentle moon.
Roll on silver moon &c.

G.W. Quidor Eng.r.
125

Parkhurst remained a star composer, and in 1866 Tremaine's "Select Catalogue of New Instrumental Music" continued to feature her as one of their "popular authors."

Parkhurst had an active career in the 1860s, producing songs in every style of the decade. During the war years she wrote abolitionist and patriotic political songs for the Union cause. Among them were pieces such as the campaign song and chorus, "Come Rally Freeman, Rally!" (1864); "Dey Said We Wouldn't Fight" (186-), written in support of the amendment emancipating Negroes who enlisted in the Union cause; and the "New Emancipation Song," which was sung by the famed Hutchinson Family;[97] and "The Sanitary Fair Polka" (1864), written for the Brooklyn Fair held by the United States Sanitary Commission, a voluntary war relief organization run by women.

Early in her career she wrote gospel tunes, setting texts of two well-known hymn writers, Mary Ann Kidder and Fanny Crosby.[98] More genteel Victorian ballads were also part of her repertoire and she herself wrote the text for one particularly morbid effort, "Angel Mary." (It begins, "You are lying alone in your grave, Mary, with the mould creeping over your face.")[99] Her comic song, "Love on the Brain," makes a nice contrast with the melancholy ballads of the 1840s. It is a straightforward piece about "sparking" and "kissing," without any of the overtones of unrequited love and victimized women that were so characteristic of songs by women composers two decades earlier. In addition, Parkhurst was an instrumental composer, turning many of her songs into variation sets and also writing a number of popular dances.

About 60 songs and 5 keyboard works from the many listed on the catalogues have been located to date.[100] In addition to those previously mentioned, other successful works include an arrangement of "Sweet Evelina,"[101] the duet "Give to Me Those Moonlit Hours," and "The Union Medley."

The earliest notice of a public appearance by Parkhurst is in a "Grand Concert of Sunday School Music" by the Methodist Church in New York in 1860, which featured her as a soloist and accompanist. After her first husband died in 1864, she became much more active, appearing in many concerts with her daughter, Effie, who was a singer. Apparently, these concerts were conceived as benefits for them, as this item from the *Brooklyn Eagle,* on December 12, 1864, indicates:

> The religious press we notice depart from their usual custom to commend the concert of Little Effie Parkhurst, which is to be given tonight. She has shown remarkable musical talent, and the concert is designed to give her a thorough musical education. Her father fell in battle last spring, and her mother has not the means to educate her daughter for the profession that she is so well qualified.

Fig. 6. The "Select Catalogue of Mrs. E.A. Parkhurst's Compositions" published by Horace Waters, 1864.

Select Catalogue of Mrs. E. A. Parkhurst's Compositions.

1864. PUBLISHED BY HORACE WATERS, 481 BROADWAY, N. Y. 1864.

NORAH DEAREST

Is a charming and popular song with chorus. It is simply arranged in the key of G.

"When the stars are brightly shining;
Far above my weary head,
Softly steal my thoughts to Norah,
Norah, sleeping with the dead."

HOW SOFTLY ON THE BRUISED HEART

Is an exquisite little ballad and should be found in every household in the land. It is simple and full of feeling, and easily arranged in the key of B flat.

"How softly on the bruised heart
A word of kindness falls,
And to the dry and parched soul
The moistening tear drop falls."

SWEET LITTLE NELL.

This is a fitting companion to "Sweet Evelina," which has been so popular, and which was one of Mrs. Parkhurst's best arrangements. It is spirited in its movement and has a charming chorus.

"Oh! talk not of daisies and violets of spring,
Of rose-buds and dew-drops or any such thing;
For the loveliest flow'ret that grows in the dell
Is the dear bonnie maiden they call Little Nell."

THE ANGELS ARE HOVERING NEAR.

This song is beautiful beyond description. The melody is low and sweet, while the Piano accompaniment has a smooth, gliding movement, very charming in its effect. It is arranged in A flat.

"When the glow of the sunset is fused in the sky,
And the creep of the twilight at evening is nigh,
When the eyelids of darkness are wet with the dew,
And the stars are ablaze in the dome of the blue,
The angels are hovering near."

THE BEAUTIFUL ANGEL BAND.

This is another ballad in A flat. The words are very beautiful and the music is finely adapted. Mrs. Parkhurst possesses a most remarkable faculty of interblending words and melody, and she was never more successful than in this song.

"Mother, dear Mother, they're calling me now;
Behold in the beautiful west,
With a bright crown decking each youthful brow,
They come from the Land of the blest."

I CAN'T FORGET.

This ballad, although simple, is very artistic in style, and is destined to be a favorite in the concert room and parlor. The melody is pure, combined with the richest harmony. Key of C.

"Do not chide if fond affection
Lingers still when hope is past,
Weeping tears of deep dejection
Where the wrecks of joy are cast."

DOST THOU EVER THINK OF ME, LOVE?

This is a song and chorus of the sentimental order, and cannot fail to be popular. It has been pronounced by good judges to be one of the prettiest ballads published. It is in the key of G.

"Dost thou ever think of me, love?
Dost thou ever think of me?
Do you still my memory cherish,
Though I'm far away from thee?"

ANGEL MARY.

This is a sweet and simple ballad in A flat. The words and music are by Mrs. Parkhurst, and are wedded in such a manner as to give a charm to both.

"You are lying low down in your grave, darling,
With the mould creeping over your face,
And sadly the green willows wave, darling,
And sigh o'er your lone resting place.
You left us when summer was throwing
O'er earth her bright mantle of flowers:
But we know in our hearts you were going
To a land that is fairer than ours."

WEEP NO MORE FOR LILY.

Song and Chorus in E flat. This is a light, sparkling melody in the solo, while the chorus is solemn and rich in its harmony. It contains all the elements of popularity.

"Lilly of the valley, modest, sweet and mild,
Ever pure and lovely was the gentle child;
Sunny hair had Lilly, eyes of azure blue,
Footstep soft and gentle as the falling dew.
Chorus.—Weep no more for Lily; Lily's gone above;
Angels came and bore her to their land of love."

MARY FAY.

This is a popular song among the Minstrel bands, and is very fine for a serenade. The chorus is particularly good. Key of B flat. 30 cents each.

"Oh! where has she gone, my Mary Fay,
My love, my joy, my pain?
I would go to the ends of the raging sea
To hear her voice again."

THE UNION MEDLEY.

This is an ingenious combination of all the best patriotic songs of the day, and will be popular. 60 cents

THE TEAR OF LOVE.

This is one of Mrs. Parkhurst's happiest efforts, and when sung by a sympathising voice cannot fail to draw the tears from every eye. It is arranged in A flat, and ranges from E to F above.

"Think not thou e'er hast won a heart,
And that heart holds thee dear,
Till it sheds for thee, and thee alone,
A pure and heartfelt tear;
For a smile of love or a spoken word
Ne'er yet affection proved;
But when we mark the starting tear,
Oh! then we are beloved."

KATY DID, KATY DIDN'T.

This is, as its name indicates, a comic song. It is designed more especially for children, and has elicited shouts of applause wherever it has been sung. It is in the key of D.

"Katy did, Katy didn't,
Katy did, Katy didn't,
Katy did, Katy didn't,
Katy didn't. She didn't, I know.
Katy had an ancient lover," &c.

THIS HAND NEVER STRUCK ME, MOTHER.

This song is founded on a very beautiful incident, and cannot fail to be popular throughout the land. It is very simple and touching. Key of C.

"Chorus.—Would that every loving sister
Could say of her darling brother,
Whether he were dead or living,
This hand never struck me, mother."

THE DYING DRUMMER.

This is a very touching song and chorus, and will be a favorite in every household, particularly those made desolate by death upon the battle-field. It is arranged in the key of D. 30 cents each.

"Chorus.—Have you come to see your darling
Die upon the battle field,
Far from home, so sad and lonely?
Have you come your boy to shield?"

The following is a list of Mrs. Parkhurst's instrumental compositions:—

"Yankee Doodle," with variations, is not difficult, but very brilliant, and has been played by Mrs. Parkhurst with great applause at over one hundred concerts.

"Morning Dreams," a collection of popular airs brilliantly varied, and especially designed for teaching purposes, viz: **"Away with Melancholy,"** rather difficult, and a great favorite among good players **"Blue Bells of Scotland,"** very showy, but not difficult. **"Sweet Evelina,"** another great favorite, and exceedingly brilliant. **"They Worked Me All the Day,"** showy and excellent practice for pupils somewhat advanced. The above pieces are 60 cents each.

"Spirit Polka." This is one of the best and most popular polkas ever published. It is excellent for dancing and possesses the charm of never growing old. It is full of melody and easily arranged in A flat.

"Summer House of Roses." A Galop very spirited and beautifully arranged. Key of C.

"Airy Castles," a Romance. This is one of those charming, silvery pieces, that once heard cannot be forgotten, and will always be a favorite with the young ladies.

"The Cloud with a Silver Lining." Another Romance of the same character as the above.

"General Scott's Farewell March." An easy March and a fine arrangement for young pupils.

"The Sanitary Fair Polka." Composed for the Sanitary Fair, and dedicated to its patrons. This is one of Mrs. Parkhurst's most successful efforts. It is simple, full of melody and exquisite harmony, and fine for dancing. The *Brooklyn Eagle* says:—

"The music is bright, sparkling, attractive and "easily whistled;" in other words, it has all the elements of popularity, and will undoubtedly extend the reputation of its accomplished author."

"The Tender Glance Schottisch." Fine for dancing, quite easy and very beautiful. 30 cents each.

New Music by Mrs. Parkhurst.—We cheerfully call attention to Mrs. Parkhurst's advertisement of new music, which appears in our columns to-day. There are some ten or fifteen compositions in all, many of which are exceedingly meritorious, while all are above the average of such works. Mrs. Parkhurst is one of our most prolific native composers, many of her songs being familiar as household words. The fair author has a happy faculty of interblending word and melody, which results in most pleasing and memorable harmony, the benefits of which our readers may share by purchasing the music and studying the composition.—*Brooklyn Eagle.*

VOCAL.

THE NEW EMANCIPATION SONG.

This is a stirring Song and Chorus, written for the Hutchinsons and sung by them throughout the land. It is well adapted to the times.

"If you wish to be commended,
Let not Slavery be extended,
But its reign quickly ended,
In these United States."

THE SOLDIER'S DYING FAREWELL.

This is another of Mrs. Parkhurst's latest productions. It has a charming melody, with a chorus beautifully harmonized, and is having a large sale.

Chorus—Don't you hear them singing, Mother,
Listen to the music's swell,
Now I leave thee, loving Mother,
God be with you, fare you well.

NO SLAVE BENEATH THAT STARRY FLAG.

This is one of the best songs of the kind ever written. The words are by the Rev. George Lansing Taylor. It has a fine chorus, and when well sung is calculated to infuse patriotism into the heart of every listener

"No Slave beneath that starry flag,
The emblem of the free,
No fettered hand, shall wield the brand,
That smites for Liberty."

DEY SAID WE WOULDN'T FIGHT.

A very amusing negro melody, with a fine chorus; It is well adapted to the times.
Chorus.—"Hi! hi! boys, we's a gwine home,
Hi! ho! now for de fray,

LITTLE JOE THE CONTRABAND.

Another mirth provoking negro melody.

THERE'S REST FOR ALL IN HEAVEN

A very beautiful song and chorus, in the key of E flat.

"We still have this sweet solace left,
There's rest for all in heaven."

COME RALLY, FREEMEN, RALLY.

A campaign song and chorus, very finely arranged. One of Mrs. Parkhurst's best.
"Hurrah, boys, hurrah, we'll work with all our might

THEY TELL ME I'LL FORGET THEE.

This is an exquisite ballad, plaintive and touching, and one of the sweetest melodies Mrs. Parkhurst has ever written. It is arranged in A flat.

"They tell me I'll forget thee, when
'Mid other scenes I stray,
That thoughts of thee will vanish as
The dew at break of day."

ONLY YOU AND I.

A charming little song, lively and very amusing. *More especially* designed for people in love.

"When'er we walk together, love,
And no one else is nigh,
It seems as if the world was made,
For only you and I."

I'M WILLING TO WAIT.

Or, The Old Maid's Song.

Another comic song, arranged with a beautiful accompaniment, very amusing.

"Twas not such a very long time ago,
At least, so it seems to me,
Since I was a maiden, just in my teens,
As pretty as I could be.
But now they call me a poor old maid,
And I'll own I'm thirty four,
But I'm willing to wait, I'm willing to wait,
With patience a year or two more."

MY JAMIE'S IN THE BATTLE FIELD.

A Scotch ballad, very pretty and taking.

"My Jamie's on the battle field,
And Oh, I miss my laddie so,
My puir lane heart so fu of pain,
I wish I had na let him go."

OUR DEAR NEW ENGLAND BOYS.

A very sweet and touching melody, with beautiful words and an excellent chorus. Key of E flat.

Chorus.—Let them rest their work is finished
Nothing now their sleep annoys,
Angels guard the unbroken slumbers,
Of our dear New England Boys.

The above pieces are 30 cents each, mailed.

WERE I BUT HIS OWN WIFE.

One of Tom Moore's beautiful songs, to sweet and appropriate music. A ... that will be a favorite.

"Were I but his own wife to guide and guard him,
'Tis little of sorrow should fall on my d...
For every kind glance my whole life w...
reward him,
In sickness I'd soothe, and in sadness cheer."

THERE ARE VOICES, SPIRIT VOI...

This is one of the best pieces Mrs. Parkhurst has ever written. It is classic... style, yet simply arranged. It has a ... beautiful chorus, with an accompanime... imitation of voices.

Chorus.—Spirit voices, hear the echo,
They are calling us away,
Where the roses never withe...
Where the crystal foun...
play."

A HOME ON THE MOUNTAIN.

A dashing spirited song in the key o... Very brilliant and beautiful.

"Let others sigh for a valley home
Where the brook runs murmurin...
I'll build my cot on the mountain's s...
Where it leans to the deep blue s...

DO THEY LOVE ME STILL AS EV...

Song and Chorus in the key of B ... Very beautiful and becoming very pop...

"Do they love me still as ever,
In the old familiar way,
Do they ne'er forget me, never,
Though afar from home I stray."

OH, SEND ME ONE FLOWER FR... HIS GRAVE.

A very touching and beautiful song, chorus finely harmonized. It is arrang... the key of A flat.

"While the merry birds sing in the branches near,
And above him the green willows w...
Still warm with the sunshine and with the dew,
Oh, send me one flower from his gr...

WAIT, MY LITTLE ONE, WAIT

This is a pathetic little ballad, that t... es the heart of every mother who has a ... one in heaven. It is simply arranged i... key of A flat.

"Wait, my little one, wait,
When you get to that beautiful
Tarry a little my darling one,
Ere you join that heavenly band.

The above pieces are 30 cents each, ma...

INSTRUMENTAL.

The Sigh in the Heart—Waltz ... mental. This is a charming piece of ... pages; brilliant, and at the same time sweet and not too difficult for ord... players. Price, 40 cents

Starlight Waltz.—A simple waltz, pretty and designed more especially for ... ers not very far advanced. Good tim... dancing.

On to Richmond Gal op—A b... spirited gallop, not very difficult, and that cannot fail to be popular. Pric... cents each, mailed.——

The SUNNYSIDE SET.

A set of easy pieces arranged from ... lar airs, especially for young beginne... "Three Roguish Chaps," (Polka); ... Country," (March); "Sunny Side Ron... "Little Bird Waltz"; "Brave McCle... (March); "What they do at the Spri... (Waltz); "They worked me all the ... (Polka); There's no such girl as mine," ... lop); "Was my brother in the b... (March); "Shall we know each other th... (Rondo); "Little Ella's an Angel," (Q... step); "Leave me with my mother, (M... "Weep no more for Lilly," (March); "... have my loved ones gone," (Schottis... "The Volunteer Polka"; "Cannon Ga... "Morning Dew," (Schottische); "... Jenny Dow," (Polka); "Sweet Eve... (Waltz); "When this dreadful war is en... (Polka); "Merry little birds are we," ... ka); "There are plenty of fish in the ... (Quickstep); "Norah Dearest," (Ma... "The Evacuation," (Dance); "F... Stubbs," (Dance); "Sweet little ... (Waltz).

The above pieces are all fingered. Pri... cents each, mailed free.

Effie popularized her mother's most famous song, the temperance ballad, "Father's A Drunkard and Mother Is Dead."[102] According to the title page of the sheet music, mother and "Little Effie" performed it at meetings all over the country.[103] Parkhurst's song was probably modeled after Henry Work's popular "Come Home, Father," written in 1864. Both are song and choruses in triple time, using a child narrator to exploit the listener's sympathies. Parkhurst's harmonic vocabulary, however, is more varied, touching on more minor chords and in particular, beginning the chorus section on B-flat minor in the first inversion. The central refrain of the song is saved for the final chorus phrase: "Dark is the night and the storm rages wild, God pity Bessie, the drunkard's lone child" (ex. 27).

Parkhurst wrote other temperance ballads that were patter songs in a comic style. These, too, were popularized by "Little Effie" at temperance meetings in New York.[104]

Her commitment to the cause was the impetus behind an article she wrote very late in her life about Stephen Foster—"Personal Recollections of the Last Days of Stephen Foster."[105] The editors prefaced it with this description:

> This is a story filled with human interest written by a lady who in her youth was known as a successful composer and who, when a young girl, took a friendly interest in Stephen Foster. She now wishes to tell the world that Foster was not altogether as dissolute as many people have supposed.

The link between the two was publisher Horace Waters, who owned a music store where Parkhurst worked in the early 1860s. Waters was also Foster's publisher in his last years, and it was at his store that Parkhust met the famous composer in 1863.

Horace Waters (1812-1893) was a figure of some importance to Foster in this period. One of the founding members of the Prohibition party and an ardent abolitionist,[106] Waters was also a fervent revivalist, active in publishing many collections of "Sunday School" hymns.[107] These hymns, in their simplicity and popular appeal, were the forerunners of the gospel hymns of the 1880s, and it may have been Waters's influence on Foster that led to the composition of the 26 Foster hymns in the early 1860s.

Parkhurst, also, was active in the church. She, too appeared as a composer in Waters's immensely successful collections of "Sunday School" songs.[107] And she also was directly involved in arranging Foster's songs in different formats for Waters, both during Foster's last years and after his death.[109]

In 1868, Susan Parkhurst married John Duer and published at least one work under a double name.[110] Her production seems to have fallen off sharply by the end of the decade, and nothing further is known of her life at this time.

Parkhurst's success came from her mastery of the popular idioms of the 1860s, which she handled with considerable ingenuity and flair. She turned the

Ex. 27.   Mrs. E.A. Parkhurst, *Father's a Drunkard and Mother is Dead*

FATHER'S A DRUNKARD, AND MOTHER IS DEAD.

Poetry by "STELLA" (of Washington)　　　　Music by Mrs E . A . PARKHURST.

One dismal, stormy night in winter, a little girl barefooted and miserably clad leaned shivering against a large tree near the President's House. "Sissie" said a passing stranger, "why dont you go home?"

She raised her pale face, and with tears dimming her sweet blue eyes, answered mournfully: "I have no home. Father's a Drunkard, and Mother is dead."

Moderato.

con espressione.

III-3

I. Out in the gloom-y night, sad-ly I roam, I have no Moth - er dear, no pleas-ant home; No bo-dy cares for me no one would cry Ev-en if poor lit-tle Bessie should die.

II. We were so hap-py till Fa-ther drank rum, Then all our sor-row and trou-ble be-gan; Moth-er grew pa - ler, and Ba - by and I were too hungry to play.

III. Oh! if the "Temp'-rance men" on-ly could find Poor, wretch-ed Fa - ther, and talk ve-ry kind— If they could stop him from drink-ing— why, then I should be so ve-ry happy a - gain!

Ex. 27, continued

4

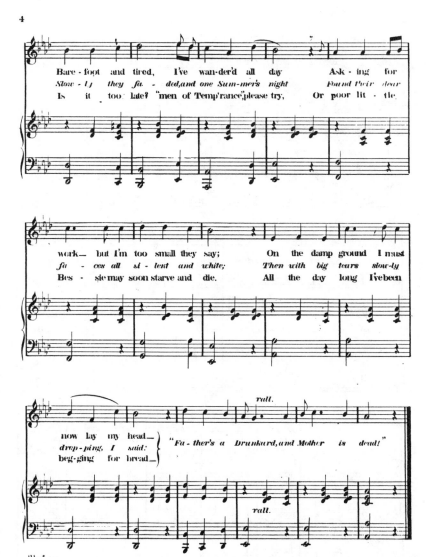

Bare - foot and tired, I've wan-der'd all day   Ask - ing for
Slow - ly they fa - ded,and one Sum-mer's night   Found their dear
Is it too late? "men of Temp'rance,please try,   Or poor lit - tle

work— but I'm too small they say;   On the damp ground I must
fa - ces all si - lent and white;   Then with big tears slow-ly
Bes - sie may soon starve and die.   All the day long I've been

now lay my head—   }
drop-ping, I said: }   "Fa - ther's a Drunkard,and Mother is dead!"
beg-ging for bread— }

rall.

111 — 5

Ex. 27, continued

formulaic song and chorus into a more ambitious unit by altering the meter and mood of the chorus section so that it provided a dramatic contrast with the solo. In "There Are Voices, Spirit Voices," for example, the solo section is in 9/8, an unusual meter, while the chorus is in 2/4 (ex. 28). In "Weep No More for Lily," the jaunty Anglo-Irish melody of the opening solo tune in 2/4 gives way to a solemn andante four-part chorus in 4/4 (ex. 29).

Her harmonic vocabulary was also more expansive and richer than most average popular songs of the period. Both of the previous examples illustrate this aspect of her style. In the first, the use of the added-sixth chord to suggest the spirit voices is picked up from the melody and used repeatedly by the piano accompaniment, especially in the little postlude that ends the song. The chromatic inflections in the four-part-harmony in the second example foreshadow the "barbershop" sound of the 1880s and '90s.

Occasionally her accompaniments reveal a pianistic imagination. In the duet "There Are Voices, Spirit Voices," the arpeggios suggest the airy land of the hereafter, and the gentle rocking motion of the 9/8 meter conveys voices floating over the chasm between the worlds of the living and the dead.

Often the little postludes that round off a Parkhurst song are far more original than the usual repetitions of the tune that sufficed for most other composers. "Don't Marry a Man If He Drinks," a song and a chorus, concludes with a miniature waltz (ex. 30).

With respect to her role as a woman composer, Parkhurst differs from the other composers in this study by virtue of her stylistic eclecticism and the topical subject matter of her songs. Perhaps the strongest point of comparison is in the personalized mode of her temperance ballads, many of which were addressed to women, and in the pattern of her career, which apparently was realized by the necessity of supporting herself after her first husband's death. This self-support depended upon her being seen, at least initially, as a widow and a mother; unfortunately, this seemed to stop after her second marriage in 1868.

Still, she seems less constricted by the notions of "accomplishment" than her predecessors or her contemporary sister composers. Certainly, her involvement in temperance gave her music a wider frame of reference than the parlor or social circle; in this respect, her work foreshadowed the later decade of the 1880s, when many women were active both as lyricists and songwriters for the temperance cause. Parkhurst was a popular composer, not an accomplished lady amateur, and her success in the 1860s foreshadows the decline that occurred in the latter part of the nineteenth century of the tradition of music as a female accomplishment.

Ex. 28.   Mrs. E.A. Parkhurst, *There are Voices, Spirit Voices*

THERE ARE VOICES--SPIRIT VOICES.

Words by FANNY CROSBY.

Music by MRS. E. A. PARKHURST.

Legato con sentimento.

1. There are voi - ces, spir - it voi - - ces, in the whis - - per of the
2. There are voi - ces, spir - it voi - - ces, I have heard............ them in my
3. There are voi - ces, spir - it voi - - ces, I have felt.............. their ten - der

breeze,...... When it wakes...... the in - fant blos - soms when it sighs...... among the
dreams,..... When in fan - - cy I have wan - der'd by the qui - et mountain
thrill....... When the heav'n - - ly dews were fall - ing and the bu - sy world was

Entered according to Act of Congress A. D. 1864, by Horace Waters in the Clerk's office of the U. S. Dist. Court for the Southern District of New York.

1040

4

trees,...... And the forms of those that love us on their view-less wings are nigh,...... In the wreath-ing clouds that lin-ger on the blue...... e-the-rial sky,

streams,.... And their mu-sic mur-mur'd light-ly 'twas a ca-rol soft and low,...... And I lis-ten'd while it min-gled with the brook-lets gen-tle flow.

still,....... O'er my tir-ed heart for-sa-ken crush'd be-neath its hea-vy chain,.... Like a rain-bow in the dark-ness dawn'd the star.... of hope a-gain.

Soprano *Accelerato.*

Spir-it voi-ces; hear the ech-o, They are call-ing us a-way.

Alto

Tenor *pp*

Spir-it voi-ces; hear the ech-o, They are call-ing us a-way.

Bass

1040

Ex. 28,   continued

Where   the ro - ses   nev - er   wither,   Where   the crystal   foun - tains play.

Where   the ro - ses   nev - er   wither,   Where   the crystal   foun - tains play.

pp accelerando.

8va

dim.   P   rall.   pp   ppp

Ex. 29. Mrs. E.A. Parkhurst, *Weep No More for Lily*

WEEP NO MORE FOR LILY.

SONG AND CHORUS.

Words by Mrs. W. V. PORTER.　　　　　　　　　Music by MRS. PARKHURST.

1. Li - ly of the val - ley, Mod - est sweet and mild,
2. Smi - ling as the sun - beam, Was her face so fair,

Ev - er pure and love - ly, Was the gen - tle child......
Pass - ing like a day dream, A zeph - yr of the air........

Entered according to Act of Congress A.D. 1864, by E. A. DAGGETT, in the Clerk's Office of the United States District Court for the Southern District of New York.

Ex. 29, continued

4

Sun - ny hair had Li - ly, Eyes of a - zure blue,......
Trip - ping o'er the heath - er, Light her foot - step fell,......

Foot - step soft and gen - tle, As the fall - ing dew........
Bear - ing ev - er with her, Fai - ry's mys - tic spell........

CHORUS. *Andante.*

Weep no more for Li - ly, Li-ly's gone a - bove,.... An - gels came and

Weep no more for Li - ly, Li-ly's gone a - bove,.... An - gels came and

Ex. 29, continued

5

Ex. 30.   Mrs. E.A. Parkhurst, *Don't Marry a Man if He Drinks*
(excerpt)

1268

man   if   he drinks,   Don't......   mar - ry   a   man   if   he drinks.

man   if   he drinks,   Don't......   mar - ry   a   man   if   he drinks.

Tempo di waltz.

3.

Just think of the sorrows and cares,
  The heart-rending sighs and the fears ;
Of the words and the blows, and the cruelest woes,
  And then think of an ocean of tears.
Think of Toodles the drunkest of men,—
  His attitudes, hiccoughs, and winks—
And then think what a dignified pair you will make,
  If you marry a man and he drinks.
    'Tis no matter, &c.

4.

Young ladies, look well to your hearts,
  Don't throw them away on a sot ;
Or a man who is given to treating his friends,
  Whate'er be his station or lot.
Though his pride may uphold him awhile,
  Yet sooner or later he sinks ;—
Then if you would be happy the rest of your days,
  Don't marry a man if he drinks.
    'Tis no matter, &c.

1268

Conclusions

We can look at the lives and work of these five notable women composers from a number of viewpoints. An overall assessment of their individual strengths as composers place Hodges, Parkhurst, and then Sullivan at the head of the group. As the first woman to become famous in the United States for her musical compositions, Augusta Browne occupies a special place in women's studies. All five of the composers differ from their contemporaries in that they produced a body of work rather than one or two isolated pieces.

The tradition of music as a feminine accomplishment affected them in a variety of ways. In keeping with the bond between accomplishment and cultivated taste, three of the five had English roots and European allegiances. Hodges and Sloman were both born and trained abroad; Browne was a true Victorian by temperament as well as musical taste. Only Parkhurst and Sullivan were directed towards a more popular indigenous style. Evidences of the female subculture supporting musical accomplishment can be found in Browne's use of ladies' magazines or in Sloman's and Hodges's connections with female seminaries. Although all, finally, wrote parlor music, the church compositions and the arias of Browne and Hodges and the political ballads of Parkhust suggest that they were less confined to the parlor genres than most of their contemporaries.

The tensions between the role of composer and that of the proper Victorian-American woman come through in details of their lives. The stereotype of the woman composer as a natural spontaneous melodist appears in Marion Dix Sullivan's descriptions of her own creativity—"unsought and unbidden"—appropriately humble rationalizations. The public performances of both Jane Sloman and Susan Parkhurst were justified in print through explanations of economic necessity. Hodges was sufficiently ambivalent about her own professional achievements to underplay them (again modesty may have been the motive) in her biography of her father. Augusta Browne wrote an extraordinary angry defense of the educated woman artist in the 1860s, the most explicit confrontation with the mores of the period.

A final noteworthy feature is the degree to which these composers used music to express their own sense of themselves as women. Sullivan's ballads, whether about nature or war, were frequently written from a female point of view or about a female subject. Hodges's most famous ballads were described in feminized terms as the "epitome of woman's life" or as full of feeling and sentiment. She also wrote two highly unusual, possibly autobiographical, songs about being single, including a protest against the restrictions placed upon her social freedoms. Parkhurst wrote many of her temperance songs addressed specifically to women and intended to be sung by a female performer.

The Emergence of a Professional Ethos for Women Composers

The "Piano Girl" is Dethroned

Attitudes towards the idea of music as a feminine accomplishment changed significantly after 1870.[1] Although statements supporting the old doctrines can be found throughout the period, attacks on the dilletantism inherent in accomplishment are more common. One example of the old attitude is an article on "The Education of Women" from the 1880s, in which an anonymous writer summed up the rationale for routine musical education for girls on familiar grounds: it was part of their training to be fit wives and mothers since it enabled them to beautify and order their households according to a cultivated standard. As for the contention that only those who were talented should study music, the author rebutted by comparing music to arithmetic: both were "practical skills" that were a necessary part of education:

> The study of music and especially the acquirement of practical skill in the making of music is sufficiently well recognized as a necessary part of a girl's education; but some question has been raised on this subject by the very persons who have most loudly complained of the defectiveness of women's education in scholastic studies. It is frequently said that only those girls who have marked ability in music, and who therefore are likely to excel in it, should be required to give time to its study. We do not argue in that way respecting the education of boys. We make all boys learn arithmetic, those who have not as well as those who have a natural aptitude for mathematics. When we reflect upon the value of musical skill to a woman as a resource for her own entertainment as a means of adding to the attractiveness of her home, and more than all, as a refining softening influence upon children, it is scarcely an exaggeration to say that a knowledge of music is as necessary to a girl as an acquaintance of arithmetic is to a boy; and as no boy not an idiot is incapable of acquiring a knowledge of arithmetic, so no girl with hands and ordinary mental capacity is incapable of acquiring skill in music.[2]

This philosophy continued to be attacked from two sides, just as it had been in the earlier decades of the century. Less cultivated people thought the emphasis on music was pretentious, the fashion for music lessons nothing more than a "strange passion." Dio Lewis, doctor, physical education teacher, and director of a girls' school in Lexington, Mass., devoted a chapter to "Piano Music" in his book on female education and health entitled *Our Girls:*

> Nothing so constantly troubled and pained me during the progress of the school at Lexington as the strange passion for the piano. Of the 140 girls present during the third year, I cannot recall more than three or four who possessed any decided musical capacity, while nearly a hundred studied music.[3]

Lewis particularly decried the snobbery, from his point of view, that motivated their lessons. Instead of good old songs like "Way Down Upon the Swanee River," they learned classical music which bored everybody, or they sang opera which communicated immoral sentiments through the lyrics.

With such opinions, Lewis can hardly be classified as a member of what the historian Joseph Mussulman calls the "cultured generation." Yet even those critics shared a sympathetic aversion to accomplishment. Mussulman writes that "almost without exception every cultured critic who wrote of parlor music at all felt constrained to deplore the debasement of cultured ideals by doting parents who forced the study of piano upon their idle young daughters to satisfy a thirst for gentility."[4] Although these critics would not have sanctioned Lewis's plebeian tastes, their common meeting ground was an attack on dilletantism.

By the end of the century cultured critics viewed the "idle young daughter" as a symbol of the philistine attitudes towards music that characterized Victorian America. She was, in James Huneker's words, the "piano girl," a stereotype that he went on to describe in telling detail:

> Passed away is the girl who played the piano in the stiff Victorian drawing rooms of our mothers. It has always seemed to me that slippery hair-cloth sofas and the "Battle of Prague" dwelt in mutual harmony. And now at the beginning of the century the girls who devote time to the keyboard merely for the purpose of social display are almost as rare as the lavender water ladies of morbid sensibilities in the Richardson and Fielding novels.... I wonder if the musical girl of the old sort may not also set down for study—the study we accord to rare and disappearing types. Yet never has America been so musical.... Here is a pretty paradox: the piano is passing and with it the piano girl—there really was a piano girl—and more music was never made before in the land![5]

Elsewhere in his discussion of the "eternal feminine" in music, Huneker defined the "piano girl," contrasting her with the "new girl."

> The piano girl was forced to practice at the keyboard, even if without talent. Every girl played the piano, not to play was a stigma of poverty. The new girl is too busy to play the piano unless she has the gift; then she plays with consuming earnestness. We listen to her, for we know that this is an age of specialization, an age when woman is coming into her own, be it nursing, electoral suffrage, or the writing of plays; so our poets no longer make sonnets to our Ladies of Ivories, nor are budding girls chained to the keyboard.[6]

The hallmark of the new age and the new girl was professionalism, or what Huneker called "specialization"—music seen as an art rather than a rudimentary skill acquired for social mobility. Perhaps what had to be conveyed above all was a sense of importance and dignity to artistic training. As Cecilia Beaux (1855-1942), the famous portrait painter, wrote in her autobiography of early education: "No kind of Art, music or other, had ever been shown to me as a toy or plaything to be taken up, trifled with and perhaps abandoned."[7]

The other aspect of professionalizing music was that it had also to be seen as a legitimate source of occupations for women. Music had to be connected to paid work outside the home. In contrast to the majority of guidebooks before the Civil War, late-nineteenth-century manuals begin to describe music as a source of employment.[8] In order to be seen as such, it had to shed the stigma of accomplishment. For Dio Lewis, the crusty doctor-author of *Our Girls*, it was a frill and a "mania," and it could not help meet the "surplus female problem."[9] But as the decades wore on, other writers were more foresighted.

Mary L. Rayne in *What Can a Woman Do; or Her Position in the Business and Literary World,* for example, listed the "profession of music" as one option. This included music teaching, of course, but she also cited the exceptional careers that could be made by women of talent. Rayne suggested singers like Adelina Patti, Modjeska, and Langtry as models,[10] but did not mention any composers. Still, she held up the professional performer as an ideal, and did not shrink from suggesting that great talent demanded realization, even if it meant appearing in public and going on the stage. All of this was a far cry from the warning against professionalism that were typical of mid-nineteenth-century etiquette books.

Similar concern for employment based on musical training can be found in Louis Lombard's *Observations of a Musician,* an extremely successful work that was later translated into French, German, and Italian.[11] He devoted one chapter to "Music as a Breadwinner for Girls." As the director of a conservatory of music in Utica, New York, Lombard was attempting to persuade "the parents of musically inclined girls" that they could not "invest money much more profitably than in the musical education of their daughters." Why? Because

> in the musical profession woman stands on a par with man. She is never underpaid simply because she is a woman.... In the course of her musical career she does not need to part with any of her womanly attributes....[12]

Lombard believed that music teaching as an open and expanding field was a suitable profession for women. In fact, Lombard overestimated the balance between demand and supply. One reason that women turned to other kinds of musical livelihood was precisely because music teaching was flooded with their sisters.

Census data between 1870 and 1900 document this trend. As table 5 indicates, the percentage of women employed in music between 1870 and 1900 rose dramatically from 26% to 56.4%. Music was, according to the 1900 census, one of the professions whose sex distribution altered most between 1880 and 1900.

Table 5.   The Increase of Women in Music and Music Teaching between 1870 and 1910, According to the U.S. Census

	Percent Female				
	1870	1880	1890	1900	1910
Musicians	2 (6,519)†	*	*	*	*
Music teachers	60 (9,491)†	*	*	*	*
Total	36	43	55	56.4	66
Total employed in profession	(16,010)†	(30,477)	(62,155)	(92,174)	(139,310)

*Not available. After 1870 the census does not distinguish between music and music teaching.
†The numbers in parentheses indicate total number of males and females in the occupation.

Equality of Creative Opportunity as the New Ideal

As the economic basis of accomplishment crumbled with the increasing number of women entering the labor force and looking for paid work, the ideology of the tradition came under a different kind of attack. The most significant change in the attacks on accomplishment in the late-nineteenth century was its source: criticism came not only from critics who had traditionally held female amateur musicians up to ridicule, but more importantly, from progressive women who perceived the shortcomings of accomplishment as a reflection of the inferior status of women in American society. It was implicit in dilettante education that women had limited creativity. Among the proponents of accomplishment there was never any talk of training women to be artists, or even of encouraging the exceptional individual to fulfill her abilities. Of course, guidebooks and etiquette books addressed the normal individual rather than the exceptional, but a consciousness of the creative equality between the sexes and the need to develop individual potential, regardless of sex, begins to emerge in this period.

In the 1870s and '80s we begin to see articles on music and women that are not addressed to "musical misses" or "musical ladies" but to women as musicians, a significant semantic shift. Fanny Ritter's paper, "Woman As a Musician,"[13] written in 1873 and later published in the *Woman's Journal* of 1876, the leading organ of the suffrage movement, is typical of this new trend. Ritter wrote her paper for the first Congress of the Association for the Advancement of Women, which began that year. The object of the association was "to receive and present practical methods for securing to women higher intellectual, moral, and physical conditions and thereby to improve all domestic and social relations."[14] It was a feminist organization, and the political climate of the meetings can be deduced from the titles of the other papers presented at Ritter's session, among them "Industrial Education for Women," "Women Suffrage," and "The Need of Women in Science."

Ritter's paper begins with a historical overview of female musicians. Their record in antiquity and folk traditions proves that their musicality existed, but their history in Western Music in Christendom is bleak because they were "banished from active musical participation in the church service"; a woman's "practical career as a public artiste only began with the invention of the opera."[15]

After naming a few outstanding singers,[16] Ritter turns to composition. She states immediately that "the list of feminine composers is a brief one, and most of its members are now living." The earliest figure mentioned is Anna Amalia of Prussia.[17] Then follows a defense:

> But women have only lately realized the depth and strength of the science of music, and what long years of severe mental discipline and scientific training are necessary in order to master the art of composition.
> ...and why should not women of sufficient intellectual and especial ability to warrant the possibility of their obtaining honorable distinction, make an effort, and discarding the absurd idea that composition is an affair of instinct, study to compose for immortality alone? There is surely a feminine side of composition, as of every other art. And I would suggest the adoption of the science of composition as an elective, if not obligatory branch of the higher course of study in ladies' colleges.[18]

One need only compare Ritter's plea for thorough professional training with the article on "The Education of Women" cited earlier[19] to realize the contrast between the two views. Essentially, Ritter was attacking the belief that music was a subject in which one might dabble. She stressed the commitment that professional composition demanded as opposed to the superficial education of the accomplishments. Music was a "science," not just a means of adding to the attractiveness of a home.

As for the lady amateur, Ritter also expands the dimensions of her sphere. Women ought to extend their influence beyond their home circle and society:

> The role of the genuine unpretending amateur, the assistant, the befriender of artists, is especially fitted to the cultivated women.... With lady amateurs then will chiefly rest the happy task of preparing... the soil which must foster the young genius of future American art.[20]

Essentially, Ritter's position was that of the Victorian ethos writ large. John Ruskin, for example, had defined women's function as "to praise, that is to serve as the inspiration and support of men of genius."[21] Ritter altered the implications of this statement by formulating the sphere in which women should inspire on a social rather than a personal scale. Her statement is a classic formulation of the philosophy behind the music club movement that gained momentum in the 1890s. Women became the cultural reformers and social consumers of music, spreading the ideals of the cultivated tradition through their clubs and their patronage of concert life and conservatories.[22]

Ritter's paper, progressive for its time, appears mild in comparison with later statements from other women. A far more dynamic work appeared about ten years later—*Women in Sacred Song*.[23] This was a large anthology of hymns, religious poems, and sacred music all written and composed "By Women." The spirit of this remarkable volume was evangelical in many respects: it grew out of the religious and temperance reform and missionary movements, in which women were particularly active, and devoted itself not only to standard denominational texts to but social problems as well. The introduction to the volume was in fact written by the president of the National Women's Christian Temperance Union, Frances Willard.

The collection contains 2,500 pieces, among them 130 songs that represented the efforts of about 50 composers. This work is the earliest known anthology of texts and music exclusively by women. Its uniqueness was well understood by the compiler and editor, Eva Munson Smith. In her preface "Woman as Musical Composer," Smith set the tone for the anthology as a whole.

> That which has been accomplished by woman in this direction, she wrote, "has been without the stimulus of encouragement, but with the irresistible impulse to place upon paper the melodies and harmonies in her heart and soul, and this too oftentimes amid a multiplicity of domestic cares."[24]

Smith cites a few women composers from the nineteenth century to "prove that women can write music"; among them were Clara Schumann, Teresa Carreno, and a "Miss Spindler, author of the famous hymn for piano, St. Agnes Eve."[25] She also singles out a number of her contemporaries. The preface concludes with a militant statement about the adverse climate in which women composers had to work, about the lack of encouragement, and about the timidity of many women who still felt it improper to publish under their own names.

If a few weeks of research has brought to light the compositions that are available of fifty or more ladies, how many more there yet must be present timidly writing under some *non-de-plume* or using their initial only and may not publish at all. The next few years will bring a revelation, showing that woman has already done much more in musical composition than is generally supposed. This volume will give but a faint idea, a dim foreshadowing of what shall be achieved in the future when she receives the stimulus born of encouragement, which is her meed. As a late writer has beautifully expressed the same idea: "The triumph of woman in sacred song is but the prelude to the triumph that awaits her."[26]

In this manner the religious and moral fervor of the social reform movements, along with their spurt of aggressive activism, was transferred to a commitment to equality of creative opportunity for women.

The composers in this volume include women from Britain. Some of the Victorian favorites are there, among them Harriet Mary Browne (Mrs. Heman's sister), represented by "Evening Song to the Virgin" and "The Messenger Bird"; Anne Fricker, "There's a Sigh in the Heart"; Virginia Gabriel, "Cleansing Fires"; Miss Lindsay, "Far Away"; and Lady Carew, "The Bridge." We also find a few of the mid-nineteenth-century Americans that we have encountered previously; these include Abby Hutchinson ("Kind Words Can Never Die") and Mrs. E.A. Parkhurst ("Father's a Drunkard and Mother is Dead").

The composer represented by the greatest number of pieces—14—is Phoebe Palmer Knapp. To the editor of this volume Knapp was the very symbol of the woman composer of sacred song. Of great importance were her religious credentials as the daughter of the evangelist Phoebe Palmer. Phoebe Palmer was herself awarded to biographical sketches as a hymn writer; these also contain descriptions of her talented daughter.[27]

Knapp is mentioned in the preface as the author of the cantata "Prince of Peace," a lady of wealth, culture, and position, who sings beautifully and writes music simply by inspiration, because she must give expression to the melody that rises a greatful incense within her.[28] A later sketch is even more effusive, claiming that "she is one of the best musical composers in America and her music is in much demand."[29] Another honor was that her "Sabbath Closing Hymn" was the first composition in the anthology.

The 14 songs by Knapp include her famous hymn "Blessed Assurance," plus "Beautiful Hour," "Consecration," and "The Cleansing Wave." An early popular home song and chorus, "Watching for Pa" (1868), is one of the few secular pieces in the collection. All are composed in four-part harmony, usually in a verse-chorus arrangement.

Other lesser known composers mentioned in the preface are Mrs. W.S. Hancock, and Episcopalian church service composer; Mrs. Clara H. Scott, author of the *Royal Anthem Book;* and Emma Pitt, author and publisher of *Gospel Light.* Also worthy of special mention is a Mrs. Cuthbert. She composed hymn tunes before the Civil War; she is one of the few women composers of sacred music known to be active before 1860.[30] She is represented here with "Howard," retitled "Providence," and arranged by Lowell Mason.

Can Women Compose?

The debates on women's education and the place of music in it that were so characteristic of the mid-nineteenth century gave way to different issues towards the end of the century. As women began to compose in greater numbers and, more importantly, in genres other than parlor music, the issue of the woman composer surfaced—could or should women aim to become serious composers? This question, whether one replied yes or no, in itself marked another step in the decline of the long Victorian tradition that produced "piano girls" as a stereotype in the mid-nineteenth century; it meant that the relationship between women and music had been focused on professional and artistic values, rather than on social and domestic ones. The era of functional domestic musical education as a priority for women was slowly coming to a close.

The debate in the 1880s began with the publication of George Upton's book *Women in Music*.[31] A prominent critic for the Chicago *Tribune,* Upton's opinions carried a great deal of weight. His work went through two editions by 1899 and was consistently referred to in articles of the period and of the 1900s. Essentially, Upton's main concern was to resolve a central paradox in nineteenth-century beliefs. If music were the art of emotions, it logically followed that women, who were more emotional than men, should excel in its creation. According to Upton, woman failed because she could not objectify emotion by translating it into any other medium. She could experience and recreate, that is, execute; but she could not create. Furthermore, music was not *all* feeling. It also depended upon the ability to think logically and to abstract— exclusively male powers:

> Every technical detail of music is charactered by science in its most rigid forms. In this direction woman, except in rare instances, has never achieved great results. It does not seem that women will ever originate music in its fullest and grandest harmonic forms. She will always be the recipient and interpreter but there is little hope that she will be the creator.[32]

Musical creativity was therefore masculine by definition because it relied on male intellectual and psychological resources. Music was, as a writer in *The Atlantic Monthly* termed it, a "masculine idea." There had never been nor could there be a great female composer:

> Women did not have recourse to greater emotional resources, because men were actually more "emotional" than women: "Much of what passes in women for true emotion is mere

nervous excitability.... Woman as the lesser man is comparatively deficient in active emotional force.... Wagner's operas and Beethoven's symphonies are good examples of the kind of music women can't write because of their lack of emotional power."[33]

These arguments were countered by veterans of the women's rights movements and their sympathizers. Alice Stone Blackwell, a leading feminist and editor of *The Women's Journal,* wrote:

> It is probably true that more women than men have received musical instruction of a sort, but not of the sort which qualifies anyone to become a composer. Girls are as a rule taught music superficially, simply as an accomplishment. To enable them to play and sing agreeably is the whole object of their music lessons. It is exceedingly rare that a girl's father cares to have her taught the underlying laws of harmony or the principles of musical composition.
>
> In Germany and Italy, the countries where the greatest musical composers have originated, the standard of women's education is especially low and the idea of woman's sphere particularly restricted. The German or Italian girl who should confess an ambition to become a composer would be regarded by her friends as out of her sphere, if not out of her mind.
>
> When women have had for for several centuries the same advantages of liberty, education, and social encouragement in the use of their brains that men have, it will be right to argue their mental inferiority if they have not produced their fair share of geniuses. But it is hardly reasonable to expect women during a few years of half liberty and half education to produce at once specimens of genius equal to the choicest men of all the ages.[34]

As for the role of patron, prophesied by Fanny Ritter in the 1870s, it, too, was attacked. The image of women as muse so precious to writers like Ruskin or George Upton, who filled his book on women in music with vignettes about composers' wives, was rejected with the kind of arguments Amy Fay, renowned pianist and teacher, used in 1900 to explain the lack of a great female composer:

> Women have been too much taken with helping and encouraging men to place a proper value on their own talent, which they are prone to underestimate and to think not worth making the most of. Their whole training from time immemorial, has tended to make them take an intense interest in the work of men and to stimulate them to their best efforts. Ruskin was quite right when he so patronizingly said that "Woman's chief function is praise." She has praised and praised and kept herself in abeyance.[35]

In the lead article for *The Etude*'s special issue on "Women in Music" (September 1901), Fanny Morris Smith specifically rebutted Upton's ideas, disparaging the looseness of most discussions of the "woman question." The contributions of women in the past were greater than Upton allowed, while their opportunities in the present were far less. The two major reasons women as a class had not composed in the nineteenth century were thus stated:

> The noble masculine spirit who cheered and upheld the fainting hopes of the feminine musical genius has yet to make his appearance in history.... The other great reason why

women did not compose was that as a class they had no *money*. They had no control of the funds necessary for a composer's education or for publication.

The significance of feminist arguments is the mode in which they rebutted nineteenth-century attitudes toward women. In effect, they used arguments about socialization and environment to counter psychological and biological determinism. In so doing, they indirectly focused on the sociological aspects of musical creativity. In opposition to the romantic notion of the creative artist in artistic isolation, feminist musicians argued about the effect of class and status on creativity. Society could not determine which individual would be gifted with genius, but it could determine which groups had access to the institutions that supported art. No one could become a musician in an Emily Dickinsonian attic. Society could also shape the expectations about the potentialities of groups that acted as self-fulfilling prophecies.

The "emancipated woman," of which the new female composer was one representative, knew better. She no longer believed that musical creativity was masculine. As Florence Sutro wrote in 1893.

> ... great intellectual effort and strong reasoning [are not] ... the proprietary right of men. Fortunately my sex has already sufficiently advanced in its revolutionary progress through mental emancipation that it no longer accepts such doctrines as those as law.
>   We have begun to think for ourselves. And we think for ourselves, we shall begin to compose.[36]

The politically charged cultural climate produced countless other articles repeating the charges of discrimination or claims of mental emancipation.[37] Certainly, the handbooks and dictionaries tended to inflate contributions of women composers, past and present. But they were provoked or countered by equally biased attacks on the music of women composers or on the women's movement in general. In a review of Ebel's *Women Composers* which appeared in *The Musical Courier* in 1903, the reviewer wrote:

> Some men and a few women, disposed to be just, have not hesitated to declare that until a woman produces a masterpiece the fair sex cannot hope to take high rank as composers. The strongminded sisterhood, on the other hand, looking as usual through lurid glasses, claim that there are some great women composers, and the reason there are not more is wholly the fault of man's selfishness and tyranny. Education and independence were denied to women for centuries after these blessed privileges were vouchsafed to men; hence why expect women to be the equal of men in all things? No one expects it, dear sisters.[38]

The "Eternal Feminine" and Sexual Aesthetics

The polemics surrounding the female composer inevitably affected the kind of music she wrote and the ways in which it was received. The conflict between her role as a woman and her role as composer was resolved through the development of sexual aesthetics, which analyzed music as a combination of masculine and feminine traits; therefore, music written by women should and did express "femininity."

As descriptive metaphors, the terms "masculine" and "feminine" were not alien to nineteenth-century music criticism. Schumann, for example, described a pair of Schubert trios in just such terms: Op. 99 was "more passive, lyric and feminine," while Op. 100 was "active, masculine and dramatic."[39] Furthermore, as metaphors used to describe the expressive range of music, such language did not *logically* need to confine the woman composer. Just as Schubert could write masculine or feminine music, so could she. However, because of the climate of prejudice against female composers, the language of romantic music criticism degenerated into the language of sexual aesthetics, in which the potentialities of the individual female composer were defined through the application of sexual stereotypes. Femininity in music was alleged to be delicate, graceful, refined, and sensitive. It was defined as the "eternal feminine" (sometimes the German phrase *ewige weibliche* was used), drawn from Goethe's concept of womanhood. (Because of the great vogue of German music in the late-nineteenth century, especially Wagnerian opera, the German term was frequently used by American critics.)

By 1900 the aesthetics of the "eternal feminine" in music had been extended to include form and style as well as emotive content. (See table 6 for a summary comparison.) Vocal music was the essence of *ewige weibliche* because it "appeals more directly to the heart."[40] Since harmony and counterpoint were "logical," they were alien subjects. Instead of musical intellect, women were supposed to rely on their "imaginations," from which "beautiful melodies could flow." The concert pianist Fanny Bloomfield-Zeisler believed in this allegedly inherent sex difference. She wrote:

> I am no "woman's emancipator." There are many fields of intellectual activity which women never do or can trespass without sacrificing their more delicate or sensitive nature, the *ewige weibliche* (ever womanly).... What we need now is not to imitate man and try to become great in a field in which he has achieved success, but to develop those qualities which specifically belong to woman... that is beautiful melodies.[41]

Clearly, these beliefs demonstrate the extent to which many of the attitudes that lay at the core of the tradition of music as a feminine accomplishment were adapted to fit the times. The idea that a *female* musician must be a *feminine* musician, which was an important part of the mid-nineteenth-century code, was reapplied to the sphere of composition; that is, that a *female* composer must write *feminine* music. Such evaluations, whether motivated by good or bad will, ultimately harmed the female composer by their insistence on a correlation between sex and emotive content of a piece.

Table 6.   Distinctions between "Feminine" and "Masculine" Music
around 1900

	The "eternal feminine" [ewige weibliche]	"Man-tone" music* (virile music)
I. Emotive content	delicate, sensitive, graceful, refined, spontaneous	powerful, broad, noble
II. Musical qualities	lyrical, melodious	intellectual, theoretical; i.e., use of harmony or counterpoint showing technical skill or structural logic
III. Genres	songs, piano pieces, the "smaller forms"	symphonies, opera, chamber music, the "higher class of compositions"
IV. Model composer	Chopin, Mendelssohn	Beethoven, Wagner

*The phrase "man-tone" comes from Rupert Hughes, *Contemporary American Composers* (New York, 1900), p. 434.

The eternal-feminine aesthetic, therefore, provided a referential vocabulary in which the music of composers could be judged by a double standard that placed them in a double bind. When they composed in the smaller "feminine" forms such as songs and piano pieces, they were thereby demonstrating their sexually derived inadequacies to think in the larger abstract forms. If, on the other hand, they attempted these forms, they were betraying their sexual identities by writing "man-tone" music. Sexual aesthetics therefore functioned as a way of keeping female composers on their traditional periphery of composition. Even Rupert Hughes, a critic sympathetic to women composers, distinguished between the eternal feminine and the "man-tone music" of symphonies and operas. He charitably allowed that "art knows no sex"; nonetheless, women writing in "man-tone" were "seeking after virility."[42] Hughes cited the songs of Margaret Lang as examples of the "supremely womanly" in art:

> Some of Miss Lang's frailer songs show the qualities many people expect in womanliness more than the works of any of these other writers.... Such a work as "The Maiden and the Butterfly" is inexpressibly sad, and therefore ought to make best. But womanliness equally marks "The Grief of Love... marks her bitterness of "Oh, What Comes Over the Sea." Her "Lament" I consider one of the greatest of songs, and proof positive of woman's high capabilities for composition.

Hughes judged Lang's work by the degree to which the emotive content of her work corresponded to his ideas about womanliness:

> Personally, I see in Miss Lang's composition such a depth of psychology that I place the general quality of her work above that of any other composer. It is devoid of meretriciousness and of any suspicion of seeking after virility....

Hughes's criticism of Lang's songs demonstrates the continuity between the tradition of music as an accomplishment for women and judgements about late-nineteenth-century women composers; both insist on correlating "femininity" with musical expression.

Acknowledging the Professional Female Composer

Despite all of this, the late-nineteenth century witnessed two constructive changes for women composers. One, a correlate of the debate over the woman question, was an enormous increase in women composers' visibility; that is to say, public acknowledgement that they existed. Even though numbers of women had published sheet music before 1870, they had never achieved comparable public status to their contemporaries in literature.

By the 1890s this was changing. In an article for *The Century Magazine,* the critic Rupert Hughes wrote:

> Only yesterday it was being said how strange it was that women could not write music. Today their compositions make up a surprisingly large portion of the total publication.... Now the manuscripts submitted by women outnumber those of the men two to one.[43]

Those in the past who had denied female creativity would no doubt change their views if they could but hear the music of American women. For it was "the very dawn of what ... is to be a great epoch of composition by women." Otto Ebel echoed these sentiments a few years later:

> Scarcely 50 years ago the subjects of harmony and counterpoint had been considered outside the province of women's education, and the acquirement of such knowledge, other than as a pastime, would have been regarded as a mental aberration.... It therefore must be considered a great point gained that it is no longer looked upon as an eccentricity for women to compose.[44]

Music journals, concert societies, and professional organizations acknowledged women composers in a variety of ways quite similar to those in the 1970s. Both *The Etude*[45] and *The Musician* instituted feature columns on women's work in music, the latter designed to celebrate "the increasing activity of women in all phases of musical life, her aggressive and authoritative entrance into spheres heretofore monopolized by men...."[46] At the annual meetings of the Music Teachers National Association in 1897, there was a "woman's department," headed by Florence Sutro. It included lectures on women's history, an exhibition, and concerts.[47] The percentage of women in the New

York Manuscript Society, a professional composers' organization, doubled between 1892 and 1898.[48] In 1895 and 1900 the society gave concerts devoted entirely to women composers.[49]

Most female composers stayed within the boundaries of the *ewige weibliche,* and concentrated on the smaller forms. Arthur Elson's book on *Women's Work in Music* listed 145 contemporary composers, only 13 of whom wrote anything but piano music or songs.[50] In this respect the majority continued the tradition that had been well established by the 1860s. Faustina Hodges and Jane Sloman were succeeded by composers like Mary Knight Wood, Mary Turner Salter, and Carrie Jacobs Bond. (Bond was one of the most successful American composers of the period, and probably the most popular woman composer in American musical history.)[51]

Onward and Upward to the "Higher Forms"

If "visibility"—public acknowledgement of their existence—was an important late-nineteenth-century change for women composers, a second change was perhaps even more significant. After 1870 a few exceptional individuals broke through the barriers of parlor music and wrote in the "higher forms"—those of orchestral pieces, chamber music, and choral works. Constance Runcie, Margaret Lang, Clara Rogers, and Amy Beach were the pioneers whose achievements were widely acknowledged in their own lifetimes. Although it is beyond the scope of this study to examine their lives and works in detail, a brief summary of their major contributions is in order.

The earliest and most enigmatic was Constance Runcie (1836-1911). Runcie, who was Robert Owen's granddaughter, founded what some writers call the first formalized women's club in the United States to be organized through a constitution and by-laws.[52] She went to study piano in Germany in the 1850s and returned to Missouri as a finished performer in 1858. Her songs were praised by William Mason and Annie Louise Cary, and she achieved a national reputation in her own lifetime. She is the only woman composer mentioned by W.S.B. Matthews in *A Hundred Years of Music in America* and one of two women composers included in the *Dictionary of American Biography in 1935.*[53]

None of Runcie's music has been located to date. She composed songs, a symphony, and chamber music—about which, however, beyond their brief mention in one reference work, nothing is known. She may have been the first American woman to write in these forms.

Margaret Lang (1867-1972) wrote the symphonic overture "Wichitis." It was played by the Boston Symphony Orchestra on April 7, 1893, the first performance of an orchestral work by an American woman.

The English-born Clara K. Rogers (1844-1931) was a well known singer as well as a composer, settling in the United States in 1873. Trained at the Leipzig

Conservatory and in Berlin, Rogers wrote a two-volume autobiography that includes some mention of her activities as a composer,[54] including this summary statement:

> From childhood up I had always a strong bent for composition—much of my thought having been quite naturally in terms of music. Themes would come to me out of the unknown at all sorts of odd times. Sometimes I would write them down and develop them, but often I allowed them to pass away unheeded. As I look back, I cannot help deploring that when I was a student in Germany there were no facilities accorded to women for learning orchestration, or, in fact, for obtaining any guidance whatever in original composition. Had I acquired early in life a good technique in writing for instruments, I really think I might have accomplished something worthwhile in orchestral composition. But, as it happened, once launched in my public career, I never had time to work at it continuously or seriously. So I had to content myself with writing music in the simpler forms, the most ambitious of my achievements—since my callow attempt at a quartette for strings when I was thirteen—being two sonatas in classic form, one for piano and violincello, the other for piano and violin.[55]

Rogers did not publish any of these compositions until 1882. Her Violin Sonata in D minor, op. 25, was performed at the first meeting of the Boston "Manuscript Club" in 1888[56] and published by A.P. Schmidt in 1893.

The most famous and by far the most important of the group was Amy Cheney Beach, known as Mrs. H.H.A. Beach throughout her long career. Beach was the first American woman to achieve an international reputation as a composer of orchestral and chamber music, in addition to her many compositions for piano and voice.[57]

The premiere of her *Gaelic Symphony* on October 30, 1896, was a controversial event. Its critical reception is a perfect example of the double standard by which the music of women composers was judged. No matter what the merits of the piece, both its virtues and its faults were alleged illustrations of the "eternal feminine." While *The Women's Journal* chronicled the event on November 6 as one that gave them "no slight satisfaction and pride," other critics were not quite so generous. The Boston critic Philip Hale, for example, attempted to avoid condescension:

> It is fortunately not necessary to say of the *Gaelic Symphony* "This is a creditable work for a woman." Such patronage is uncalled for, and it would be offensive.... This symphony is the fullest exhibition of Mrs. Beach's indisputable talent.

Nevertheless, despite his praise for the "elemental swing, force and grandeur of the finale," he still related the defects of the orchestration to her sex:

> Occasionally she is noisy rather than sonorous. Here she is eminently feminine. A woman who writes for orchestra thinks "I must be virile at any cost...." The only trace of women I find in this symphony is this boisterousness....[58]

What Hale meant by virility was excessively heavy orchestration. The implication is that because of prejudice against women composers, Beach overcompensated by overwriting. The moral was obvious. Women who sought after "virility" by writing in the higher forms defeated themselves. Reviewing a performance of the symphony, a critic for *The Musical Courier* wrote:

> The symphony of Mrs. Beach is too long, too strenuously worked over and attempts too much. Almost every modern composer has left a trace in her score, which in its efforts to be Gaelic and masculine ends in being monotonous and spasmodic.
> ...there is no gainsaying her industry, her gift for melody...or her lack of logic. Contrapuntally she is not strong. Of grace and delicacy there are evidences in the Siciliano [*sic*], and there she is at her best: "but yet a woman."[59]

Ironically, the composer George Chadwick, who was a personal friend of Beach's, allegedly had the opposite reaction. According to a story in *The Etude* (Feb., 1904):

> When George Whitefield Chadwick first heard Mrs. Beach's symphony "Gaelic," [*sic*] he is said to have exclaimed: "Why was not I born a woman?" It was the delicacy of thought and finish in her musical expression that had struck him, an expression of true womanliness, absolute in its sincerity....

The critical reception of Beach's symphony symbolizes the ambiguities and tensions that accompanied the emergence of the woman composer from the parlor into the professional world of music as art. Women composers had to combat the stereotypes of dilettante and "piano girl" that were the legacy of the tradition of musical accomplishment for women. Still, the piano girl slowly gave way, or at least found a strong competitor in the "new woman." The tradition declined under social and economic pressures and a healthier, freer climate for creative American women. No doubt one could trace its vestiges today, and certainly its influence was not limited to women but affected men as well, in ways that still have yet to be explored. Beach's music stands on its own artistic merits. But her achievements and those of her generation shine even brighter in historical context, for they created options for other women who had remained within the traditional world of parlor music. By the turn of the century, women shared a vision of a future in which economic and social self-determination would have deep artistic parallels:

> This same force that will make some of them financiers, scientists, investers, litterateurs, will make of them composers, and not composers that will mince around on the outskirts of music satisfied to present here and there an oversentimental melody which is a composite of everything that has ever been written, but those who will write music which is as deep as anything that has ever been called great.[60]

Such a vision was needed to sustain women in their confrontation with a tradition of inferior education and double standards that had deep and complex roots in 100 years of American musical life.

The "outskirts of music" was, of course, parlor music, and the militant fervor of this vision conjures up an image of the woman composer as an Ibsen heroine, a Nora, reassessing the room that has been a home and now appears to be a prison.

One can measure the amount of change that occurred in the nineteenth century by these remarks. To Almira Phelps, who yearned for an American Mrs. Hemans, the creativity of the American woman had no other purpose than to serve virtue. Since virtue and domesticity were synonymous, "sleeping lyres" should awaken primarily to serve the home and family.

The early history of American woman composers is a record of the intimate connection between social change and the creative process. Their achievements as composers before 1870 depended first on creating an acceptable "sphere" and then, ironically, transcending it. Parlor music was the medium for this process. By the mid-nineteenth century, women composers established themselves through this loosely defined genre and enough creative temperaments flourished within it to allow a musical Nora to leave the room whose dimensions had been so painstakingly expanded by the collective efforts of anonymous ladies and a few brave professionals, and close the door.

Appendix

Selected Compositions Published by Women in the U.S. before 1870

The following is a selected list of compositions published by women composers in the United States before 1870. In the list, the letter (E) denotes English nationality. The names of lyricists are in parentheses. Libraries are indicated by the abbreviations below:

BPL	Boston Public Library
Cty	Yale University
DLC	Library of Congress
HC	Harding Collection, Bodleian Library, Oxford University
LIHS	Long Island Historical Society
LL	Lester Levy (private collection)
ncl	no copy located
NN	New York Public Library
NYHS	New York Historical Society
PFL	Philadelphia Free Library
SCaU	University of South Carolina
VaU	University of Virginia

Ablamowicz, Anna, arr., "The Vale of Avoca," Louisville: G.W. Brainard & Co., 1852.   NN

Abrams, Harriet (E), "Crazy Jane," (G.M. Lewis), Boston: P.A. Von Hagen & Co., 1799-1802.   NN

——. "A Smile and a Tear," (M.P. Andrews), New York: J & M Paff [1800].   NN

Adelene, "Why Ask Me Now?" (composer), Baltimore: F.D. Benteen, 1845.   NN

Armstrong, Miss, "Poor Juna," Boston: Henry Tolman, 1865.   BPL, LL

Baker, Mrs. Sophia M., "The Burial of the Indian Girl," (Mrs. L.H. Sigourney), Boston: Keith's Music Publishing House, 1845.   ncl

Barnard, Charlotte Allington (Claribel-E), "Five O'clock in the Morning," (composer), Boston: Oliver Ditson & Co. [1860].   NN

——. "I Cannot Sing the Old Songs," (composer), New York: Wm. A. Pond & Co. [1865].   LL, NN

——. "Only a Lock of Hair," Philadelphia: Lee & Walker [1856].   NN

——. "Take Back the Heart," (composer), New York: S.T. Gordon [1865].   NN

Bellchambers, Julliet, "The Spell Is Broken," New York: J.F. Atwill, 1842.   BPL, NN

Blake, Mary, "Beautiful Star of the Twilight," (composer), Boston: Oliver Ditson & Co., 1857.   LL

Browne, Augusta, "The American Bouquet," Philadelphia: Osbourn's Music Saloon [1844].   BPL, DLC

_____. "The Babes in the Wood," New York: C. Holt, Jr. [184-].   HC

_____. "Caledonia" (or "Caledonian Bouquet"), New York: C.G. Christian, 1841.   NN

_____. "The Chieftain's Halls," Boston: Henry Prentiss, 1844.   Cty

_____. "The De Meyer Grand Waltz," New York: Firth & Hall, 1846.   HC, PFL

_____. "The Ethereal Grand Waltz," New York: Firth, Hall & Pond, n.d.   LIHS

_____. "The Family Meeting," (Charles Sprague), New York: Wm. Hall & Son, 1842.   HC, NN

_____. "The Fisher Boy's Song," New York: Firth & Hall, n.d.   HC

_____. "Grand Vesper Chorus," (Bishop Heber), New York: Wm. Dubois [1842].   NN

_____. "Hear Therefore O Israel," Brooklyn, N.Y.: 1842.   NN

_____. "The Reply of the Messenger Bird," (Edward Young), Philadelphia: A. Fiot, 1848.   NN

_____. "The Seaman's Night Song," Boston: C. Bradlee [184-].   BPL

_____. "Song of Mercy," (Bunyan's *Pilgrim's Progress*), New York: Firth, Pond & Co., 1851.   NN

_____. "A Song for New England," (H.W. Elsworth), New York: Firth & Hall [1844].   NN

_____. "The Warlike Dead in Mexico," (Mrs. Balmanno), New York: C. Holt Jr., 1848.   NN

Browne, Harriet (E), "The Captive Knight," (Mrs. Hemans), New York: Bourne [1827-32].   LL, NN

_____. "Evening Song to the Virgin," (Mrs. Hemans), Boston: C. Bradlee [1835-36].   LL, NN

_____. "The Messenger Bird," (Mrs. F. Hemans), Boston: C. Bradlee [1835-36].   NN

_____. "Pilgrim Fathers," (Mrs. Hemans), Baltimore: F.D. Benteen [1839-53].   LL, NN

_____. "Tyrolese Evening Hymn," (Mrs. Hemans), New York: Bourne [1827-32].   LL, NN

Burnham, Georgiana, "O Worship Not the Beautiful," (Lucy Linwood), Boston: Oliver Ditson, 184-.   BPL

Burtis, Mrs. Sarah R., "The Lady's Book Polka," Philadelphia: T.C. Andrews & Son, 1852.   NN

_____. "Morning Star and Evening Star Polkas," Philadelphia: T.C. Andrews, 1853.   NN

Carew, Lady (E), "The Bridge," (H.W. Longfellow), Boston: Oliver Ditson & Co. [1858-76].   NN

Clark, Caroline, "Lafayette's March," Boston: author, 1824.   NN

Cowell, Augusta, arr. (E?), "Thy Name was Once a Magic Spell," (Mrs. Norton), Baltimore: Miller and Beacham, 1866.   NN

_____. "We Have Been Friends Together," (Mrs. Norton), New York: James L. Hewitt & Co. [1836-37 or 1842-43].   NN

Daly, Julia, "Dying Camille," (Wm. K. McCurdy), Philadelphia: Lee & Walker, 1856.   NN

DeLisle, Estelle, "Cape Cottage Waltz," Philadelphia: J.E. Gould, 1856.   NN

Deming, Mrs. L.L., "I Cannot Sing Tonight," (composer), Boston: Henry Tolman & Co., 1854.   NN

Disbrow, Mrs. Wm. H., "The Forsaken One," (Alfred Wheeler), New York: C. Holt Jr., 1848.   NN, VaU

Dana, Mary S.B., arr., "Flee As a Bird," Boston: Oliver Ditson & Co., 1857.   NN

_____. arr., "The Ruler's Daughter," Boston: Oliver Ditson & Co., 1858.   NN

Dole, Mrs. Caroline, "Answer to the Messenger Bird," (American Quaker Lady), Boston: C.H. Keith, 1848.   NN

Durham, Miss M.T., "The Promised Land," *The Southern Harmony* ed. William Walker (New Haven, Conn., 1835).   NN

_____. "Star of Columbia," (Dr. Dwight), *The Southern Harmony,* ed. William Walker (New Haven, Conn., 1835).   NN

Fitzgerald, Mrs. Edward (E?), "The Dying Girl to her Lover," (Winthrop M. Praed, Esq.), New York: Firth & Hall [1832/1834-42/1844-47].   LL, NN

_____. "I Remember How My Childhood Fleeted By," (Winthrop M. Praed), New York: Atwill [1843-47].   LL, NN

Fitzhenry, Marceline, "Clara Polka," Philadelphia: Couenhoven & Duffy, 1854.   NN

Flower, Eliza (E), "My Native Land, Good Night," (Lord Byron), New York: Torp & Unger [1838-39].   NN

_____. "My Native Shore, Adieu," (Lord Byron), New York: Wm. Dubois [1817].   NN

Fricker, Anne (E), "There's a Sigh in the Heart," (composer), Boston: Oliver Ditson [c. 1853].   LL, NN

Gabriel, Virginia (E), "The Forsaken," (H. Aide), New York: Wm. A. Pond & Co. [c. 1866].   NN

Garrett, Mrs. William, "The Emily Polka," Boston: Russell & Richarson, 1857.   NN

Gerard, Miss, "The Fire Polka," New York: Dressler & Clayton, 1854.   NN

Groom, Mrs. (E), "Over the Sea," Boston: Oliver Ditson & Co. [1857-71].   BPL, NN

Habicht, Mrs. C.E., "The Sun is in the West," (composer), Boston: G.P. Reed, 1848.   NN

Hagen, Catherine Elizabeth Van, "The Country Maid or l'Amour est un enfant trompeur," n.d.

Hart, Imogene, "Gaily Smiles the Earth," (composer), Boston: Oliver Ditson & Co., 1859.   NN

Hewitt, Estelle, "The Snowdrop Waltz," Baltimore: F.D. Benteen, 1847.   NN

Hill, Martha, "The Ghost of Uncle Tom," (composer), New York: Horace Waters, 1854.   LL, NN

Hodges, Faustina Hasse, "The Alp-Horn," (Miss C.J. Warner), New York: Firth, Pond & Co., n.d.   NN

_____. "Because I'm 25," (composer), New York: S.T. Gordon, 1850.   NYHS

_____. "Dreams," (H.C.L.), New York: G. Schirmer, 1868.   BPL, NN

_____. "The Holy Dead," (Klopstock, trans. Prof. Longfellow), New York: Firth, Pond & Co. [1861].   NN

_____. "The Indigent Spinster," (composer), New York: W. Hall, 1867.   NN

_____. "Lake Shore Dream," New York: Beer & Schirmer, 1868.   NYHS

_____. "The Rose-Bush," (trans. from the German by W. Caldwell), New York: Beer & Schirmer, 1859.   BPL, NN

_____. "Still O'er the Waters," New York: Wm. Hall & Son, 1852.   NN

_____. "Suffer Little Children," Cincinnati: J. Church, 1860.   ncl

Hohnstock, Adele, "Agnes Polka," Charleston, S.C.: Geo. Oates, 1850.   SCaU

_____. "The Celebrated Concert Polka" (or "Hohnstock Concert Polka"), Philadelphia: A. Fiot, 1849.   NN

Horn, Kate, "Woman's Rights," (composer), Boston: Geo. P. Reed & Co., 1853.   Cty, NN

Hutchinson, Abby, "Kind Words Can Never Die," Boston: Oliver Ditson, 1855.   NN

Hutet, Josephine, "Sigma Waltz," Albany: L.F. Newland, 1848.   NN

Jordan, Dorothy Bland (E), "The Blue Bells of Scotland," New York: W. Hall & Son [1808-1809].   NN

Kerby, Carolina, "The Thornless Rose," (S. Wild), Philadelphia: R.H. Hobson, 1829.   NN

King, Frances Isabella, "Fly, Fly Away," (composer), New York: Horace Waters, 1853.   BPL, LL, NN

Knapp, Mrs. J.F., "Consecration," and "Jesus' Jewels," Boston: D. Lothrop, 1885.   NN

_____. "Watchin' for Pa," New York: Wm. A. Pond, 1867.   NN

A Lady, "Jerusalem," Philadelphia: G. Willig [1818-19].   NN

A Lady, (E?), arr. Henry R. Bishop, "And Ye Shall Walk in Silk Attire," (Susan Blamire), New York: Dubois & Stodart, 1825.   NN

A Lady, "The Match Girl," Philadelphia: Carr and Co. [1793].

A Lady, "Oft in a Stilly Night with Variations for the Piano Forte," Philadelphia: G. Willig, 1827.   NN

A Lady, "Thou Hast Wounded the Spirit That Lov'd Thee," (composer), Balitmore: F.D. Benteen, 1846.   DLC, NN

Lady of Baltimore, "Titus March," Baltimore: J. Cole, 1824.   NN

Lady of Charleston, "United States Marine March," Boston: Oliver Ditson [1814-15].   NN

Lady of Philadelphia, "The Cheerful Spring Begins Today," Philadelphia, 1793.   DLC

Lady of Richmond, Virginia, "God Will Defend the Right," (composer), New Orleans: A.E. Blackmar [1861].   BPL

Lady of Virginia, "Tis Sweet to Muse O'er Memory's Page," (composer), New York: Wm. Hall & Sons, 1849.   NN

Lady of Virginia, "Lady Jane Grey," (Miss Leslie), Baltimore: G. Willig, Jr., 1844.   VaU

Lady of Virginia, "Wild Ashe Deer. Brilliant Variations for the Piano," Baltimore: Miller and Beachem, 1854.   VaU

Lady of South Carolina, "Keowee Waltzes," Charleston, S.C.: Geo. Oates, 1847.   SCaU

Lane, Alice, "The Stars of Our Banner," (M.F. Bigney), New Orleans: A.E. Blackmar, 1861.   SCaU

Lindsay, Miss M. (Bliss, Mrs. J. Worthington) (E), "The Bridge," (Henry W. Longfellow), Boston: Oliver Ditson & Co., 1861.   BPL

_____. "Too Late, Too Late," (Tennyson), Boston: Oliver Ditson & Co., [1858-76].   BPL, NN

Livingston, Hattie, "The Young Folks at Home," (Frank Spencer), New York: T.S. Berry, 1852.   NN

Loud, Emily L., "Kohinor. The Mountain of Light Waltz," Penn.: composer published, 1851.   NN

Luyster, Mrs. A.R., "Mary, Dear Mary," (composer), New York: F. Riley & Co., 1847.   Cty

Mary, "Adieu Sweet Companion," (Eliza C. Hurley), New York: Firth, Pond & Co., 1849.   NN

_____. "Oh, Leave Me Not in Sorrow," (Miss Hurley), New York: Firth, Pond & Co., 1848.   NN

_____. "The Ring My Mother Wore," (Louis Dela), Philadelphia: Beck & Lawton, 1860.   LL

_____. "Rosebud Quickstep," New York: Firth, Pond & Co., 1848.   DLC, NN

Millard, Mrs. P. (E), "Alice Gray," New York: Bourne, 1828.   LL, NN

More, Isabella Theaker (E), "The Walls of My Prison," Philadelphia, [1793-95].

Morton, Nellie, "Ida May," Philadelphia: Wm. H. Coulston, 1856.   LL

Mott, Mrs. Valentine, "Forget Thee, Ah Never," (V.D.M.), New York: Firth, Hall & Co., 1846.   NN

Myers, Emma, "Capital March," Philadelphia: Lee & Walker, 1850.   NN

Norton, Caroline (E), "Fanny Grey," (composer), Boston: Parker & Ditson, 1836-37.   NN

_____. "Fairy Bells," (composer), Boston: C. Bradlee [1827-34].   NN

_____. "Juanita," (composer), New York: S.T. Gordon [1855].   NN

_____. "O Take Me Back to Switzerland," (composer), New York: Atwill [1834-47].   NN

_____. "Would I Were With Thee," (composer), New York: James L. Hewitt & Co. [1836-37].   NN

Parker, Mrs., "Malibran Waltz," Boston: H. Prentiss, 1841.   NN

Parkhurst, Mrs. E.A., "Angel Mary," (composer), New York: Horace Waters, 1863.   LL, NN

_____. "The Angels are Hovering Near," (H.W. Adams), New York: Horace Waters, 1862.   NN

_____. "Come Rally Freeman, Rally," (John Adam), New York: Horace Waters, 1864.   NN

_____. "Dey Said We Wouldn't Fight," (Mrs. M.A. Kidder), New York: Horace Waters, 1864.   NN

_____. "Don't Marry a Man If He Drinks," (Mrs. M.A. Kidder), New York: C.H. Tremaine, 1866.   NN

_____. "Father's a Drunkard and Mother is Dead," (Stella), Washington, D.C.: John F. Ellis, 1866.   LL, NN

_____. "Girls, Wait for a Temperance Man," (Mrs. M.A. Kidder), New York: C.W. Harris, 1867.   NN

_____. "Give to Me Those Moonlit Hours," (Francis B. Murtha), New York: Wm. Hall, 1865.   NN

_____. "A Home on the Mountain," (Rev. Sidney Dyer), New York: Horace Waters, 1865.   NN

_____. "I'm Willing to Wait," (Mrs. M.A. Kidder), New York: Horace Waters, 1864.   NN

_____. "Sweet Evelina," ("M; melody by "T"), New York: Horace Waters, 1863.   LL, NN

_____. "There Are Voices, Spirit Voices," (Fanny Crosby), New York: Horace Waters, 1864.   NN

_____. "The Union Medley," New York: Horace Waters, 1863.   NN

_____. "Weep No More for Lily," (Mrs. W.V. Porter), New York: Horace Waters, 1864.   NN

Pownall, Mary Ann (E), "Jemmy of the Glen," (composer), New York: Hewitt & Pownall, 1794. NN

_____. "Kisses Sue'd For," (Shakespeare), New York: G. Gilfert & Co. [1795]. NN

_____. "Lavinia," New York: Hewitt & Pownall, 1794. NN

_____. "The Straw Bonnet," New York: Hewitt & Pownall, 1794. NN

Richards, Grace, "Orphan Nosegay Girl," (Mrs. Rowson), Boston: G. Graupner [1800]. BPL, NN

Sandford, Lucy A, "Stars of the Summer Night," (Henry W. Longfellow), New York: W. Hall, 1849. NN

Scott, Miss M.B., "Bird of Beauty," (Ella of Woodlawn), Boston: Oliver Ditson, 1856. NN

Siegling, Marie R., "La Capricieuse," Baltimore: G. Willig, 1845. SCaU

_____. "La Gracieuse," Baltimore: G. Willig, 1845. SCaU

Sloman, Ann, "The Bridal Wreath," *Columbian Ladies' and Gentleman's Magazine* VIII/6 (Dec. 1847), 282.

Sloman, Jane, "The Ericcson Schottisch," New York: W. Hall, 1853. PFL, NN

Sloman Torry, Jane, "La Farfalletta," (The Butterfly), trans. E.C. Sebastiani, New York: Wm. Hall & Son, 1861. Cty, NN

Sloman, Jane, "Forget Thee?" (composer), Boston: W.H. Oakes, 1843. BPL, NN

_____. "I'll Make Him Speak Out," (composer), Boston: W.H. Oakes, 1843. NN

_____. "The Maiden's Farewell," (composer), Boston: Wm. H. Oakes, 1842. DLC

_____. *The Melodist*. New York: Wm. Hall & Son, 1850. NN

_____. "Roll On, Silver Moon," arr. by N. Barker, New York: Firth, Pond, 1848. NN

Sloman Torry, Jane, "Take Back the Ring," (composer), New York: Wm. Hall & Son, 1860. NN

Smith, Miss, "A Place in Thy Memory Dearest," (the author of The Collegians), New York: James L. Hewitt & Co. [1836-43]. NN

Stith, Mrs. Townshend, "Our Friendship," Philadelphia: G. Willig, 1830. NN

_____. "We Parted in Silence," Philadelphia: G. Willig, 1835. Cty, NN

Sullivan, Marion Dix, "Bible Songs," harmonized by Mr. B.J. Lang, Boston: Nathan Richardson, 1856. DLC

_____. "The Blue Juniata," (composer), Boston: Oliver Ditson, 1841. NN

_____. "The Fanny Bell Polka," Boston: Oliver Ditson, 1846. NN

_____. "The Field of Monterey," (composer), Boston: Oliver Ditson, 1846. NN

_____. "Jessie Cook," (composer), Boston: Henry Prentiss, 1844. NN

_____. *The Juniata Ballads*. Boston: Nathan Richardson, 1855. DLC

_____. "Marion Day," (composer), Boston: Oliver Ditson, 1844. NN

_____. "Oh! Boatman Row Me Oer the Stream," (composer), Boston: Oliver Ditson, 1844. NN

_____. "We Cross the Prairie as of Old," (J.G. Whittier), Boston: E.H. Wade, 1854. BPL

Temple, Mrs. A Niecieska, "Rutledge Waltz," Boston: Oliver Ditson, 1855. SCaU

Vane, Florence, "Are We Almost There," (composer), Boston: Oliver Ditson & Co., 1845. LL, NN

Notes

Chapter 1

1. Susanna Rowson, *Miscellaneous Poems* (Boston, 1804), pp. 109-10. Cited also in Nicholas Tawa, "Secular Music in the Late-Eighteenth-Century Home," *Musical Quarterly* LXI/4 (Oct. 1975), 511.

2. Mark Twain, *Life on the Mississippi* (New York, 1883), p. 403.

3. Charles Dickens, *The Life and Adventures of Martin Chuzzlewit* (New York: Alfred Knopf, 1947), p. 260.

4. "Young Ladies' Musical Education," *Musical Reporter* January 1841, p. 22.

5. See chap. 5, below.

6. Arthur Loesser, *Men, Women and Pianos* (New York: Simon and Schuster, 1954), p. 267.

7. The composers mentioned are included in contemporary reference works, histories, or music anthologies. Specific references are given in chaps. 5, 6, and 7.

8. Anne Firor Scott, "Women in American Life," in *The Reinterpretation of American History and Culture,* ed. by William Cartwright and Richard Watson (Washington, D.C.: National Council for the Social Studies, 1973), pp. 151-63, discusses the development of women's studies in American history. For the current renaissance of scholarship in nineteenth-century American music, see for example, *Sonneck Society Newsletter* II/2 (June 1976) and II/3 (Sept. 1976).

9. Charles and Mary Beard, *The Rise of American Civilization* (New York: The Macmillan Co., 1930), II, p. 457.

10. Mary Beard was also the author of *Women as Force in History: A Study in Traditions and Realities* (New York: The Macmillan Co., 1946). This is one of the first significant twentieth-century histories with a feminist viewpoint.

11. Richard Crawford, *American Studies and American Musicology: A Point of View and A Case in Point,* I.S.A.M. Monographs, No. 4 (New York: Institute for Studies in American Music, 1975), p. 4.

12. The arguments on the next few pages owe a good deal to two essays by Gerda Lerner, "New Approaches to the Study of Women in American History," and "Placing Women in History," both in *Liberating Women's History,* ed. by Berenice A. Carroll (Urbana: University of Illinois Press, 1976), pp. 349-67.

13. Patricia Meyer Spacks, *The Female Imagination* (New York: Alfred A. Knopf, Inc., 1972), p. 3.

14. Francis Hopkinson, *Seven Songs for the Harpsichord or Forte Piano* (Philadelphia, 1788). Facsimile ed. by Harry Dichter (Philadelphia: Musical Americana, 1954).

15. Lerner, *Liberating Women's History,* p. 355.

16. See Ann Sutherland Harris and Linda Nochlin, *Women Artists: 1550-1950* (New York: Alfred A. Knopf, 1977).

17. Elaine Showalter, "Women Writers and the Double Standard," *Women in a Sexist Society,* ed. by Vivian Gornick and Barbara Moran. (New York: Basic Books, 1971), pp. 452-79.

18. Ann Douglas, "The 'Scribbling Women' and Fanny Fern: Why Women Wrote," *American Quarterly* XXIII/1 (Spring 1971), 4.

19. Ann Douglas, *The Feminization of American Culture* (New York: Alfred A. Knopf, 1977).

20. This phrase was coined by Barbara Welter, "The Cult of True Womanhood: 1820-1860," *American Quarterly* XVIII (Summer 1966), 151-74, to describe Victorian-American attitudes towards female identity and woman's nature.

21. Frank Rossiter, *Charles Ives and His America* (New York: Liveright, 1975).

22. Gilbert Chase, *America's Music* (New York: McGraw-Hill Co., 1966), pp. 283-300.

23. Ibid., pp. 286-88.

24. Ibid., p. 285.

25. Joseph Mussulman, *Music in the Cultured Generation* (Evanston: Northwestern University Press, 1971).

26. Ibid., p. 170 ff.

27. Ibid., p. 171.

28. Ibid., pp. 174, 223.

29. Ibid., p. 173.

30. Rossiter, *Charles Ives,* pp. 33-35.

31. For a discussion of this work see Lerner, "Placing Women in History: A 1975 Perspective," in *Liberating Women's History,* p. 359; and Donna Gerstenberger and Carolyn Allen, "Women Studies/American Studies, 1970-1975," *American Quarterly* XXIX/3 (1977), 263-79.

32. Thomas Woody, *A History of Women's Education in the United States* (New York: The Science Press, 1929).

33. Arthur Schlesinger, *Learning How to Behave* (New York: Macmillan Co., 1947).

34. Eleanor Thompson, *Education for Ladies 1830-1860* (New York: King's Crown Press, 1947).

35. The most recently published is *A Season in New York, 1801. Letters of Harriet and Maria Trumbull,* ed. by Helen M. Morgan (Pittsburgh: University of Pittsburgh Press, 1969). Harriet was the pupil of James Hewitt.

36. Frances Hall Johnson, *Music Vale Seminary, 1835-1876* (New Haven: Yale University Press, 1934).

37. William Reichel, *A History of the Rise, Progress and Present Condition of the Moravian Seminary for Young Ladies at Bethlehem, Pa.* (Philadelphia: J.B. Lippincott & Co., 1870).

38.   Julia Cherry Spruill, *Women's Life and Work in the Southern Colonies* (Chapel Hill, North Carolina, 1938, reprinted New York: W.W. Norton & Co., Inc., 1972).

39.   Linda Grant DePauw and Conover Hunt, *Remember the Ladies: Women in America 1750-1815* (New York: The Viking Press, 1976).

40.   Mary Sumner Benson, *Women in Eighteenth-Century America* (Port Washington, N.Y.: Kennekot Press, 1935).

41.   Nicholas Tawa, *Sweet Songs for Gentle Americans* (Bowling Green, Ohio: Bowling Green University Popular Press, 1980). The article is in *Musical Quarterly* LXI/4 (Oct. 1975), 511-27.

42.   Oscar Sonneck, *A Bibliography of Early Secular American Music* (Rev. W.T. Upton, 1945, reprinted New York: Da Capo Press, 1964), pp. 6-7.

43.   Charles Kaufmann, *Music in New Jersey, 1655 through 1860* (Teaneck: Fairleigh Dickinson University Press, 1980). Katherine Mahan, *Showboats to Soft Shoes: A Century of Musical Development in Columbus, Georgia from 1828 to 1928.* Columbus, Georgia, 1968. See also Emma K. Crews, "A History of Music in Knoxville, Tennessee, 1791-1910," (Ed.D. dissertation, Florida State University, 1961).

44.   Don L. Hixon and Don Hennessee, *Women In Music* (Metuchen, N.J.: The Scarecrow Press, 1975), pp. 132, 206.

45.   Waldo Pratt, *American Supplement to Grove's* (New York: The Macmillan Co., 1930).

46.   *Bio-bibliographical Index of Musicians from Colonial Times to Present* (Washington, D.C.: Music Division, Pan American Union, 1956).

47.   Charles Claghorn, *A Biographical Dictionary of American Music* (West Nyack, N.Y.: Parker Pub. Co., 1973). Also included are Caroline Richings Bernard, Mary Dana, Caroline Gilman, Eliza Murden, and Mary Weir.

48.   *Variety Music Cavalcade,* compiled by Julius Mattfeld (New York: Prentice-Hall, 1952). The pieces are "Tyrolese Evening Hymn," 1828, and "The Pilgrim Fathers" (1830), m. Augusta Browne Garrett; "The Blue Juniata," M.D. Sullivan, 1844; "Roll On, Silver Moon," melody attributed to one Sloman (R. Sloman? 1847); "The Bridge," Miss M. Lindsay, 1850; "The Young Folks at Home," Hattie Livingston, 1852; "Flee As a Bird," Mrs. M.S.B. Dana, 1857; "The Bridge," Lady Carew, 1867.

49.   Sigmund Spaeth, *A History of Popular Music in America* (New York: Random House, 1948). Mentioned are Miss M. T. Durham's "Star of Columbia"; Mrs. Winchell's "Niagara Falls"; Claribel mentioned as "popular in 1860's" (p. 143); Margaret Weir's "Dixie Doodle"; Augusta Browne, "The Warlike Dead in Mexico"; Marion Dix Sullivan, "The Field of Monterey"; Maria Seguin, "The American Stamp Polka."

50.   Tawa, *Sweet Songs for Gentle Americans.* See "Alice Gray," Mrs. P. Millard; "The Blue Juniata," and "The Field of Monterey," Sullivan; "Pilgrim Fathers" and "Tyrolese Evening Hymn," Miss Browne; and "The Knight Errant" Hortense de Beauharnais. All of these composers but Sullivan are foreign.

51.   Michael Turner, *The Parlour Songbook* (London: Michael Joseph Ltd., 1972), p. 252, "Father's A Drunkard and Mother Is Dead."

52.   *Civil War Songbook,* ed. Richard Crawford (New York: Dover Press, 1977), p. 137.

53.   *Piano Music in America.* Volume 1 (New York: Vox Records SUBX 5302, 1974), performed by Neely Bruce.

54.   Otto Ebel, *Women Composers* (Brooklyn, New York: F.H. Chandler, 1902). Included are Faustina Hodges and Phoebe Knapp.

55.   Arthur Elson, *Women's Work in Music* (Boston: L.C. Page & Co., 1903). Included are Phoebe Knapp, Mrs. C.F. Chickering, and Caroline Richings Bernard.

56.   See. H. Earle Johnson, *Musical Interludes in Boston, 1795-1830* (New York: Columbia University Press, 1943); Oscar Sonneck, *Early Concert Life in America* (Leipzig: Breitkopf & Härtel, 1907, reprinted New York: Musurgia, 1949); Julian Mates, *The American Musical Stage Before 1800* (New Brunswick, N.J., 1962; Elizabeth Dexter, *Career Women of America, 1776-1840* (Francestown, N.H.: M. Jones, 1950).

57.   Tawa, *Sweet Songs for Gentle Americans,* p. 3.

58.   Grace Yerbury, *Song in America from Early Times to About 1850* (Metuchen, N.J.: The Scarecrow Press, Inc., 1971), p. 215.

59.   The most important and earliest music dictionary is John W. Moore's *A Dictionary of Musical Information* (Boston: Oliver Ditson & Co., 1876) and his *Appendix to the Encyclopedia of Music* (Boston, 1875). See chap. 7 for a list of entries about early American women composers contained in these works.

60.   For example, Sarah J. Hale's *Woman's Record, or Sketches of all Distinguished Women* (New York: Harper & Brothers, 1852). Works like these emphasized literary women. Those composers who were also poets or writers were more likely to be included.

61.   Adrienne Fried Block and Carol Neuls-Bates, *Women in American Music: A Bibliography* (Westport, Conn: Greenwood Press, 1979).

62.   Phyllis Mackowitz Bruce, "A Preliminary Investigation of American Women Song Composers of the Nineteenth and Early Twentieth Centuries" (undergraduate honors thesis, Wesleyan University, Middletown, Conn., 1977). App. B, "A Listing of American Women Composers," pp. 53-64; app. C, "Songs by Women Composers Collected for this Study," pp. 65-82.

63.   Figures from estimates made by the staff of the Music Division in 1976. Information supplied by Richard Jackson. It should be noted, however, that the shelflist is incomplete.

64.   U.S. Board of Music Trade, *Complete Catalogue of Sheet Music and Musical Works, 1870.* Reprinted with an introduction by Dena J. Epstein (New York: Da Capo Press, 1973). Epstein describes it as "the best presently available music bibliography for the years between 1825 and 1891" (p. ii). We shall refer to this reference work as the *Complete Catalogue.*

65.   Richard Harwell, *Confederate Music* (Chapel Hill: University of North Carolina Press, 1950).

66.   Dena J. Epstein, *Music Publishing in Chicago Before 1871: The Firm of Root & Cady, 1858-1871* (Detroit: Information Coordinators, Inc., 1969).

67.   Harry Dichter and Elliott Shapiro, *Early American Sheet Music—Its Lure and Lore, 1768-1889* (New York: R.R. Bowker Co., 1941).

68.   Sonneck, *A Bibliography of Early Secular American Music;* and Richard J. Wolfe, *Secular Music in America, 1801-1825* (New York: New York Public Library, 1964).

69.   *Early American Imprints, 1639-1800,* ed. Clifford K. Shipton (American Antiquarian Society microprint editions, New York: Readex Co., 1952).

70.   Information supplied by Lenore Coral, music librarian, University of Wisconsin.

71. *Complete Catalogue,* p. xx.

72. *Home Musical Library* (Boston: Oliver Ditson & Co., ca. 1850). This series contains nine volumes of parlor songs and keyboard works: *The Silver Chord, Gems of German Song, The Shower of Pearls, Gems of Sacred Songs, Gems of Scottish Song, The Musical Treasure, Wreath of Gems, Operatic Pearls, The Silver Wreath.* Not all have been located but are listed as a series on the cover of *Shower of Pearls,* 1859.

73. *Franklin Square Song Collection.* Selected by J.P. McCaskey (New York: Harper & Bros., 1884-92), Vols. 1-8.

74. For example, *Crown Jewels.* A Collection of Living Gems transcribed for the Piano (Boston: Oliver Ditson, 1861). All titles issued as separate imprints.

75. Charles Wunderlich, "A History and Bibliography of Early American Musical Periodicals, 1781-1852" (Ph.D. University of Michigan, 1962) has an appendix containing a list of all music in periodicals after that date.

76. Ladies' magazines are discussed in chap. 6. No one has yet surveyed their music, although the incomplete "Index to Early American Periodicals" (New York University, microfilm of incomplete manuscript, n.d.) does include pieces from *Godey's Lady's Book, Peterson's Home Magazine,* and *Ladies' Companion.*

Chapter 2

1. Robert Gerson, *Music in Philadelphia* (Philadelphia: Theodore Presser, 1940), p. 9.

2. Ibid. The date of the advertisement was March 5, 1730.

3. John Bennett, *Letters to a Young Lady* (Worcester, Mass., 1798), Letter XVIV. The first edition of this work was published in 1792. Bennett was the curate of St. Mary's in Manchester, England.

4. Ibid., pp. 23-24.

5. Ann Sutherland Harris and Linda Nochlin, *Women Artists 1550-1950* (New York: Alfred A. Knopf, 1977), pp. 24, 108, discuss music as one of the arts for the Italian woman in the Renaissance. See also Arthur Loesser, *Men, Women and Pianos* (New York: Simon and Schuster, Inc., 1954), pp. 267-83.

6. *The Ladies' Calling, In Two Parts, By the Author of the Whole Duty of Man.* This work is described by Julia Spruill, *Women's Life and Work in the Southern Colonies.* (New York: W.W. Norton Co., 1972. Reprint of the 1938 ed.), p. 214.

7. *The Ladies' Calling,* quoted in Spruill, *Women's Life and Work,* p. 215.

8. Ibid.

9. Cotton Mather, *The Ornaments for the Daughters of Zion* (Cambridge, 1692).

10. Ibid., p. 20.

11. Percy Scholes, *The Puritans and Music in England and New England* (New York: Oxford University Press, 1934), p. 270. See also the chapter on instrumental music and the New England community for secular music.

12. Mather, *The Ornaments* (pagination illegible).

13. This interpretation of Mather is based on Page Smith, *Daughters of the Promised Land. Women in American History* (Boston-Toronto: Little, Brown and Co., 1970), p. 47-9ff.

14.   H. Wiley Hitchcock, *Music in the United States: A Historical Introduction,* 2nd ed. (Englewood Cliffs, N.J., 1974), p. 21.

15.   Most women's studies scholars tend to regard the "fashionable woman" as diminishing the role of women in society from one of equal as economic participation to that of artificiality and uselessness. See Page Smith, *Daughters of the Promised Land* Boston: Little, Brown & Co., 1970), pp. 57-59ff; and Mary Ryan, *Womanhood in America* (New York: New Viewpoints, 1975), p. 106.

16.   "For middle- or upper-class young ladies some demonstrable ability in singing and at the keyboard was a fashionable accomplishment and a necessary component of a genteel education." Nicholas Tawa, "Secular Music in the Late-Eighteenth-Century American Home," *The Musical Quarterly* LXI/4 (Oct. 1975), 512.

17.   *The Spectator* [Connecticut], September 26, 1801 quoted in Helen Morgan, ed., *A Season in New York, 1801. The Letters of Harriet and Maria Trumbull* (Pittsburgh, 1969), p. 36n.

18.   Hitchcock, *Music in the United States,* p. 34.

19.   Ryan, *Womanhood,* pp. 107-8.

20.   John Burton, *Lectures on Female Education* (New York, 1974), p. 97.

21.   John Gregory, *A Father's Legacy to His Daughter* (London, 1774), pp. 26-28. Between 1775 and 1799, this work went through two American editions.

22.   Ibid., p. 31.

23.   Ibid., p. 51.

24.   Ibid.

25.   See the article from *Mirror of Taste and Dramatic Censor* (Philadelphia, 1810) quoted in Loesser, *Men, Women and Pianos,* pp. 456-57.

26.   *The Spectator* [Connecticut], September 26, 1801, quoted in Morgan, *A Season in New York, 1801,* p. 37.

27.   Elizabeth Griffiths, *Letters Addressed to Young Married Women* (Philadelphia, 1796), pp. 42-45.

28.   *Dictionary of National Biography,* ed. Leslie Stephen and Sidney Lee. (London: Oxford University Press, 1959), IV, p. 58.

29.   Hester Chapone, *Letters on the Improvement of the Mind, Addressed to a Young Lady* (Boston, 1783), p. 117.

30.   Bennett, *Letters,* Letter LXVI.

31.   *National Index of American Imprints Through 1800—The Short-Title Evans.* ed., Clifford K. Shipton and James E. Mooney (Barre, Mass.: American Antiquarian Society, 1969), p. 75.

32.   Chapone, *Letters on the Improvement of the Mind,* p. 117.

33.   *The Polite Lady; or a Course of Female Education* (Philadelphia, 1798), p. 30.

34.   Tawa, "Secular Music," p. 512.

35.   Charles Brockden Brown, *Ormond* (New York, 1799), p. 27, quoted in Tawa, ibid.

36.   Brissot de Warville, *New Travels in the United States of America, 1788,* quoted in Thomas Woody, *A History of Women's Education in the United States* (New York, 1929), I, p. 157n.

37. Quoted in Tawa, "Secular Music," pp. 514-15. See also Gilbert Chase, *America's Music* (revised 2nd ed. New York: McGraw-Hill Book Co., 1966). Chase devotes a chapter to the "gentlemen amateurs" of the late-eighteenth century.

38. John Aikin, *Letters from a Father to His Son* (Philadelphia, 1794), pp. 273-85.

39. Woody, *A History of Women's Education,* I, 96.

40. Timothy Dwight, *Travels in New England and New York, New Haven, 1821-1822.* ed. Barbara Solomon (Cambridge, Mass.: Harvard University Press, 1969), I, p. 371.

41. Woody, *A History of Women's Education,* I, pp. 301 ff.

42. Benjamin Rush, *Thoughts Upon Female Education* (Philadelphia, 1787), p. 15.

43. Benjamin Rush, *Essays, Literary, Moral and Pilosophical* (Boston, 1798), p. 75ff, quoted in Woody, *A History of Women's Education,* I, p. 303.

44. The *Strictures* were first published in England and then in America one year later. Three more editions were in print by 1813. The American publication of More's complete works that ran to seven volumes went through eight editions between 1818 and 1868. Sarah J. Hale claimed in *A Woman's Record* (New York, 1852), that More was "probably read more in America then England."

45. Quoted in Woody, *A History of Women's Education,* I, p. 51.

46. Quoted in Margaret Coxe, *The Young Lady's Companion* (Columbus, Ohio, 1846), p. 180.

47. For a discussion of More, see Smith, *Daughters of the Promised Land,* p. 100.

48. Woody, *A History of Women's Education,* I, pp. 31 and 51n.

49. Quoted in ibid. I, p. 442.

50. Hannah Foster, *The Boarding School* (Boston, 1798), p. 39-47.

51. *Charlotte Temple* was published in 1794 and went through 104 editions in the nineteenth century. Fred Louis Pattee, *The First Century of American Literature 1770-1870* (New York, 1935), pp. 86-90.

52. Elias Nason, *A Memoir of Mrs. Susanna Rowson* (Albany, 1870), p. 102.

53. O.G.T. Sonneck, *Bibliography of Early Secular American Music,* rev. by W.T. Upton (Washington, 1945), pp. 108, 188, 207, 233, 234, 386, 438, and 446.

54. Susanna Rowson, *Mentoria* (Philadelphia, 1794), II, p. 64.

55. Susanna Rowson, *Miscellaneous Poems* (Boston, 1804), pp. 109-10. Also quoted in Tawa, "Secular Music," p. 511.

Chapter 3

1. Rush is cited in the following: "The Use of Vocal Music," *Euterpeiad* (May 1, 1830), 1; *The Family Minstrel* (July 15, 1835); *Southern Literary Messenger* (Sept. 1839), 597; "Female Education," *Boston Musical Gazette* (Jan. 9, 1839), 149.

2. Charles Butler, *The American Lady* (Philadelphia, 1836), p. 59; See also Almira Phelps, *The Female Student* (New York, 1836), p. 373: "[Music could] not only console her in trouble, but [could] soften and elevate the tone of her mind and smooth the asperities of her own temper."

3.   Lydia Sigourney, *Letters to Young Ladies* (New York: Harper & Bros., 1844), p. 111. For the same tale about a minister and his amiable singing daughters, see also "The Power of Music," *Arthur's Illustrated Home Magazine* (Oct. 1852), 128.

4.   "Women and Music," *Dwight's Journal of Music* (Jan. 5, 1861), 324, called "The Professor's Story," by Dr. Holmes, and excerpt from a short story published in *The Atlantic Monthly*.

5.   Caroline Gilman, *Recollections of a Southern Matron,* (New York, 1837; reprinted 1852), p. 141. Gilman was also a songwriter. See Charles Claghorn, *Biographical Dictionary of American Music* (West Nyack, N.Y.: Parker Pub. Co., 1975), p. 172.

6.   "Fashionable Music," *The Singer's Companion* (New York, 1854), 51.

7.   "A School Incident," *New York Mirror* (Apr. 13, 1839).

8.   Charles Butler, *The American Lady* (Philadelphia, 1836), p. 142.

9.   Fanny Forrester, "Dora, A Slight Etching," *New York Weekly Mirror,* (Nov. 23, 1844), 97.

10.   Barbara Welter, "The Cult of True Womanhood, 1820-1860," *American Quarterly* XVIII (Summer 1966), 151-74.

11.   James S. Hart, *The Popular Book* (London: Oxford University Press, 1950, 2nd ed. 1961), p. 133.

12.   Sigourney, *Letters to Young Ladies,* p. 105.

13.   Ibid., p. 112.

14.   Ibid., p. 118.

15.   Phelps was the sister of Emma Willard, a pioneer in women's education. She also founded the Patapsco Female Seminary in Baltimore in 1841. Thomas Woody, *A History of Women's Education in the United States* (New York, 1929), I, pp. 317ff.

16.   Almira Hart Phelps, *The Female Student,* or *Lectures to Young Ladies on Female Education* (New York, 1833), p. 376.

17.   Ibid., p. 369.

18.   The quotation from More is cited in chap. 2, n. 46, above. Margaret Coxe, *The Young Lady's Companion.* (Columbus, Ohio, 1846), p. 181.

19.   Ibid., p. 369.

20.   "Musical Wives," *Godey's Lady's Book* (Mar. 1835), 119-20.

21.   "The Musical Wife," Thomas Haynes Bayley (Philadelphia: L.A. Meignen & Co., 1832). Also published in *Godey's Lady's Book* (June 1843). *The Complete Catalogue of Sheet Music and Musical Works, 1870* (published by the Board of Music Trade, 1871, reprinted New York: Da Capo Press, 1973), p. 86, lists two songs with the same title, one by Parry, the other by Schmitz.

22.   Gail Hamilton, *Gala Days* (Boston: Ticknor and Fields, 1863), p. 276.

23.   "Household Music," *Arthur's Illustrated Home Magazine,* (Oct. 1852), 128; "Home Music," *New York Musical World,* (Jan. 3, 10, 17, 1857), 2-3, 17-18, 33-34; "Woman's Influence," *Western Musical World* (May 1866), 68.

24.   Sarah J. Hale, *Happy Homes and Good Society All the Year Round* (Boston: J.E. Tilton & Co., 1868, reprinted New York: Arno Press, 1972), p. 177.

25. "Home Music," *Western Musical World* (February 1867), 20.

26. "Woman's Influence," *Western Musical World* (May 1866), 68.

27. See n. 5, above.

28. Phelps, *The Female Student*, p. 370.

29. This phrase was part of the title of *The Ladies' Companion* and *Graham's Lady's and Gentleman's Magazine.*

30. Nicholas Temperly, "Domestic Music in England between 1800 and 1860," *Proceedings of the Royal Music Association* LXXXV (1958-59), 35.

31. Quoted in Judith Tick, "Women as Professional Musicians in the United States, 1870 to 1900," *Yearbook for InterAmerican Musical Research* (1973), 99.

32. Ibid.

33. Wilson Flagg, "Parlor Singing," *Atlantic Monthly* (October 1869), 410-20. Quoted in Joseph Mussulman, *Music in the Cultured Generation* (Evanston: Northwestern Univerity Press, 1971) p. 174.

34. Phelps, *The Female Student*, p. 374.

35. Coxe, *The Young Lady's Companion*, p. 183.

36. Phelps, *The Female Student*, p. 374.

37. "Young Ladies' Musical Education," *Boston Musical Reporter* (Jan. 1841), 22-24.

38. John Dwight, "Musical Amateurs of the Period," *Dwight's Journal of Music* (Nov. 20, 1869), 138.

39. "A Hint to Musical Ladies," *Boston Musical Visitor* (July 16, 1844), p. 113.

40. "Mems for Musical Misses," *Harpers New Monthly Magazine* (Sept. 1851) 489.

41. Loesser, *Men, Women and Pianos*, p. 509.

42. Hitchcock, *Music in the United States*, p. 53.

Chapter 4

1. Lydia Sigourney, *Letters to Young Ladies* (New York: Harper and Brothers, 1844), p. 111.

2. Virginia Penny, *The Employments of Women* (Boston: Walker, Wise & Co., 1863), p. 44.

3. This is the impression given by writers of the period and, as we shall see, in regional studies that discuss music at private boys' schools. However, research in the history of music education at private schools for boys and at co-ed institutions remains to be done.

4. "Musical Culture," *Western Musical World* (June 1866), 85.

5. For example, Lloyd Sunderman, *Historical Foundations of Music Education in the United States* (Metuchen, N.J.: The Scarecrow Press, 1971) moves directly from singing schools to public schools with no mention of seminary activity.

6. Ibid., I, 44.

7. Thomas Woody, *A History of Women's Education in the Unitd States*, 2 vols (New York and Lancaster, Pa.: The Science Press, 1929) p. 544.

8. Arthur Loesser, *Men, Women and Pianos* (New York: Simon and Schuster, 1954), p. 508.

9. R.B. Harwell, *Confederate Music* (Chapel Hill: University of North Carolina Press, 1950), p. 29.

10. Gilbert Chase, *America's Music,* rev. 2nd ed. (New York: McGraw-Hill, 1966), p. 179.

11. Emma Crews, "A History of Music in Knoxville, Tennessee, 1791-1910,"(Ed.D. dissertation, Florida State University, 1961).

12. Ibid., p. 79.

13. Ibid., p. 37. See also, Katherine H. Mahan, *Showboats to Soft Shoes. A Century of Musical Development in Columbus, Georgia, from 1828 to 1928* (Columbus, Ga., 1968) for similar accounts of the activities of female seminaries. By 1840 there were three in the area and Glenville Female College opened with 17 pianos, a melodeon, and equipment for a full orchestra (pp. 17 ff). Occasionally music was taught at a male school, but typically music was extracurricular and centered around bands (pp. 26f).

14. The back cover of George Root's *The Festival Glee Book* (New York: Mason Bros., 1857) has a category "For Academies and Seminaries" listing this cantata.

15. Whittlesey was the founder of Music Vale Female Seminary; see n. 48, below. Nothing further is known about the Masi piece except that it is cited in the *Complete Catalogue,* p. 465.

16. This review of the seminary is taken from Woody, *A History of Women's Education,* I, 415.

17. Ibid., I, 395.

18. Source: Ibid., I, 415.

19. Source: Ibid., I, 563.

20. Source: Ibid., I, 559-60.

21. George Webb, *Young Ladies' Vocal Classbook,* (Boston: Jenks and Palmer, 1843), preface.

22. George Webb, *The American Glee Book* (Boston, 1841), preface.

23. T. Bissell, *The American Music Class Book* (Boston, 1859); George Bristow, *The Cantilena* (New York, 1865); C. Butler, *The Silver Bell* (Boston, 1866); J.A. Getze, *Tara's Harp* (Philadelphia, 1858); George Root, *The Young Ladies' Choir* (New York, 1846); Jane Sloman, *The Melodist* (New York, 1850).

24. For example, Allen Britton, "Music Education: An American Specialty," *One Hundred Years of Music in America,* ed. by Paul Henry Lang (New York: G. Schirmer, Inc., 1961), p. 214, notes the blandness of music in these vocal classbooks.

25. Bristow, *The Cantilena,* preface.

26. Catalogues located in the collection of the New York Public Library, Annex Division. Emma Willard is the author of the famous poem, "Rocked in the Cradle of the Deep," set to music by Joseph Knight (New York C.H. Horn, 1840).

27. Louisa Maria Ackley, "Diary 1831-1832, My Record, Geneva Female Seminary," unpublished manuscript, New York Public Library, Manuscript and Rare Books Division.

28. *Complete Catalouge,* p. 312, lists seven sets of variations of this tune by the following composers: Ulmo, Spindler, Valentine, Darley, Meinecke, Welch, and Wallace.

29. *The Family Minstrel,* July 15, 1835, n.p., reviews of W. Nixon, *A Guide to Instruction on the Piano Forte.* Designed for the use of both parents and pupils, with a series of short essays. Dedicated to the young ladies of the musical seminary. (Cincinnati: J. Drake, 1834).

30. *A Season in New York 1801. Letters of Harriet and Maria Trumbull,* ed. Helen M. Morgan (Pittsburgh: University of Pittsburgh Press, 1969). The author thanks Amy Aaron for bringing this book to her attention.

31. Another New York piano teacher, Angelica Martin, also advertised three lessons a week for quarter terms. See Richard J. Wolfe, *Secular Music in America, 1801-1825,* (New York: New York Public Library, 1964), II, 544.

32. Morgan, *A Season in New York,* p. 116.

33. Ibid., pp. 135, 145.

34. William C. Reichel, *A History of the Rise, Progress and Present Condition of the Moravian Seminary for Young Ladies at Bethlehem, Pennsylvania* (Philadelphia: J.B. Lippincott & Co., 1870), p. 141.

35. Eliza Southgate Bowne, *A Girl's Life Eighty Years Ago.* (New York: Charles Scribner's Songs, 1887), letter dated August 9, 1803.

36. "Musical Education for Young Ladies," *The Musical World and Times* (Feb. 19, 1853), 118.

37. Ibid., September 2, 1854, p. 2.

38. From the Cherry Valley Seminary (N.Y.) catlogue of 1854.

39. Ibid.

40. Ibid.

41. "Musical Progress," *The Musical World and Times* IX (Aug. 5, 1854), 161.

42. Henri Herz, *My Travels in America,* trans by. H.B. Hill (Madison, Wisconsin: State Historical Society, 1963), p. 91.

43. Ibid.

44. *Dwight's Journal of Music* (July 10, 1852), 111.

45. *Dwight's Journal of Music* (Aug. 6, 1853), 142.

46. Concert held July 27, 1853. *Dwight's Journal of Music* (Aug. 6, 1853), 142.

47. "That Monster Concert by Young Ladies," *Dwight's Journal of Music* (Oct. 15, 1853), 20.

48. Frances Hall Johnson, *Music Vale Seminary, 1835-1876.* (New Haven: Yale University Press, 1934), p. 16.

49. Sunderman, *Historical Foundations,* p. 50.

50. Johnson, *Music Vale,* p. 11.

51. Sunderman, *Historical Foundations,* p. 230.

52. Johnson, *Music Vale,* p. 11.

53. Ibid., p. 16.

54. Ibid.

55. *The Musical World and Times* (Feb. 1853), 131-32.

56.   Johnson, *Music Vale,* p. 12.

57.   *The Musical World and Times* (Feb. 1853), 131-32.

58.   For example, "Music Vale Seminary Quickstep" (New York: Horace Waters, 1855).

59.   Johnson, *Music Vale,* p. 15.

60.   Susan Lyman Leslie, *Recollections of my Mother* (Boston, 1886), p. 89.

61.   Letitia Burwell, *A Girl's Life in Virginia Before the War* (New York, 1895), p. 33.

62.   "The Philosophy of a Ball-Room," *The Columbian Lady's and Gentleman's Magazine* (Oct. 1845), 201-4.

63.   Ibid., 203.

Chapter 5

1.   The two biographies of American secular music before 1825 are Oscar G.T. Sonneck, *A Bibliography of Early Secular American Music.* Rev. W.T. Upton (1945: reprint ed., New York: Da Capo Press, 1964) and Richard J. Wolfe, *Secular Music in America, 1801 to 1825,* 3 vols. (New York: New York Public Library, 1962). The figure of 6,800 is a conservative estimate calculated in the following manner. Wolfe's *Index of Titles* (Vol. 3, pp. 1037-86) contains approximately 5,500 entries. Wolfe (preface, p.xx) estimates that the volume of music in his bibliography represents perhaps four times the volume recorded in Sonneck-Upton, which is thereby approximately 1,325 pieces. We might add that the collection of titles in the Americana Collection of the Music Division of the New York Public Library for approximately the same time period (through 1830) has been estimated at about 4,900 entries.

2.   Information supplied by Richard Crawford.

3.   Richard Crawford, "An Overview of Sacred Music Imprints in the United States through 1810" (paper presented at the meetings of the Sonneck Society, Queensboro College, May 1976), cited 4,600 works by about 300 American composers, all men.

4.   Sonneck, *Bibliography,* p. 168. The song was also published in an important early collection, *The American Musical Miscellany* (1798; reprint ed., New York: Da Capo Press, 1972), pp. 158-59, without a composer attribution. Galli was active in London between 1743 and 1780.

5.   Moller and Capron eds., *Monthly Numbers,* Nos. 1 and 3 (Philadelphia, 1793). Sonneck, *Bibliography,* pp. 34, 7.

6.   Boston: G. Graupner, ca. 1803-1806. This imprint does not bear any composer attribution; however, the song appears in Oliver Shaw's *A Selection of Progressive Airs* (Dedham, 1810), p. 5, under Richard's name. In 1859 it was republished by S. Brainard & Co., and it is listed in the *Complete Catalogue of Sheet Music and Musical Works, 1870,* (1871; reprint ed., New York: Da Capo Press, 1973), p. 101.

7.   On the Pietists see J.F. Sachse, *Music of the Cloister* (Philadelphia, 1900) II, pp. 128-60. On the Shakers see Edward Andrews, *The Gift to be Simple* (New York, 1940; reprint ed., 1962).

8.   Carl Holliday, *Woman's Life in Colonial Days* (1922; reprint ed., Williamstown, Mass.: Corner House Publishers, 1968), p. 34.

9.   Linda Grant De Pauw and Conover Hunt, *Remember the Ladies, Women in America 1750-1815* (New York: The Viking Press, 1976), p. 78.

10.   Miss M.T. Durham published "Star of Columbia" and an arrangement of "The Promised Land" in *The Southern Harmony,* ed., William Walker (Philadelphia, 1835), pp. 51, 160.

11. Holliday, *Woman's Life,* p. 68.

12. They are Harriet Abrams, Frances Alsop, Charlotte Anley, Elizabeth Anspach, Miss Bannister, Maria Bland, Anne Cantelo, Georgianna Spencer Cavendish, Maria Dickons, Eliza Flower, Isabelle Theaker More, Jane Quest Miles, and Mary Ann Pownall.

13. Charles Hamm, *Yesterdays. Popular Song in America* (New York: W.W. Norton & Co., 1979), p. 60, gives a thorough penetrating account of English and American secular song composers in the 1780s and '90s. See chap. 2 and 5 in particular.

14. This account of Pownall's life is based on information in Oscar Sonneck's studies, *Early Opera in America* New York: G. Schirmer, 1915) and *Early Concert Life in America* (Leipzig: Breitkopf and Hartel, 1907), and Julian Mates, *The American Musical Stage before 1800* (New Brunswick, N.J.: Rutgers University Press, 1962). The songs by Pownall in the *Six Songs*... include "Jemmy of the Glen," "The Straw Bonnet," and "Lavinia." "The Straw Bonnet" has recently been published in Elwyn A. Weinandt, *The Bicentennial Collection of America Music,* Volume I, 1698-1800 (Carol Stream, Ill.: Hope Pub. Co., 1974), pp. 159-62.

15. The only other extant song is "Kisses sue'd for," New York: G. Gilfert & Co., (1795).

16. Charles Odell, *Annals of the New York Stage* (New York: Columbia University Press, 1927-31), I, p. 366.

17. Sonneck, *Bibliography,* pp. 93-94, lists both the Davis and Abrams version. Wolfe, *Secular Music,* p. 1, lists two Abrams imprints and three collections containing her version.

18. "My Native Land Goodnight!" sung by Mrs. French, arranged by Miss Fowler [*sic*] (New York: Torp & Unger, ca. 1839) is an edition of the professional or complex version; "My Native Shore, Adieu," words by Lord Byron composed by Miss Fowler [*sic*] (New York: Wm. Dubois, ca. 1817) is a simple version. Brown and Stratton, *British Musical Biography* (Birmingham, 1897), p. 148 state that Eliza Flower (1803-1846) was mistakenly published as "Fowler" in the United States. Wolfe, *Secular Music,* I, p. 283 lists her as "Miss Fowler, unidentified composer, probably English." "My Native Land, Goodnight" (New York: W. Dubois, 1818-1821) was also published as "My Native Shore, Adieu," (New York: John Paff, 1811-1817). *The U.S. Board of Music Trade, op. cit.,* p. 89 lists it in print in 1870 in the catalogues of three publishers. Eliza Flower's sister, Sarah Jane Flower Adams, wrote the hymn "Nearer My God To Thee."

19. For information on singers and instrumentalists active in this period, see H. Earle Johnson, *Musical Interludes in Boston, 1795-1835* (New York: Columbia University Press, 1943) and Julian Mates, *The American Musical Stage Before 1800.* For further references see the comprehensive and indispensable guide, *Women in American Music, A Bibliography of Music and Literature* eds., Adrienne Fried Block and Carol Neuls-Bates (Westport, Conn: Greenwood Press, 1980).

20. John Rowe Parker, *A Musical Biography* (Boston: Stone and Fovell, 1824), lists the following: Mrs. Storace; Madama Mara Lee Schnelling; Mrs. Billington; Angelica Catalani; Miss Stephen; Mrs. Salmon; Miss Broadhurst; Mrs. Oldmixon; Mrs. Ostinelli; Miss Eustaphiève. The last two were American pianists.

21. We should also mention the models provided by women of famous families, among them Martha Jefferson, wife of the president, and Eleanor Parke Custis, a step grand-daughter of George Washington.

22. They are Catherine Bauer, Caroline Clark, Marthesie Demillière, Elizabeth Van Hagen, Annette Mariott, Angelica Martin, Grace Richards, Sally Sully, and Mary Weir.

23. Angelica Martin taught music in New York in the 1820s and '30s and in New Jersey in the 1840s. Sully was a professor of music in Richmond, Virginia. Elizabeth Van Hagen was an organist, pianist, and teacher, and a member of a prominent family of musicians in Boston, around 1800. See Wolfe, *Secular Music,* 1, p. 332; 2. pp. 544, 890.

24. Hamm, *Yesterdays,* p. 23. Hamm's analysis of stylistic trends from 1790 through 1870 inform this chapter.

25. Boston: G. Graupner (ca. 1803-1806). This imprint does not bear any composer attribution; however, the song appears in Oliver Shaw's *A Selection of Progressive Airs* (Dedham, 1810), p. 5, under Richard's name. The 1859 imprint was published by S. Brainard & Co., *Complete Catalogue of Sheet Music and Musical Works, 1870* (U.S. Board of Music Trade, 1871; New York: Da Capo Press, 1973), p. 101. We shall refer to this catalogue as the *Complete Catalogue.*

26. Words by Mrs. Rowson. One imprint even attributes Carr's melody to a lady (Boston, P.A. Van Hagen, ca. 1800); however, Wolfe, *Secular Music,* p. 104, says this version is identical with other imprints under Carr's name.

27. Wolfe, *Secular Music,* I, pp. 295-96 lists seven songs with this kind of attribution.

28. The list includes works through 1830, thanks to a survey made by B.A. Wolverton, "Keyboard Music and Musicians in the Colonies and the United States of America Before 1830," (Ph.D. dissertation, University of Indiana, 1966).

29. Odell, *Annals,* I, p. 311.

30. Johnson, *Musical Interludes,* p. 163.

31. *Complete Catalogue,* pp. 530-31.

32. Copyright protection was extended to music by American composers by 1831.

33. *The Welcome Guest* (Boston: Henry Tolman & Co., 1830).

34. Wolfe, *Secular Music,* III, p. 962.

35. *The Parlor Companion* (Boston: Oliver Ditson, 1850), p. 86.

36. *Complete Catalogue,* p. 324.

Chapter 6

1. The criteria for determining popularity are discussed in the introduction. See also appendix, "Selected Compositions Published by Women in the U.S. before 1870." All individual pieces cited in the text will be accompanied only by a date since full bibliographical information is in the appendix. Complete citations will accompany only those works that are not in the appendix.

2. The lives and work of these composers are discussed in the next chapter.

3. Hutchinson's songs are discussed later in this chapter.

4. Baker has one song to her credit, "The Burial of an Indian Girl," w. Mrs. L.H. Sigourney, Boston, 1845. No copy located, but listed in Harry Dichter, *Handbook of American Sheet Music* (Philadelphia, 1947), p. 68. Also listed in the *Complete Catalogue,* p. 17, attributed to the Baker Family.

5.   Mentioned in Richard B. Harwell, *Confederate Music* (Chapel Hill: University of North Carolina Press, 1950), p. 112; See George Odell, *Annals of the New York Stage* (New York: Columbia University Press, 1927-31), VII, p. 181, for information on her acting career.

6.   Works listed in Harwell, *Confederate Music*, p. 153; "We Have Parted," "My Mother's Voice," and "A Few More Days and We Shall Part," all published in Blackmar's *Selection of One Hundred Beautiful Songs and Pieces* (New Orleans, 186-). She is described as a singer on the title page of John Hill Hewitt's "The Young Volunteer" (Macon, Ga.: J.C. Schreiner, 1863); Harwell, *Confederate Music*, p. 80.

7.   Madame Ablamovicz is listed in concert notices in Louisville newspapers in 1853. See Edward Barret, "Items from the *Louisville Journal, Louisville Democrat,* and the *Daily Cincinnati Gazette,* 1853" unpublished list accompanying the paper "Louisville Kentucky, 1853," delivered at the national meetings of the American Musicological Society, November 5, 1976.

8.   All of her works were published by Root and Cady, and none have been located to date. Listed in Dena Epstein, *Music Publishing in Chicago Before 1871: The Firm of Root & Cady, 1858-1871* (Detroit: Information Coordinators, Inc., 1969) are "The Valentine; or the Spirit of Song" (1858) and "Songs of Affection" (186-). Higgins was a member of a singing troupe "The Columbians."

9.   Stith's song "Our Friendship" (1830) and Pettigrew's "Birdling, My Messenger" (1854) were both dedicated to pupils. Miss Jackson published "Two Brilliant Waltzes" (New York, 1839) dedicated to a pupil, Miss Alcott, from Albany.

10.   See appendix for a list of works published by Ladies or Ladies from a particular locale.

11.   Cited in Harwell, *Confederate Music,* p. 132. The piece may have been borrowing titles from the Wilkie Collins novel *Woman in White.*

12.   E.g., "Dearest One, When Thou Art Absent," "I'm Thinking of You, Dear One Tonight," "American Banner March," and "Cataract Quickstep," *Complete Catalogue,* pp. 27, 60, 514, 516.

13.   John Tasker Howard, *America's Troubadour* (New York: Thomas Y. Crowell Co., 1934, rev. eds. 1953, 1962), pp. 189-90, cites this song as one of Foster's "descents into the depths of the saccharine." According to Howard, Foster's sister wrote of learning this song in 1836.

14.   The concordance between this tune and the Moore melody comes from an anonymous researcher who left this information in a clipping attached to the Foster Piece in the collection of the New York Public Library.

15.   Pieces by Adeline and Mary are in the appendix. Published "The Heath Polka" in *Peterson's Magazine* XXXIX (June 1861) 265. Other first names include Werline, "I'm Going to Sleep," (Boston: Henry Tolman, 1864) and "The Mississippi Regiment March," listed in the *Complete Catalogue,* p. 525; Leonore, "Be Kind to Thy Mother," *Complete Catalogue,* p. 13; Lelia, "The Gunboat Quickstep" and the "Midnight March," *Complete Catalogue,* pp. 520, 525.

16.   Claribel was Charlotte Allington Barnard, and Dolores was Ellen Dickson.

17.   Septimus Winner published many works as Alice Hawthorne, among them "Listen to the Mocking Bird." Joseph E. Winner published a pirated edition of "Little Brown Jug" (New York: S.T. Gordon, 1869) as "Betta."

18.   Sarah J. Hale, *Society and Manners, or Happy Homes and Good Society All the Year Round* (Boston: J.E. Tilton and Co., 1868, reprinted New York: Arno Press, 1972), p. 180. Quoted

also in Phyllis Mackowitz, "A Preliminary Investigation of American Women Song Composers of the Nineteenth and Early Twentieth Centuries," (M.A. thesis, Wesleyan University, April 1977), p. 50.

19. *The New World* V (September 17, 1842), 193, had a notice of a ballad, "The Departed,"words by Park Benjamin, music, Miss Ellen Blundell (Philadelphia: W.R. Bayley, 1842), and wrote that the music was "...quite worthy of the words which accompany it: the fair composer could desire no higher praise." Another example is a notice that the *Brooklyn Eagle* published, praising "The Sanitary Fair Polka" of Mrs. E.A. Parkhurst (1864), in which she was similarly described.

20. Both E.G. White and Benjamin Lang provided harmonizations.

21. Listed in Epstein, *Music Publishing in Chicago,* p. 269.

22. *The New World* (Jan. 8, 1842), 31.

23. *The New World,* Oct. 30, 1841, p. 287. Professional female writers often justified their work with "feminine" rationalizations. See the analysis is Ann D. Wood, "The Scribbling Women" and Fanny Fern, "Why Women Wrote," *American Quarterly* XXIII/2 (Spring 1971), 4-24. On the amateur pose of lady poets, see E. Douglas Branch, *The Sentimental Years 1835-1860* (New York: D. Appleton-Century Co., 1934), p. 135, who writes, "It was feminine not feminist to be a humble dilettante, and it also saved the poetess from the labor of revising her verses."

24. Charles Grobe, ed., *The Musical Almanac for 1861,* op. 1300 (Philadelphia: Lee & Walker, 1861), pp. 43-44.

25. For the most recent and most important discussion of Anglo-American home songs see Charles Hamm, *Yesterdays. Popular Song in America.* (New York: W.W. Norton & Co., 1979). Also worthy of mention is William W. Austin, *"Susanna," "Jeanie," and "The Old Folks at Home"* (New York: Macmillan Co., 1975), chap. 7. Most discussions of the period mention English men, particularly Henry Russell. For a recent study from an English point of view, see Ronald Pearsall, *Victorian Popular Music* (Detroit: Gale Research Co., 1973), chap. 5, "Music in the Home." The subject of Victorian music in America is a fertile area for research, since English composers remained a presence in American music through the entire century. A helpful work for the music historian is Daniel Walker Howe, ed., *Victorian America,* (Philadelphia: University of Pennsylvania Press, 1976); in particular, Howe's overview, "Victorian Culture in America," and David Hull's "The Victorian Connection."

26. Hamm, *Yesterdays,* p. 184, calls Barnard "one of the most skillful and sensitive writers of the entire nineteenth century in Great Britain."

27. Composer attributions on nineteenth-century imprints refer to her as "Mrs. Hemans sister" as well as Miss Browne, and usually place the poet's name in a more prominent position.

28. Austin, *"Susanna,"* p. 144, mentions Mrs. Hemans as one of the major contributors to the home-song tradition, but does not refer to the musical settings made by Harriet Mary Browne.

29. See chap. 7, below.

30. Almira Phelps, *The Female Student* (New York, 1836), p. 372.

31. "The Captive Knight," "The Messenger Bird," "Evening Song to the Virgin," "Tyrolese Evening Hymn," and "Pilgrim Fathers" are in the *Parlour Companion* (New York, 1836) and the *Franklin Square Song Collection* (New York, 1884-1892). They were all printed by six to eleven different publishers in the *Complete Catalogue,* pp. 19, 33, 82, 106, 137. "Pilgrim

Fathers" and "The Messenger Bird" are in George Kingsley, *The Social Choir* (Boston, 1838), pp. 40, 140; "The Messenger Bird" and "Evening Song..." were both transcribed for piano, the former by Charles Grobe and the latter included in *Crown Jewels* (Boston, 1861). "Tyrolese Evening Hymn" is listed with an incorrect attribution to Augusta, in Julius Mattfeld, *Variety Music Cavalcade 1620-1950* (New York: Prentice-Hall, 1952), p. 38, for 1828. Nicholas Tawa, *Sweet Songs for Gentle Americans* (Bowling Green, Ohio: Bowling Green University Popular Press, 1980), cites "Tyrolese Evening Hymn," "Pilgrim Fathers," and "Captive Knight" as among the most popular songs in the collections he examined. The Hutchinson Family sang "Ave Sanctissima" [Evening Song to the Virgin] in a quartet arrangement. See Carol Brink, *Harps in the Wind,* p. 294. Mary Dana also used this tune for one of her arrangements in *The Northern Harp* (Boston, 1841), p. 28. "Pilgrim Fathers" is also in *The Hesperian Harp,* ed. William Hauser (Philadelphia, 1848), p. 551, in a shape-note setting.

32. Sarah J. Hale, *Woman's Record; or Sketches of All Distinguished Women* (New York: Harper & Brothers, 1852), p. 761.

33. Jane Grey Perkins, *The Life of the Honourable Mrs. Norton* (New York: Henry Holt and Co., 1909), p. 25.

34. Harwell, *Confederate Music,* p. 96, cites her as one of the two great favorites among foreign song wrtiers, for "Juanita," which went into four editions; "Ringer on the Rhine," and "Would I Were with Thee" were two other popular numbers. Lubov Keefer, *Baltimore's Music* (Baltimore: J.H. Furst Co., 1962), p. 102 n, cites Norton as a poet, rather than composer.

35. "Take Me Back..." in *The Musical Annual* (Philadelphia, 1847). "Juanita" in *The Home Melodist* (Boston: Oliver Ditson, 1859), p. 9. "Officer's Funeral" in *The Silver Chord* (Boston: Oliver Ditson, 1862); and "Gems of Sacred Song," p. 22. All in print in the *Complete Catalogue,* pp. 18, 34, 67, 95, 102. Also in *The Home Circle. A Collection of Beautiful Duos by Eminent Composers* (Boston: Oliver Ditson, 1858-76). Hamm, *Yesterdays,* p. 485, cites "Juanita" as among the most popular foreign songs in the century.

36. For information on ladies' magazines, see Bertha Stearns, "New England Magazines for Ladies, 1830-1860," *New England Quarterly* II (Oct. 1930), 627-56; "Philadelphia Magazines for Ladies, 1830-1860," *Pennsylvania Magazine of History and Biography* LXIX (July 1945) 207-19; "Early Western Magazines for Ladies," *Mississippi Valley Historical Review* XVIII (1931-32), 319-30.

37. Caroline J. Garnsey, "Ladies Magazine to 1850," *Bulletin of the New York Public Library* LVIII (1954), 74-88. This article includes a checklist of 110 ladies' magazines published by 1850.

38. The others include the following: *Boston Miscellany of Fashion, The Bouquet and Ladies' Musical Portfolio, The Casket, Godey's Lady's Book, Columbian Ladies' and Gentlemen's Magazine, Ladies' Garland and Family Wreath, The Ladies' Pearl, The New York Mirror and Ladies' Literary Gazette, Arthur's Illustrated Home Magazine, The Home Monthly, The Evergreen, Peterson's Magazine.*

39. For some examples see the following: "Fairy Bells" w. Caroline Norton, m. her sister, *The Ladies' Companion* VII (May 1837), 48; "The Fair Puritan," Mrs. T.H. Bayly, *Ladies Companion* IV (Apr. 1836), 284; "I'll Speak of Thee," Maria Hawes, *Ladies' Companion* XVII (Jan. 1842), 160; "Thou Art Lovlier," *Graham's Literary and Ladies Magazine* XXXVI (Mar. 1850), 226; Mrs. Fitzgerald, "The Dying Girl to her Lover," *New York Mirror and Ladies' Gazette* XIV (Oct. 22, 1836), 136; "Bye Gone Hours" by Mrs. Norton and Mrs. Price

Blackwood, *Graham's Literary and Ladies' Magazine* XIX (1841), 185; "The Bridal Morn," Miss Clarkson, advertised as the first American reprint in *The Dollar Magazine* (July 1841), 223; Claribel, "I Cannot Sing the Old Songs," *Peterson's Magazine* LV (Apr. 1869).

40. *Godey's Lady's Book*, (Jan. 1852).

41. Composed by Mrs. S.R. Burtis. *Complete Catalogue*, p. 462.

42. See, for example, "No More" by a Young Lady, *Godey's Lady's Book* (Jan. 1840), 34; "The Fascination Schottische," a Lady, *Peterson's Magazine* (Oct. 1861).

43. "The Heath Polka," Nita, *Peterson's Magazine* (June 1861), 265.

44. "The Rose of the Prairie Waltz," Ada Bolton, *Peterson's Magazine* (Aug. 1858). "The Spirit's Whisper," Clare Beames, *Columbian Lady's and Gentleman's Magazine* (July 1847).

45. "Our Friendship," Mrs. Townshend Stith (Philadelphia: G. Willig, 1830), in *Godey's Lady's Book* (1830), 277; "The Spell is Broken," Juliet Bellchambers (New York: Atwill, 1842), in *Graham's Literary and Lady's Magazine* XXVIII (1846).

46. Works include "The Chain that Links My Heart to Thine" (Feb. 1844), 94; "The Parting" (Feb. 1845) 93; "Wo's Me" (Apr. 1845), 191; "Sometimes Remember Me" (June 1845), 280; "While Through the Toilsome Roads of Life" (Aug. 1845), 94; "The Gondolier" (Oct. 1845), 188; "Good Night" (Dec. 1845), 280; "Thou Shalt Sing to Me" (Nov. 1847), 28; "The Bridal Wreath" (Dec. 1847), 282.

47. See chap. 7, below.

48. Pieces by Mrs. C.L. Hull include "The Lover's Farewell" (Jan. 1845) and "Love's First Step is Upon the Rose" (Oct. 1844), 190.

49. For a coy but interesting description of music by both men and women in these magazines, see Paul Fatout, "Threnodies of the Ladies' Books," *Musical Quarterly* XXXI/4 (Oct. 1945), 464-78.

50. Howe, "Victorian Culture in America," *Victorian America*, p. 26. "One useful approach to the history of women in the nineteenth century is to study their particular subculture of Victorianism. The innovations in printing and in women's education brought with them the emergence of an enormous new audience of women readers who were served to a large extent by a new group of women writers. There was a woman's communication network in middle-class Victorian society."

51. Hans Nathan, *Dan Emmett and the Rise of Negro Minstrelry* (Norman: University of Oklahoma Press, 1962), p. 230.

52. Tawa, *Gentle Songs*, p. 122.

53. From Tuckerman's introduction to *The Works of Felicia Hemans*, ed. Rufus Griswald (Philadelphia: John Ball Co., 1850).

54. Lubov Keefer in her study *Baltimore's Music, The Haven of the American Composer* (Baltimore: J.H. Furst Co., 1962), pp. 101-2, lists a number of ballads by women from the 1840s, among them "the popular Julia Fowle, the numerous distaff members of the Hewitt and Carusi clans, and the prolific society belles, many of them loath to reveal their identities." She concludes that "the ballad opened wide the doors to woman ... from the passive object of pity or adulation, equally unprofitable, she enters now man's arena as poet and composer."

55. Nicholas Tawa, "The Ways of Love in the Mid-Nineteenth Century American Song," *Journal of Popular Culture* X/2 (Fall 1976), 337-51. Other songs by women cited in this

article include "No More" by a Young Lady of Georgia, "The Sun is in the West" by Mrs. C.E. Habicht, and "Thou Hast Wounded the Spirit that Loved Thee" by a Lady.

56. Ibid., p. 340.

57. "The Female World of Love and Ritual: Relations Between Women in Nineteenth-Century America," *Signs* I/ 1 (1975), 1-29.

58. Ada Parker, "Letters" (Boston, 1863), unpublished ms., New York Public Library, includes the letter of August 24, 1938, to Mrs. Emily Greene: "At this time there are a large number of young females within the circuit of a few miles. Most of us meet to sing, and in this way we form very happy acquaintances."

59. Cincinnati: F.W. Rauch, 1859.

60. Tawa, *Sweet Songs for Gentle Americans*, pp. 5-7.

61. See n. 5, 6, above.

62. In print in the *Complete Catalogue*, p. 103. Stith wrote other ballads in the 1830's: "Didst Thou Ever Think of Me" (Philadelphia, 1831) and "We Parted in Silence" (Philadelphia, 1835), also in print in the *Complete Catalogue*, p. 142.

63. *Godey's Lady's Book* (1830), 277.

64. New York: Atwills, 1842, described as "a celebrated ballad, as sung in public and private circles with the most distinguished success. Simplified arrangement by "L.T.H." Listed in the *Complete Catalogue*, p. 122, in the catalogues of three publishers. Bellchambers also wrote an "Answer to Spell is Broken," listed in the *Complete Catalogue*, p. 8. Maeder's arrangement was part of a series *Gems of Ballads* (Boston: Wm. H. Oakes, 1843).

65. *Complete Catalogue*, p. 14. In Charles Butler, *The Silver Bell* (Boston: H. Tolman, 1866), p. 96; *Forget Me Not*, ed. Horace Waters (New York, 186-), pp. 188-89; and in *the Day School Bell*, ed. Horace Waters (New York, 1861), p. 188. Also included in *One Hundred Beautiful Songs and Pieces* (New Orleans: A.E. Blackmar, 186-). Also in *Peterson's Magazine*, July 1867, published anonymously.

66. Smith's piece was transcribed for guitar by Carusi (Philadelphia, 1837-39); the *Complete Catalogue*, p. 106, lists it in the catalogues of eight different publishers. Mary Dana Shindler used the tune for one of her contrafacta in *The Northern Harp* (Boston, 1841), p. 36, retitled "Mary at the Tomb" and in *Good Old Songs* (Boston: Oliver Ditson, 1887), Vol. I, p. 63. Both reprinted in Charles Jarvis, *The Young Folk's Glee Book* (New York: S.T. Gordon, 1854), pp. 56-57.

67. This song spawned an "Answer to 'Thou Hast Wounded the Spirit' " by the composer Ratcliffe, cited in the *Complete Catalogue*, p. 8; it was in print in 1870 and in the collection *Good Old Songs* (Boston: Oliver Ditson 1895), II, p. 67, and in *The Wreath of Gems* (Boston: Oliver Ditson, 1868), p. 87. See also Henry de Marsan, *New Comic and Sentimental Singer's Journal* (New York: 1868-71), No. 3, p. 18.

68. Traces of Irish mannerisms also appear in "The Ring My Mother Wore" (1860), a "song for hearts bereaved" composed some years later by "Mary." This song was listed in the *Complete Catalogue*, p. 110; also in de Marsan, *New Comic*, No. 5 (1868-71), n.p., lyrics only.

69. Carol Brink, *Harps in the Wind* (New York: Macmillan Co., 1947), p. 275; the author describes Abby in Victorian terms: "Abby had never made any pretense of being a composer, as her brothers had; yet out of the fullness of gentle heart, she had made the music for several songs: they were 'Ring Out, Wild Bells' and 'Rock Me to Sleep, Mother.' " "Kind Words . . . "

was arranged for four-part chorus in *The Sabbath Bell* ed. Horace Waters (New York, 1859-60), p. 24.

70. Listed as one of the hits of 1852 in Mattfeld, *Variety Music Cavalcade*, p. 88. In print in the *Complete Catalogue*, p. 153. There is no musical connection to the Foster tune.

71. Original date unknown but listed in Lee and Walker's *Musical Almanac* (Philadelphia, 1869), as a song and chorus. Other songs and choruses include Werline's song cited in n. 15: Phoebe Palmer Knapp's *Watching for Pa* (New York, 1867); Martha Hills "The Ghost of Uncle Tom, as sung by the Hutchinson's" is attributed to them in the *Complete Catalogue*, p. 42.

72. There is a review of Mary Dana's *Temperance Lyre* in *Brother Jonathan*, July 2, 1842.

73. See the next chapter for a discussion of her work.

74. Cited in Epstein, *Music Publishing in Chicago*, p. 115. Since this study concentrates on commercial sheet music, it overlooks pieces in collections; it is quite likely that women contributed music for these movements through political songsters and collections.

75. See, for example, the "Continental Polka Mazurka," Mrs. E. Blessey (New Orleans, 1862), "the proceeds to be sent to the Continentals now in active service in Virginia." Cited in Harwell, *Confederate Music*, p. 109.

76. Works listed in Harwell, *Confederate Music*, pp. 109ff. The last two also mentioned in Lota Spell, *Music in Texas* (Austin, 1936; reprint New York: AMS Pub. Co., 1973), pp. 61-62. Both in print in 1870, *Complete Catalogue*, pp. 43, 123.

77. A thorough examination of the vast repertory of nineteenth-century religious song is far beyond the scope of this study. The remarks below are intended as starting points for others.

78. Barbara Welter, "The Feminization of American Religion: 1800-1860," *Clio's Consciousness Raised. New Perspectives on the History of Women*, ed. Mary Hartman and Lois W. *Banner* (New York: Harper Torchbooks, 1974), pp. 141, 154 n. Welter surveyed 15 hymnals.

79. James Downey, "The Music of American Revivalism," (Ph.D. dissertation, Tulane University, 1968), contains a survey of pieces from revival collections through 1840.

80. William Walker, *The Sourthern Harmony* (Philadelphia, 1835), pp. 51 and 160. First piece also in Hauser, *The Hesperian Harp*, p. 154; second piece in *Original Sacred Harp*, p. 51. See also, the hymns by Sarah Lancaster, "The Last Words of Copernicus," "I'm On My Journey Home," and "Sardis" and Miss P.R. Lancaster, "Oh Sing With Me" in the *Original Sacred Harp*. Denson Revision (Cullman, Alabama, 1971), pp. 112, 345, 374, 460.

81. The Shaker repertory contains many pieces by women. As it was a religious movement led by a woman (Mother Anne), this is understandable.

82. Charles Claghorn, *Biographical Dictionary of American Music* (West Nyack, N.Y.: Parker Publishing Co., 1973), p. 257.

83. "Blessed Assurance," w. Fanny Crosby (New York: Wm. A. Pond & Co., 1873); "Open the Gates..." w. Fanny Crosby (New York: Wm. A. Pond & Co., 1892). The first hymn is, according to Robert Stevenson, "probably the all-time favorite in Billy Graham revivals." ("Church Music: A Century of Contrasts," *One Hundred Years of Music in America* (New York: G. Schirmer Inc., 1961), p. 88n.

84. Claghorn, *Biographical Dictionary*, p. 257. Both texts were by the composer's mother, Phoebe Palmer.

85. Moore, *A Dictionary of Musical Information*, p. 202.

86. *Women in Sacred Song* (Boston: D. Lothrop, 1885). For more information about Knapp and this important collection, see chap. 8. Knapp's included "Consecration," p. 470; "Blessed Assurance," p. 542; "Watchin' for Pa," p. 680; "Jesus' Jewels," p. 408. Also mentioned is a cantata, *Prince of Peace,* about which nothing further is known (p. 470).

87. Ira Sankey, *Gospel Hymns* Nos. 1 to 6 Complete (New York, 1894), 739 hymns, seven written by women. Knapp is represented with "Blessed Assurance" (No. 304), "Nearer the Cross" (No. 320), and "Jesus Christ is Passing By" (No. 620).

88. Timothy L. Smith, *Revivalism and Social Reform in Mid-Nineteenth Century America* (New York: Abingdon Press, 1957), p. 82.

89. For a list of female hymn writers, the most famous of which was Fanny Crosby, see John Julian, *A Dictionary of Hymnology* (2nd ed. 1907; reprinted New York: Dover Press, 1957), pp. 60f.

90. This song and "Messenger Bird" are in *Gems of Sacred Song* (Boston: Oliver Ditson Co., 1867).

91. Emma Willard, m. Joseph Knight (Boston: C.F. Chickering, 1840); cited in Tawa, *Sweet Songs for Gentle Americans,* p. 194, as the song that began the vogue for sacred song.

92. See Richard Jackson's notes to "Flee as a Bird," *Angel's Visits* (New York: New World Records, 1977), NWR 220.

93. For biographical information, see Hale, *Women's Record,* p. 836, and Julian, *A Dictionary of Hymnology,* p. 1055.

94. *The Northern Harp* (Boston: Oliver Ditson, 1842). Listed in the *Complete Catalogue,* p. 572, are two other unlocated collections, *The Western Harp* and *Songs of the People.*

95. "The Ruler's Daughter" is listed in the *Complete Catalogue,* p. 112. Boston: Oliver Ditson, 1858. Also in *The American Vocalist,* ed. Rev. D.H. Mansfield (Boston: W.J. Reynolds & Co., 1849), p. 259.

96. Recorded in *Angel Visits, The Northern Harp,* p. 72, listed in J. Mattfeld, *Variety Music Cavalcade,* p. 100, as one of the hit songs of 1857, in its arrangement by George Root. In print, *Complete Catalogue,* p. 359. In the following collections: *Franklin Square Song Collection,* Vol. II, p. 64 *Good Old Songs* (Boston, 1887), p. 147, as arranged by George Root; *The Silver Chord* (Boston, 1862), p. 87; Ira Sankey, *The Male Chorus,* 1888 (four-part settings of hymns), p. 104; *Gems of Sacred Song* (Boston, 1866), p. 87; arranged in piano transcription by Moelling in *Cluster of Brilliants.* Also in *Heart Songs* (New York: World Syndicate Co., 1909), p. 154.

97. For a similar collection and preface, see *Parlour Melodies,* ed. Miss M.E. Bailey and Mrs. M.B. Lloyd (New York: Harper & Bros., 1842).

98. Hale, *Woman's Record,* p. 836.

99. Andrew C. Minor, "Piano Concerts in New York City 1849-1865" (master's thesis, University of Michigan, 1947), p. 472, mentions five "better women pianists, all foreign-born and foreign-trained." None of the concerts he surveyed included music by women composers with the exception of one Eugenie Barmetche, who on April 28, 1863, played a recital that included two of her own works, an "Impromptu" and a "Caprice Basque" (p. 388).

100. Copy in the collection of Lester Levy. Carrēno played this piece at her debut on November 25, 1862. See Marta Milinowski, *Teresa Carreno* (New Haven: Yale University Press, 1940, reprinted, New York: Da Capo Press, 1977), p. 9.

101.   Early keyboard performers include Sophie Hewitt, the organist for the *Handel and Haydn Society* in 1820; and a Miss Sterling, whose concerts are cited by Loesser, *Men, Women and Pianos*, p. 472. In 1849 the child prodigy Wilhemina Neruda (a great violinist from Europe) played with the New York Philharmonic Orchestra. A review in *The Spirit of the Times* of her concerts was favorable (New York: July 14, 1849, Vol. 19, p. 224). Cited in Riegel, *American Women*, p. 193. No pieces by these women have been located to date. Two church organists, Maria Burdick and Mrs. Clark, are listed in Joyce Mangler, *Rhode Island Music and Musicians*, 1733-1850 (Detroit: Information Service, Inc., 1975), p. 9.

102.   *Grove's Dictionary of Music and Musicians* (2nd ed., 1904-10). American Supplement, ed. Waldo Selden Pratt. (New York: The Macmillan Co., 1920), p. 25. Described as "Adelaide Hohnstock (d. 1856)," the sister of Carl Hohnstock, a pianist and teacher active in Philadelphia, and "associated with him."

103.   Listed anonymously under that title in the *Complete Catalogue*, p. 451.

104.   Stephen Foster, *Social Orchestra*, (New York, 1854, reprinted, New York: Da Capo Press, 1973), p. 5.

105.   Program from the Cherry Valley Library, New York, reprinted in chap. 4.

106.   Hitchcock, *Music in the United States*, p. 76.

107.   Both listed in Epstein, *Music Publishing in Chicago*.

108.   *Complete Catalogue*, p. 347, attribution to a Lady.

109.   *Complete Catalogue*, p. 429.

110.   In print in 1870. *Complete Catalogue*, p. 464, 457. Recorded by Neely Bruce, *Piano Music in America*, Vol. I: 19th-Century Popular Concert and Parlor Music (Vox, SVBX 5302).

111.   Charleston, South Carolina: George Oates, 1847.

Chapter 7

1.   John W. Moore, *Appendix to the Encyclopedia of Music* (Boston: Oliver Ditson & Co., 1875).

2.   John W. Moore, *A Dictionary of Musical Information* (Boston: Oliver Ditson & Co., 1876).

3.   Moore, *Appendix*, p. 22. For the full text of Moore's entry, see p. 10.

4.   Moore, *Dictionary*, pp. 138, 146, 140, 202, 204.

5.   Arranged and edited by Mrs. M.B. Lloyd and Miss M.E. Bailey (New York: Harper and Brothers, 1842). The collection includes four works by women composers: An American, Miss Smith, and two English women, Miss Brown (Mrs. Heman's sister) and Mrs. Norton. The original tunes are unidentified. This was a collection of sacred songs.

6.   W.S.B. Matthews, ed. *A Hundred Years of Music in America* (Chicago: A.L. Howe, 1889). Matthews does include Constance Runcie (1836-1911), who was not active in the United States before 1870.

7.   Frederick Louis Ritter, *Music in America* (New York: Charles Scribner's Sons, 1883).

8.   "Music in America. The Woman Composers," *Godey's Lady's Book* (Jan. 1896), 38.

9.   *Index of Marriages in the Massachusetts Centinel and Columbia Centinel 1784 to 1840.* Compiled by the American Antiquarian Society (Boston, 1961), as follows: Sullivan, J.W. of

Boston married Marianne [sic] M. Dix, daughter of late Colonel Timothy Dix of Boscawen, N.H. in Littleton, Mass. Dec. 17, 1825.

10. Boston: Oliver Ditson, 1844. In print in the *Complete Catalogue*, p. 15. Nicholas Tawa, *Sweet Songs for Gentle Americans* (Bowling Green, Ohio; Bowling Green University Popular Press, 1980), p. 198, includes it in his appendix of "The Most Popular Songs in the Extant Collections of Music." Also in Julius Mattfeld, *Variety Music Cavalcade* (New York: Prentice-Hall, 1962), p. 65. It is one of three compositions by her listed in Fr. Pazdirek, *Universal Handbook of Music Literature* (Vienna, 1910), p. 1196; the others are "O Boatman, Row Me Oer the Stream" and "The Evening Bugle." She is listed as M.D. Sullivan here.

11. In E.L. White and T. Bissell, *The Seminary Class Book* (Boston, 1852), p. 72; C. Jarvis, *The Young Folk's Glee Book* (New York: S.T. Gordon, 1854), p. 55; *Our Familiar Songs* (New York, 1881), p. 279; *The Good Old Songs* (Boston, 1887), p. 93; *Crown Jewels*, A Collection of Living Gems transcribed for the piano. (Boston: Oliver Ditson, 1861); *Heart Songs* (New York: 1909), p. 154.

12. *Complete Catalogue*, p. 288.

13. *The Autobiography of Mark Twain*. Ed. Charles Neider (New York: Harper & Row, 1959), p. 61.

14. Boston: Oliver Ditson, 1846. Also listed in N. Tawa, *Sweet Songs for Gentle Americans*, p. 199; mentioned as a popular song in Lota Spell, *Music in Texas* (Austin, 1936; reprint New York: AMS Editions, 1973), p. 50; *Franklin Square Song Collection*, Vol. 7; Also in *Heart Songs* (New York, 1909), p. 318; "Oh! Boatman..." in *Franklin Square Song Collection*, VI, 10; *Gems of Sacred Song* (Boston: Oliver Ditson, 1866), p. 38.

15. *Godey's Lady's Book*, XL (March 1850). Cited in Paul Fatout, "Threnodies of the Ladies' Books," *Musical Quarterly* XXXI (Oct. 1945), 473.

16. *Dwight's Journal of Music* (Aug. 6, 1853), 142, printed the program of the concert. All other songs are published by Oliver Ditson. "When the Bright Waves..." is a duet.

17. Marion Dix Sullivan, *Bible Songs* (Boston: Nathan Richardson, 1856). The collection contains 24 sacred songs. Sullivan wrote in the preface that "To all for whom Christ died, the Bible Songs are trustfully offered." This collection cited in Moore.

18. Marion Dix Sullivan, *Juniata Ballads* (Boston: Nathan Richardson, 1855), preface. This song is not included in the collection as the author says "it is not now my property."

19. *The Complete Catalogue*, p. 570.

20. Moore, *Appendix*, p. 22.

21. Works in the holdings of the New York Public Library, Long Island Historical Society, New York Historical Society, University of North Carolina, Boston Public Library, the Free Library of Philadelphia, and the University of Virginia. The Harding Collection at the Bodleian Library contains several songs. Jean Geil kindly supplied this information.

22. See the appendix for a list of these pieces.

23. Simeon Cheney, *The American Singing Book* (Boston: White, Smith & Co., 1879), p. 310. Incorrect attribution also in William Hauser, ed. *The Hesperian Harp* (Philadelphia: T.K. and P.G. Collins, 1848), p. 551. This confusion persists in modern reference works, including Mattfeld, *Variety Music Cavalcade*, p. 42.

24. Her biography of her brother, *Hamilton, the Young Artist* (Philadelphia: T.S. Arthur, 1851), p. 16, supplies information about the family.

25. Ibid., p. 26.

26. Her name changed to Garrett around 1855. Her book, *Precious Stones of the Heavenly Foundation* (New York: Sheldon & Co., 1859) includes a poem by the late John Walter B. Garrett "and is dedicated to the memory of one asleep in hope of a joyful reunion in the Great Day of Awakening."

27. Mrs. Hemans, *Godey's Lady's Book*, Vol. XXII (Jan. 1841) 38-39.

28. *New York Mirror*, Vol. XIX (Sept. 25, 1841) 311. Piece unlocated to date. No further information about her appears in this magazine.

29. Title page of the song, "The Family Meeting" (New York: Wm. Hull & Son, 1842).

30. Title page of "The Voice of Spring" (Philadelphia: G.E. Blake, ca. 1840). The Logierian system was named for John Bernard Logier, the author of a popular piano method. He was apparently one of her heroes for she wrote a short story about him, "The Musician's Adventure," *Columbian Lady's and Gentleman's Magazine* III (June 1845), 234.

31. Title page of "A Song for New England" (New York: Firth & Hall, 1844).

32. "Grand Vesper Chorus." Designed for the Church and Social Circle. The first verse written by Bishop Heber. The music composed, harmonized by Miss Augusta Browne, Organist of the Rev. Dr. Cox's Church (New York: Wm. Dubois, 1842-1844). According to the *Complete Catalogue*, p. 45, in print at William A. Pond Co.

33. Information from print of anthem made for the centennial service of the First Presbyterian Church, March 10, 1922.

34. Charles Odell, *Annals of the New York Stage* (New York: Columbia University Press, 1927-34) IV, 601—April 11, 1842, at the Lyceum; June 27, 1843, at Dr. Cox's church concerts.

35. Ibid., IV, 593. John Braham (1777-1856) was a great English tenor, especially famous for his song recitals and oratorio. He and his son Charles toured America between 1840 and 1842.

36. For information on ladies' magazines, see chap 6. Also, Charles Wunderlich, "A History and Bibliography of Early American Musical Periodicals, 1782-1852" (Ph.D. dissertation, University of Michigan, 1962), p. 207, says there was "a tremendous wave of interest in musical periodicals in the 1840s with 30 new publications."

37. Music: "New England Churches," I (March 1844), 143; "The Columbian Quickstep" II (Dec. 1844), 284; "Wake, Lady Mine" w. Mrs. Balmanno, IV (Sept. 1845), 142; "German Air with Variations," IV (Nov. 1845); "Pleasure! Naught but Pleasure w. M.B.H., VI (July 1846), 44; "The Persian Lover's Song," VII (June 1847), 281. Articles: "Musical Thoughts," III (Jan 1845), 68-9; "The Musician's Adventure," III (June 1845), 239; "The Music of America," IV (July 1845, 37-8; "The Divine Origin of Music," IV (July 1845), 37-8; "Music from Heaven," IV (Sept. 1845), 110; "The Enchanted Piper," VI (July 1846), 57; "Reveries of a Musician," VIII (July, Oct. 1847), 26, 185.

38. Wunderlich, "A History and Bibliography," pp. 557, 589.

39. *New York Musical Review* XV (Dec. 17, 1864), 307-8, 323, 403-4.

40. *New York Musical World and Times* (Feb. 20, 1855), 63.

41. Ibid. (May 1852), 76.

42. Ibid. (Jan. 1857), 38. See also, "The Music of Our Neighborhood Morning," *Sartain's Union Magazine of Literature and Art III* (Dec. 1848), 253-58; "The Music of Our Neighborhood," *Brainard's Western Musical World* Feb., 1867.

43. See "The Divine Origins of Music," *Columbian Ladies' and Gentleman's Magazine* (July 1845), 37.

44. Letter, A.B. Garrett to Henry Pierrepont, September 25, 1874, Manuscript Division, New York Public Library. (Pierrepont was a delegate to the Episcopal General Convention.)

45. Untitled review in *New York Musical World and Times* (Aug. 6, 1853), 211.

46. Article in *The Musician and Intelligencer of Cincinnati, 1848,* cited in G. Chase, *America's Music* (rev. 2nd ed., New York: McGraw Hill, 1955), p. 183.

47. New York: Wm. B. Dubois, M.D. (184-), located in the University of Virginia library.

48. Thomas Moore, *A Selection of Irish Melodies,* with Symphonies and Accompaniment, by Sir John Stevenson (London: 1807-1811).

49. "The Warlike Dead in Mexico" (New York: C. Holt, Jr., 1848), located at the New York Public Library; "The Indian Chief," located at Brown University. For Braham's song, see Michael Turner, *The Parlour Song Book* (New York: The Viking Press, 1972), pp. 296-305. "The Death of Nelson" (1811) is listed in Julius Mattfeld, *Variety Music Cavalcade,* p. 19, as one of the most popular songs for that year.

50. Augusta Browne, "A Woman on Women," *Knickerbocker Magazine* (Jan. 1863), 10-20.

51. Robert Riegel, *American Women* (Cranbury, New Jersey: Associated University Presses, 1970), pp. 215f.

52. Browne "A Woman on Women," p. 11.

53. Ibid., p. 19.

54. Ibid., p. 17.

55. Ibid., p. 18.

56. Ibid., p. 20.

57. A number of piano works and songs are located at the New York Historical Society.

58. *Grove's Dictionary of Music and Musicians,* 5th ed., ed. Eric Blom. (New York: St. Martin's Press, 1954), IV, 310. *s.v.* "(Edward Hodges)."

59. Faustina Hodges, *Edward Hodges* (New York, 1896, reprinted New York: AMS Editions, 1970).

60. Ibid., pp. 10, 59, 69, and epilogue.

61. Ibid., p. 237.

62. Ibid., p. 240.

63. Ibid.

64. *Grove's Dictionary of Music and Musicians,* 3rd ed. (ed. H.C. Colles, New York: Macmillan Co., 1927-33), p. 647; and *Baker's Dictionary of Music* (New York: G. Schirmer, 1919), p. 405. *Baker's* and the *American Supplement to Grove's* (ed. W.S. Pratt, New York, 1935), p. 241, both give an incorrect death date of 1896 instead of 1895.

65. Hodges, *Edward Hodges,* n.p., postscript. According to an obituary notice in *The Philadelphia Public Ledger,* February 6, 1895, Hodges died on February 4, 1895.

66. "Music in America—The Woman Composers," *Godey's Lady's Book* CXXXII (Jan. 1896), 30-40.

67. For a discussion of the influence of German song style in the United States in the 1850s and '60s, see Charles Hamm, *Yesterdays. Popular Song in America* (New York: W.W. Norton & Co., 1979), pp. 192 ff. On the use of waltz rhythms in popular song, see p. 198.

68. It was published in *Songs of All Nations* (Milwaukee: H.N. Hempsted, n.d.); *Home Delights* (New York, n.d.); *Parlor Gems* (Macon, Ga.: John C, Schreiner & Son, n.d.); and *Music of the Day. Blackmar and Company's Selection of 100 Beautiful Songs and Pieces* (New Orleans, 1863-1864). According to the *Complete Catalogue,* p. 30, it was listed in the catalogues of eleven publishers.

69. Otto Ebel, *Women Composers,* p. 69, reported that "it has sold over 100,000 copies." It was also arranged for four-part chorus in George Root, *The Diapason* (New York: Mason Bros., 1860), p. 82.

70. Mrs. R.C. Waterson, *Adelaide Phillipps* (Boston: A. Williams & Co., 1883), p. 99. This review appeared in a newspaper, the *Indiana Sentinel,* but no date is given for the concert.

71. For a reproduction of this painting, see Karen Peterson and J.J. Wilson, *Women Artists, Recognition and Reappraisal from the Early Middle Ages to the Twentieth Century,* (New York: Harper & Row, 1976), p. 60. Stephen Foster also wrote a song on the *vanitas* theme: "Ah, May the Red Rose Live Always." Other songs by Hodges along these lines include "Farewell to North Maven" (1864), "Three Roses" (1874), "Yearnings" (1893), and "As the Hours Pass On" (1882).

72. *A Biographical Sketch of Jane Sloman, the Celebrated Pianist* (Boston: Dutton and Wentworth, 1841), pp. 7, 18.

73. Ibid., p. 18.

74. The earliest known work under the name Sloman Torry is "La Farfalletta," (New York: Wm. Hall & Son, 1862). The song "Titania" was published in 1902.

75. Jane Sloman, ed., *The Melodist* (New York: Wm. Hall & Son, 1850). See Fig. 1.

76. Moore, *Dictionary,* p. 140.

77. Cheney, *The American Singing Book,* p. 103.

78. *Complete Catalogue,* pp. 39, 79, 476.

79. Ebel, *Women Composers,* p. 138. Ebel described her as an "American composer of a number of piano pieces and songs," and he singles out these songs. He also attributes "Barbara Frietchie" to her, but that work was composed by Elizabeth Sloman (w. John Greenleaf Whittier. New York: Wm. A. Pond & Co., 1874). Copy located in DLC.

80. Foster, *The Social Orchestra,* p. 11; *Complete Catalogue,* p. 332; Mark Twain, *Life on the Mississippi* (New York, 1883), p. 403.

81. *Complete Catalogue,* p. 111.

82. Mattfeld, *Variety Music Cavalcade,* p. 72. According to Mattfeld, Joseph Turner made a second arrangement in which no composer is given and claims, "the Turner arrangement is found in most collections." However, Harry Dichter and Elliott Shapiro, *Early American Sheet Music* (New York: R.R. Bowker Co., 1941), p. 150, cite the Sloman-Barker arrangement in his "Famous Songs" category. There is also the possibility that Charles Sloman, the British music-hall singer, wrote the tune, but it is unlike the style of his narrative ballads or his patter comic songs.

83. *A Biographical Sketch of Jane Sloman, the Celebrated Pianist.*

84. Ibid., p. 11.

85. Ibid., p. 17, "... the rudiments of composition and a correct knowledge of 'thorough bass' was acquired by reading and studying without the assistance of any second person."

86. Ibid., p. 10.

87. Ibid., p. 19.

88. Cited in Odell, *Annals of the New York Stage,* IV, 521.

89. Odell, *Annals of the New York Stage,* IV, pp. 522-23, and IV, p. 533.

90. Ibid., V, p. 593.

91. Her works include "Forget Thee?" (Boston: W.H. Oakes, 1843); "La Farfalletta"; "Queen of the Night" [Del Ciel Regina] (Boston: White & Smith, 1873); "So Far Away" (New York: Wm. Hall, 1868).

92. "The Maiden's Farewell" (Boston: W.H. Oates, 1843); "Take Back the Ring" (New York: W.H. Hall, 1860); "I'll Make Him Speak Out" (New York: W.H. Hall, 1852).

93. See the liner notes by Richard Jackson for "Angel's Visits," *Recorded Anthology of American Music* (New York: New World Records, 1977), NW. He describes her as "a prolific composer who merits a thorough investigation of her life and work."

94. Her marriage to John Duer in 1868 is listed in Marriage Register No. HD 62/1868, Marriage License Bureau, Borough of Brooklyn, Office of the City Clerk, New York City. Her birthdate of June 5, 1836, is in *Vital Records of Leicester, Mass. to the End of the Year 1849* (Worcester, Mass., 1903), p. 62. Her deathdate of May 4, 1918, is documented through the Certificate of Death No. 11024, Bureau of Records, Dept. of Health, New York City.

95. "Beautiful Hands" (Chicago: Root & Cady, 1868), published as Mrs. E.A. Parkhurst Duer. No copy has been located, but the work is listed in Dena Epstein, *Music Publishing in Chicago* (Detroit: Information Coordinators, Inc., 1969), p. 113. Epstein states that the firm usually published music of local composers, but occasionally handled works outside of the midwest, if the composer's reputation was national.

96. A notice from the *Brooklyn Eagle* reprinted on the back page of "Our Dear New England Boys" (New York: Horace Waters, 1864) reads: "New Music by Mrs. Parkhurst: We cheerfully call attention to Mrs. Parkhurst's advertisement of new music, which appears in our columns to-day. There are some ten or fifteen compositions in all, many of which are exceedingly meritorious, while all are above the average of such works. Mrs. Parkhurst is one of our most prolific native composers, many of her songs being familiar as household words. The fair author has a happy faculty of interblending words and melody, which results in most pleasing and memorable harmony."

97. The song is reprinted in Richard Crawford, ed., *Civil War Songs* (New York: Dover Press, 1977), p. 137.

98. "There Are Voices, Spirit Voices" w. Fanny Crosby. Mrs. M.A. Kidder wrote the texts for many of Parkhurst's gospel and secular songs; among them "Dey Said We Wouldn't Fight," "Don't Marry a Man If He Drinks" (New York: C.M. Tremaine, 1866), and "Love on the Brain" (New York: Wm. Demorest, 1865).

99. "Angel Mary" (New York: Horace Waters, 1863).

100. For a list of these pieces, see the appendix. Most of her keyboard works are located in the American Antiquarian Society. The largest selection of vocal works is in the New York Public Library.

101. "Sweet Evelina" (New York: H. Waters, 1863). Harwell, *Confederate Music,* p. 6, cites this as one of the most popular songs among Confederate soldiers. It is also listed in Harry Dichter and Elliott Shapiro, *Early American Sheet Music,* p. 152, in the group of "Famous Songs."

102. Written with "Stella" [Nellie Bradley] (Washington, D.C.: John F. Ellis, 1866). That edition was also carried by seven other publishers. Anthologized in *Women in Sacred Song* (Boston, 1885), p. 600, as "the first original temperance song published in the city of Washington," with the date given as 1858, it was also included in William Bradbury and N.J. Stearns, eds., *Temperance Chimes,* rev.ed. (New York: National Temperance Society and Publication House, 1887), p. 46; and in the following twentieth-century anthologies: Philip Jordan and Lillian Kessler eds., *Songs of Yesterday* (New York: Doubleday, 1941), p. 171, and Michael Turner, ed., *The Parlour Song Book,* p. 252. It has been recorded on *The Hand that Holds the Bread* (New York: New World Records, 1977), NW 267.

103. Odell, *Annals,* 8: 97, lists concerts by Effie in New York at Dodworth's Hall on December 22, 1865, at the Athenaeum in Brooklyn on January 18, 1866, in Williamsburgh on November 22, 1865, and on Staten Island on November 19, 1866.

104. Other songs include "Don't Marry a Man If He Drinks" cited in n. 98; "Girls, Wait for a Temperance Man," w. Mrs. M.A. Kidder (New York: C.W. Harris, 1867), described as sung by "little Effie Parkhurst at the great temperance meetings in New York"; and "I'll Marry No Man If He Drinks" (New York: C.M. Tremaine, 1866).

105. *The Etude Magazine* (Sept. 1916), 625. Also quoted in John Tasker Howard, *America's Troubadour,* p. 328.

106. Samuel J. Rogal, "The Gospel Hymns of Stephen Collins Foster," *The Hymn* 21/1 (Jan. 1970), 8.

107. Rogal lists these collections: *The Golden Harp* (1863); *The Athenaeum Collection* (1863); and *The Anniversary and Sunday School Music Book* (1859), all of which contained hymns by Foster.

108. Hymns by Parkhurst appear in *The Anthenaeum* and *The Golden Harp,* as well as *Zion's Refreshing Showers* (New York, 1867).

109. Parkhurst arranged Foster's "The Pure! The Bright! The Beautiful!" which had appeared as a hymn in *The Athenaeum* as sheet music for Waters in 1864. She also fitted Foster's "Merry Little Birds" with new words for the same collection. In *Zion's Refreshing Showers,* Foster's "Under the Willow She's Sleeping" became the chorus section "Save, Jesus Save" in the hymn that begins "There is a Fountain Filled with Blood."

110. Odell, Annals, VII, 556, lists her as "Mrs. Duer (late Mrs. Parkhurst), performing at a concert in Staten Island with her daughter on Sept. 30, 1868." The work is "Beautiful Hands" see n. 95, above.

Chapter 8

1. Sections of this chapter first appeared in my article "Women as Professional Musicians in the United States, 1870-1900," *Yearbook for Inter-American Research* IX (1973), 95-133.

2. George Cary Eggleston, "The Education of Women," *Harper's Magazine* LVIII (July 1883), 294.

3. Dio Lewis, *Our Girls* (New York: *Harper and Bros,* 1871), p. 199.

4. Joseph Mussulman, *Music in the Cultured Generation* (Evanston: Northwestern University Press, 1971), p. 171. Mussulman quoted from "Music and Drawing at Home," *Century Magazine,* July 1878, p. 437:

    the acquisition of the proper rank in gentility involves the necessity of "piano-lessons" for the girls. The instrument is bought after much saving and stinting in other matters. Nelly is brought, through sore tribulations, to hammer out a dozen dashing marches or waltzes, and that is the end of it. After she marries, she neither plays for her own pleasure nor for her husband's, and she is not competent to teach her own daughter. But the piano is there, a big assertant token of social rank.

5. James Huneker, *Overtones* (New York: Charles Scribner's Sons, 1904), p. 285.

6. Ibid., p. 292.

7. Cecilia Beaux, *Background with Figures* (1930), p. 24, quoted in Judith E. Stein, "Profile of Cecilia Beaux," *Feminist Art Journal* (Winter 1975/6), 26. Beaux received her early music and art education from her Aunt Eliza who was a "finished musician" and had studied with a pupil of Mendelssohn.

8. Virginia Penny, *The Employments of Women: A Cyclopedia of Woman's Work* (Boston: Walker, Wise & Co., 1863), pp. 75-76, is one of the earliest sources to cite music as an occupation: "Music teacher is a suitable profession and one in which many women are engaged."

9. Lewis, *Our Girls,* p. 131.

10. Mary L. Rayne, *What Can a Woman Do; or Her Position in the Business and Literary World* (Peterborough, New York, 1893), cited in Page Smith, *Daughters of the Promised Land* (Boston: Little, Brown and Co., 1970), p. 278.

11. Louis Lombard, *Observations of a Musician* (Utica, New York, 1893). The translations appeared by 1904.

12. Ibid., p. 73.

13. Also reprinted as a separate pamphlet. Fanny Ritter, *Woman as a Musician* (New York: Edward Schuberth, 1876).

14. "Historical Account of the Association for the Advancement of Women, 1873-1893," 21st Women's Congress (World Colombian Exposition, Chicago, 1893).

15. Ritter, *Woman As a Musician* p. 8.

16. Ibid. They were Vittoria Archilei, Faustina Bordoni, Madame Mara, and Mrs. Billington.

17. Ibid., p. 11. Others were Leopoldine Blahetka, Josephine Lang, Louise Farrenc, Fanny Hensel, Louisa Puget, Clara Schumann, Madame Dolby, and Virginia Gabriel.

18. Ibid., p. 12.

19. See n. 2, above.

20. Ritter, *Woman as a Musician,* p. 17.

21. John Ruskin, "Of Queens Gardens," *Works* XVIII (London, 1905), 122.

22. Charles and Mary Beard, *The Rise of American Civilization* (New York: The Macmillan Co., 1930), II, p. 457.

23. Eva Munson Smith, compiler and editor, *Women in Sacred Song.* A Library of Hymns, Religious Poems and Sacred Music by Women (Boston: D. Lothrop, 1885).

24. Ibid., p. vii.

25. Ibid., p. viii.

26. Ibid.

27. Ibid., pp. 306, 494.

28. Ibid., p. viii.

29. Ibid., p. 494.

30. "Howard" also appears in *The American Vocalist,* ed. Rev. D.H. Mansfield (Boston: J. Reynolds & Co., 1849), p. 89.

31. George Upton, *Women in Music* (Boston: J.R. Osgood & Co., 1880, second ed. Chicago: A.C. McClury & Co., 1887 and 1899).

32. Ibid., p. 23.

33. Edith Brower, "Is the Musical Idea Masculine?" *Atlantic Monthly* (March 1894), 332-39. Other critics of a similar persuasion included Havelock Ellis and Lawrence Gilman. See Gilman's chapter "Women and Modern Music," *Phases of Modern Music* (New York: Harper, 1904), pp. 93-101, which also cites Ellis.

34. *The Women's Journal* (Aug. 29, 1891).

35. Amy Fay, "Women and Music," *Music* (Oct. 1900), 505-7.

36. Florence Sutro, "Women in Music and Law," (New York, 1875), p. 10. Paper first read for the Clef Club in 1893. Sutro later became the first president of the National Federation of Music Clubs.

37. For example, John Towers, *Women in Music* (Winchester, Va., 1987); Otto Ebel, *Women Composers. A Biographical Handbook of Women's Work in Music* (Brooklyn, N.Y. 1902); Adolph Willharitz, *Some Facts About Women in Music* (Los Angeles, 1902).

38. "Women Composers of All Lands," *The Musical Courier* (Jan. 1903), 19.

39. R. Schumann, *On Music and Musicians.* Trans. P. Rosenfeld (New York: McGraw-Hill, 1964), p. 121.

40. T.L. Krebs, "Women as Musicians," *Swanee Review* II (1893), 77.

41. Fanny Bloomfield-Zeisler, "Women in Music," *American Art Journal* (Oct. 17, 1891).

42. Rupert Hughes, *Contemporary American Composers,* (New York, 1900), pp. 434f.

43. Rupert Hughes, "Women Composers," *The Century Magazine* (Mar. 1898), 768-79. This estimate was from an unnamed "prominent publisher."

44. Ebel, *Women Composers,* preface.

45. *The Etude* began its series in 1901.

46. *The Musician* V (Mar. 6, 1900).

47. *Proceedings of the Nineteenth Annual Meeting of the Music Teachers National Association,* June 24-28, 1897, p. 171-2.

48. It went from 6% (5 out of 82) in 1892 to 13% (19 out of 130) in 1898. This statistic was computed from membership lists in the scrapbook on the Manuscript Society in the New York Public Library.

49.   The program on Dec. 18, 1895, was entirely by "the women composers who were members of the society and it was interpreted by women." Sumner Salter, "Early Encouragements to American Composers," *The Musical Quarterly* XVIII/1 (Jan. 1932), 76-105.

50.   Arthur Elson, *Women's Work in Music* (Boston: L.C. Page, 1903). They were Helen Andrus, Amy Beach, Laura Collins, Laura Danziger, Marie von Hammer, Helen Hood, Helen Hopekirk, Clara Korn, Margaret Lang, Grace Marckwald, Margueritte Melville, L.E. Orth, Clara Rogers, Emma Steiner, Alicia Van Buren, Margaret Williams, and Mary Knight Wood.

51.   Russel Nye, *The Unembarrassed Muse* (New York: The Dial Press, 1970), p. 316. For a reassessment and full study of Bond, see Phyllis Ruth Bruce, "From Rags to Roses. The Life and Times of Carrie Jacobs Bond, an American Composer," (master's thesis, Wesleyan University, 1980).

52.   Floyd C. Shoemaker, *Missouri, Day by Day* (St. Joseph, Mo.: State Historical Society of Missouri, 1942), p. 43. The sketch of Runcie states that she was a pioneer club woman and organized the Minerva Club in New Harmony, Indiana.

53.   W.S.B. Matthews, *A Hundred Years of Music in America* (Chicago: G.F. Howe, 1889). *Dictionary of American Biography*, XVI, pp. 224-25. For additional information on Runcie see Stella Reid Crothers, "Constance Faunt le Roy Runcie," *Musical America* (Aug. 21, 1909) 15; and Ernst C. Krohn, *Missouri Music* (St. Louis, 1924, reprinted Da Capo Press, 1971). Runcie also wrote an autobiography, *Divinely Led* (New York, 1895). Barton Cantrell, a scholar with a special interest in Runcie, believes that the symphony predates that of Amy Beach, and may have been the first symphony composed by an American woman. He has not located the manuscript to date.

54.   Clara K. Rogers, *Memories of a Musical Career* and its sequel, *The Story of Two Lives* (Norwood, Mass.: The Plimpton Press, 1932). Rogers was at the Leipzig Conservatory in 1857 but did not study composition, for "there was no composition class for my sex, no woman composer having yet appeared on the musical horizon, with the exception of Fanny Hensel...and Clara Schumann" (Vol. I, p. 108). She wrote a string quartet in Leipzig in 1859 (Vol. I, p. 159).

55.   Rogers, *The Story of Two Lives*, pp. 80-81.

56.   Ibid., p. 187.

57.   For information see Burnet Tuthill, "Mrs. H.H.A. Beach," *Musical Quarterly* XXVI/3 (1940), 297-310, and E. Lindsay Merrill, "Mrs. H.H.A. Beach: Her Life and Work" (Ph.D. dissertation, University of Rochester, 1963). A new study of Beach would be welcome. In the last few years a number of recordings of her work have been issued, among them the Piano Quartet in F-sharp Minor, op. 67, the Trio for Violin, Cello, and Piano, op. 150, the Piano Concerto in C Minor, and the Sonata for Violin and Piano in A Minor.

58.   Philip Hale, *Musical and Drama Criticism 1892-1900,* Microfilm collection, New York Public Library. Also, "Beach's Gaelic Symphony," *Boston Tribune* (Nov. 1, 1896), and "Women as Symphony Makers," Nov. 4, 1896.

59.   Anon review, *Musical Courier* (Feb. 23, 1898).

60.   Emilie Bauer, "Women as Composers in the Future," *Etude Magazine* (Sept. 1901), 321.

Bibliography

Books and Articles

Ackley, Louisa Maria. "My Record, Geneva Female Seminary, 1831-32." New York Public Library, Manuscript Division.

Aikin, John. *Letters from a Father to His Son.* Philadelphia, 1794.

Austin, William W. *"Susanna," "Jeanie," and "The Old Folks at Home."* New York: Macmillan, 1975.

Bennett, John. *Letters to a Young Lady.* Worcester, Mass., 1798.

A Biographical Sketch of Jane Sloman, the Celebrated Pianist. Boston: Dutton and Wentworth, 1841.

Blackwell, Alice Stone. "Women in Literature and Art," *The Woman's Journal,* August 29, 1891.

Block, Adrienne Fried, and Carol Neuls-Bates, eds. *Women in American Music. A Bibliography of Music and Literature.* Westport: Greenwood Press, 1979.

Bode, Carl. *The Anatomy of American Popular Culture 1840-1861.* Berkeley and Los Angeles: University of California Press, 1959.

Bowne, Eliza Southgate. *A Girl's Life Eighty Years Ago.* Selections from the Letters of E.S.B. New York: Charles Scribner's Songs, 1887.

Branch, E. Douglas. *The Sentimental Years 1836-1860.* New York: D. Appleton-Century Co., 1934.

Brower, Edith. "Is the Musical Idea Masculine," *Atlantic Monthly* (March 1894), 332-39.

Browne, Augusta. *Hamilton, the Young Artist.* Philadelphia: T.S. Arthur, 1851.

———. "Musical Thoughts," *Columbian Lady's and Gentleman's Magazine* (Jan. 1845), 68.

Browne Garrett, Augusta. *Precious Stones of the Heavenly Foundation.* New York: Sheldon & Co., 1859.

———. "Reveries of a Musician, Part II," *Columbian Lady's and Gentleman's Magazine* (Oct. 1847), 185.

———. [Review of Henry Herz] *New York Musical World and Times* (Aug. 6, 1853), 211.

———. "A Woman on Women; With Reflections on the Other Sex," *Knickerbocker Magazine* (Jan. 1863), 10-20.

Brown, Herbert Ross. *The Sentimental Novel in America, 1789-1860.* Duke U. Press, 1940; 2nd ed. reprinted Freeport, New York: Books for Libraries Press, 1970.

Burton, John. *Lectures on Female Education.* New York, 1794.

Burwell, Letitia. *A Girl's Life in Virginia Before the War.* New York, 1895.

Butler, Charles. *The American Lady.* Philadelphia, 1836.

Carpenter, Hoyle. "Salon Music in the Mid-Nineteenth Century," *Civil War History* (Sept. 1958), 291-99.

Carroll, Berenice, A., ed. *Liberating Women's History.* Urbana: University of Illinois Press, 1976.

[Catalogues] for Cherry Valley Female Seminary and Troy Seminary, New York Public Library.

Chapone, Hester M. *Letters on the Improvement of the Mind, Addressed to a Young Lady.* Boston, 1783.

Chase, Gilbert. *America's Music,* rev. 2nd ed. New York: McGraw-Hill, 1966.

Claghorn, Charles. *Biographical Dictionary of American Music.* West Nyack, N.Y.: Parker Pub. Co., 1973.

The Columbian Lady's and Gentleman's Magazine. New York: Israel Post, 1844-49.

Complete Catalogue of Sheet Music and Musical Works, 1870. U.S. Board of Music Trade, 1st ed., 1871; reprinted New York: Da Capo Press, 1973.

Coxe, Margaret. *The Young Lady's Companion.* Columbus, Ohio, 1846.

Crews, Emma K. "A History of Music in Knoxville, Tennessee, 1791-1910." Ed.D. dissertation, Florida State University, 1961.

Davison, Sister Mary Veronica. "American Music Periodicals, 1853-1899." Ph.D. dissertation, University of Minnesota, 1973.

DePauw, Linda Grant, and Conover Hunt. *Remember the Ladies: Women in America 1750-1815.* New York: The Viking Press, 1976.

Dexter, Elizabeth Anthony. *Career Women of America, 1776-1840.* Francetown, N.H.: Marshall Jones Co., 1950.

Dichter, Harry, and Elliott Shapiro. *Early American Sheet Music, Its Lure and Its Lore. 1768-1889.* New York: R.R. Bowker Co., 1941.

Douglas, Ann. *The Feminization of American Culture.* New York: Alfred A. Knopf, 1977.

Dwight, John S. "A Monster Concert by Young Ladies," *Dwight's Journal of Music* (Aug. 6, 1853), 142.

_____. "Musical Amateurs of the Period," *Dwight's Journal of Music* (Nov. 20, 1869), 138.

_____. "Musical Education Down South," *Dwight's Journal of Music* (July 10, 1852), 111.

Dwight, Timothy. *Travels in New England and New York,* ed. by Barbara Solomon. Cambridge, Mass.: Harvard University Press, 1969.

Ebel, Otto. *Women Composers. A Biographical Handbook of Woman's Work in Music.* Brooklyn, N.Y.: F.H. Chandler, 1902.

Eggleston, George Carey. "The Education of Women," *Harper's Magazine* LVIII (July 1883), 292-96.

Elson, Arthur. *Woman's Work in Music.* Boston: L.C. Page & Co., 1903.

Epstein, Cynthia. *Woman's Place.* Options and Limits in Professional Careers. Berkeley: University of California Press, 1971.

Epstein, Dena. *Music Publishing in Chicago Before 1871: The Firm of Root & Cady, 1858-1871.* Detroit: Information Coordinators, Inc., 1969.

The Etude XIX/9 (Sept. 1901), "Woman's Number."

Fatout, Paul. "Threnodies of the Ladies' Books," *Musical Quarterly* XXXI/4 (Oct. 1945), 464-78.

Fay, Amy. "Women and Music," *Music* (Oct. 1900), 505-7.

"Female Education," *Boston Musical Gazette* (Jan. 9, 1839), 149.

Flagg, Wilson. "Parlor Singing," *Atlantic Monthly* XXIV (Oct. 1869), 410-20.

Forrester, Fanny. "Dora' A Slight Etching," *New York Weekly Mirror* (Nov. 23, 1844), 97.

Foster, Hannah. *The Boarding School;* or Lessons of a Preceptress to her Pupils. Boston, 1798.

Garnett, James M. *Seven Lectures on Female Education.* Richmond, Va., 1824.

Garnsey, Caroline John. "Ladies' Magazines to 1850: The Beginnings of an Industry," *Bulletin of the New York Public Library* LVIII (1954), 74-88.

Gilman, Caroline Howard. *Recollections of a Southern Matron.* New York: G.P. Putnam & Co., 1852.

Gerson, Robert. *Music in Philadelphia.* Philadelphia: Theodore Presser, 1940.

Gerstenberger, Donna, and Carolyn Allen. "Women Studies/American Studies, 1970-1975," *American Quarterly* XXIX/3 (1977), 263-79.

Gregory, John. *A Father's Legacy to His Daughter.* London, 1774.

Griffiths, Elizabeth. *Letters Addressed to Young Married Women.* Philadelphia, 1796.

Grobe, Charles, ed. *The Musical Almanac for 1861,* Op. 1300. Philadelphia: Lee & Walker, 1861.

Hale, Philip. *Musical and Drama Criticism, 1892-1900.* Microfilm collection, Music Division, New York Public Library.

Hale, Sarah J. *Happy Homes and Good Society All the Year Round.* Boston: J.E. Tilton and Co., 1868; reprinted New York: AMS Press, 1972.

_____. *Woman's Record;* or, Sketches of All Distinguished Women. New York: Harper & Brothers, 1852.

Hamilton, Gail [Mary Abigail Dodge]. *Gala-Days.* Boston: Ticknor and Fields, 1863.

Hamm, Charles, *Yesterdays.* Popular Song in America. New York: W.W. Norton & Co., 1979.

Hanaford, Phebe A. *Daughters of America;* or Women of the Century. Augusta, Me.: True and Co., 1882.

Harris, Ann Sutherland, and Linda Nochlin. *Women Artists: 1550-1950.* New York: Alfred A. Knopf, 1977.

Hart, James D. *The Popular Book.* A History of America's Literary Taste. London: Oxford University Press, 1950; 2nd ed., 1961.

Harwell, Richard B. *Confederate Music.* Chapel Hill: The University of North Carolina Press, 1950.

Herz, Henri. *My Travels in America* (Mes voyages en Amerique. Paris, 1866), trans. H.B. Hill. Madison, Wisc.: State Historical Society, 1963.

"A Hint to Musical Ladies," *Boston Musical Visitor* (July 16, 1844), 113.

Hitchcock, H. Wiley. *Music in the United States. A Historical Introduction,* 2nd ed. Englewood Cliffs, N.J.: Prentice-Hall, Inc., 1974.

Hixon, Don L., and Don Hennessee. *Women in Music. A Biobibliography.* Metuchen, N.J.: The Scarecrow Press, Inc., 1975.

Hodges, Faustina. *Edward Hodges.* New York, 1896; reprinted New York: AMS Editions, 1970.

"Home Music," *New York Musical World* (Jan. 3, 10, 17, 1857), 2-3, 17-18, 33-4.

"Home Music," *Western Musical World* (May 1866), 68.

Howe, Daniel Walker, ed. *Victorian America.* Philadelphia: University of Pennsylvania, 1976.

Hughes, Rupert. "Music in America—The Woman Composers," *Godey's Lady's Book* (Jan. 1896), 30-40.

Huneker, James. *Overtones.* New York: Charles Scribner's Sons, 1904.

Index of Early American Periodicals, Bobst Library, unpublished manuscript, microfilm, New York University [1940].

Johnson, H. Earle. *Musical Interludes in Boston, 1795-1830.* New York: Columbia University Press, 1943.

Johnson, Frances Hall. *Music Vale Seminary, 1835-1876.* Committee on Historical Publications, Yale University Press, 1934.

Jones, M.G. *Hannah More.* Cambridge, England: University of Cambridge Press, 1952.

Jordan, Philip D., and Lillian Kessler. *Songs of Yesterday.* A Song Anthology of American Life. New York: Doubleday, 1941.

Julian, John. *A Dictionary of Hymnology,* 2nd ed., 1907; Dover Reprint, 1957.

Kaufman, Charles. "Music in New Jersey, 1655-1860." Teaneck, N.J.: Fairleigh Dickinson University Press, 1980.

Keefer, Lubov. *Baltimore's Music.* The Haven of the American Composer. Baltimore: J.H. Furst Co., 1962.

Kingsley, George, ed. *The Social Choir.* Boston: Crocker & Brewster, 1838.

Krohn, Ernst C. *Missouri Music.* St. Louis, 1924; reprinted New York: Da Capo Press, 1971.

_____. *Music Publishing in the Middle Western States Before the Civil War.* Detroit: Information Coordinators, Inc., 1972.

Lang, Paul Henry, ed. *One Hundred Years of Music in America.* New York: G. Schirmer Inc., 1961.

Lesley, Susan L. *Recollections of My Mother*. Boston, 1886.

Lewis, Dio. *Our Girls*. New York: Harper and Bros., 1871.

Loesser, Arthur. *Men, Women and Pianos*. New York: Simon and Schuster, 1954.

Mackowitz, Phyllis Ruth. "A Preliminary Investigation of American Women Song Composers of the Nineteenth and Early Twentieth Centuries," M.A. thesis, Wesleyan University, April, 1977.

Mahan, Katherine Hines. *Showboats to Soft Shoes. A Century of Musical Development in Columbus, Georgia, from 1828 to 1928*. Columbus, Georgia, 1968.

Mangler, Joyce E. *Rhode Island Music and Musicians 1733-1850*. Detroit Studies in Music Bibliography, No. 7. Detroit: Information Service Inc., 1965.

Mates, Julian. *The American Musical Stage Before 1800*. New Brunswick, N.J.: Rutgers University Press, 1962.

Mather, Cotton. *Ornaments for the Daughters of Zion,* or The Character and Happiness of a Virtuous Maiden. Cambridge, 1692.

Mattfeld, Victor. *Variety Music Cavalcade 1620-1950*. New York: Prentice-Hall, 1952.

"Mems for Musical Misses," *Harper's New Monthly Magazine* (Sept. 1851), 488-89.

Moore, John W. *Appendix to Encyclopedia of Music*. Boston: Oliver Ditson & Co., 1875.

───. *A Dictionary of Musical Information*. Boston: Oliver Ditson & Co., 1876.

Moore, Thomas. *A Selection of Irish Melodies,* with Symphonies and Accompaniments by Sir John Stevenson. London, [1807-11].

Morgan, Helen, ed. *A Season in New York 1801. Letters of Harriet and Maria Trumbull*. Pittsburgh: University of Pittsburgh Press, 1969.

More, Hannah. *Strictures on the Modern System of Female Education*. Philadelphia: Thomas Dobson, 1800.

Mott, Frank Luther. *A History of American Magazines,* Vol. I, 1741-1850; Vol. II, 1850-1865. Cambridge, Mass.: Harvard University Press, 1957.

"Musical Culture," *Western Musical World* (June 1866), 85.

"Musical Education for Young Ladies," *New York Musical World and Times* (Feb 19, 1853), 118.

"Musical Wives," *Godey's Lady's Book* (March 1835), 119-20.

Mussulman, Joseph. *Music in the Cultured Generation*. Evanston: Northwestern University Press, 1971.

National Index of American Imprints Through 1800—The Short-Title Evans, ed. Clifford K. Shipton and James E. Mooney, 2 vls. Barre, Mass.: American Antiquarian Society and Barre Publishers, 1969.

Notable American Women 1607-1950. A Biographical Dictionary, eds. Edward T. James and Janet Wilson James. Cambridge: Harvard University Press, 1971.

Nye, Russel. *Society and Culture in America, 1830-1860*. New York: Harper & Row, 1974.

Odell, George. *Annals of the New York Stage*. New York: Columbia University Press, 1927-31.

Parkhurst-Duer, Mrs. E.A. "Personal Recollections of the Last Days of Stephen Foster," *The Etude Magazine* (Sept. 1816), 625.

Pattee, Fred L. *The First Century of American Literature, 1770-1870*. New York: D. Appleton-Century Co., 1935.

Pearsall, Ronald. *Victorian Popular Music*. Detroit: Gale Research Co., 1973.

Penny, Virginia. *The Employments of Women*. A Cyclopedia of Woman's Work. Boston: Walker, Wise & Co., 1863.

Perkins, Jane Grey. *The Life of the Honourable Mrs. Norton*. New York: Henry Holt & Co., 1909.

Phelps, Almira. *The Female Student; or Lectures to Young Ladies on Female Education*. New York, 1836.

The Polite Lady; or a Course of Female Education. Philadelphia, 1798.

Pond, Jean Sarah. *Bradford. A New England School*. Sesquicentennial edition. Revised and supplemented by Dale Mitchell. Bradford, Mass., 1954.

Rayne, Mary L. *What Can a Woman Do*. Peterborough, New York, 1893.

Reichel, William C. *A History of the Rise, Progress, and Present Condition of the Moravian Seminary for Young Ladies at Bethlehem, Pa.* Philadelphia: J.B. Lippincott & Co., 1870.

Riegel, Robert. *American Women. A Story of Social Change.* Cranbury, N.J.: Fairleigh Dickinson University Press, 1970.

Ritter, Fanny. *Woman As a Musician.* New York: Edward Schuberth, 1876.

Rogers, Clara K. *Memories of a Musical Career.* Norwood, Mass.: The Plimpton Press, 1932.

———. *The Story of Two Lives.* Norwood, Mass.: The Plimpton Press, 1932.

Rossiter, Frank. *Charles Ives and His America.* New York: Liverwright, 1975.

Rowson, Susannah. *Mentoria.* Philadelphia, 1794.

———. *Miscellaneous Poems.* Boston, 1804.

Rush, Benjamin. *Thoughts Upon Female Education.* Philadelphia, 1787.

Ryan, Mary P. *Womanhood In America.* New York: Franklin Watts, Inc., 1975.

Schlesinger, Arthur M. *Learning How to Behave.* A Historical Study of American Etiquette Books. New York: The Macmillan Co., 1947.

Scholes, Percy. *The Puritans and Music in England and New England.* London: Oxford University Press, 1934.

"A School Incident," *New York Mirror,* April 13, 1839.

Scott, Anne Firor. "Women in American Life," in *The Reinter Pretation of American History and Culture.* eds., Wm. Cartwright and Richard Watson (Washington, D.C.: National Council for the Social Studies, 1973)

Shipton, Clifford K., ed. *Early American Imprints, 1639-1800.* American Antiquarian Society microprint editions. New York: Readex Co., 195-.

Sigourney, Lydia. *Letters to Young Ladies.* New York: Harper & Bros., 1844.

Smith, Page. *Daughters of the Promised Land.* Boston: Little, Brown and Co., 1970.

Smith, Timothy L. *Revivalism and Social Reform in Mid-Nineteenth Century America.* New York and Nashville: Abingdon Press, 1957.

Sonneck, Oscar G.T. *A Bibliography of Early Secular American Music.* Rev. W.T. Upton, 1945; New York: Da Capo Press, 1964.

———. *Early Concert Life in America.* Leipzig: Breitkopf & Härtel, 1907; reprinted New York: Musurgia, 1949.

Spaeth, Sigmund. *A History of Popular Music in America.* New York: Random House, 1948.

Spell, Lota M. *Music in Texas.* Austin, Texas, 1936; reprinted New York: AMS Editions, 1923.

Spruill, Julia Cherry. *Women's Life and Work in the Southern Colonies,* 1938; reprinted New York: W.W. Norton & Co., 1972.

Stern, Madeleine B. *We the Women.* Career Firsts of Nineteenth-Century America. New York: Schulte Publishing Co., 1963.

Stoutamire, Albert L. "A History of Music in Richmond, Virginia, from 1742 to 1865," Ed.D. dissertation, Florida State University, 1960.

Sunderman, Lloyd. *Historical Foundations of Music Education in the United States.* Metuchen, N.J.: The Scarecrow Press, Inc., 1971.

Tawa, Nicholas. *Sweet Songs for Gentle Americans.* The Parlor Song in America, 1790-1860. Bowling Green, Ohio: Bowling Green University Popular Press, 1980.

———. "Secular Music in the Late-Eighteenth-Century American Home," *Musical Quarterly* LXI/4 (Oct. 1975), 511-27.

———. "The Ways of Love in the Mid-Nineteenth-Century American Song," *Journal of Popular Culture* X/2 (Fall 1976), 337-51.

Temperly, Nicholas. "Domestic Music in England, 1800-1860," *Proceedings of the Royal Music Association* LXXXV (1958-59), 31-47.

Thompson, Eleanor Wolf. *Education for Ladies, 1830-1860;* Ideas on Education in Magazines for Women. New York: King's Crown Press, 1947.

Twain, Mark. *Autobiography,* ed. by Charles Neider. New York: Harper & Row, 1959.

Upton, George P. *Women in Music.* Boston: J.R. Osgood & Co., 1880; 2nd ed. Chicago: A.C. McClury & Co., 1899.

Waterson, Mrs. R.C. *Adelaide Phillipps.* Boston: A. Williams and Co., 1883.

Welter, Barbara, "The Cult of True Womanhood: 1820-1860," *American Quarterly* XVIII (Summer 1966), 151-74.

_____. "The Feminization of American Religion: 1800-1860," *Clio's Consciousness Raised,* ed. Mary Hartman and Lois W. Banner (New York: Harper & Row, 1974), 137-57.

Whittlesey, Oramel. "Salem Normal School," *New York Musical World and Times* V (Feb. 1853), 131-2.

Wolfe, Richard J. *Secular Music in America, 1801-1825.* New York: New York Public Library, 1964.

Wolverton, Byron Adams. "Keyboard Music and Musicians in the Colonies and United States of America Before 1830," Ph.D. dissertation, Indiana University, 1966.

"Woman's Influence," *Western Musical World* (May, 1866), 68.

Wood, Ann D. "The 'Scribbling Women' and Fanny Fern: Why Women Wrote," *American Quarterly* XXIII/1 (Spring 1971), 4-23.

Woody, Thomas. *A History of Women's Education in the United States,* 2 vols. New York and Lancaster, Pa.: The Science Press, 1929.

Wunderlich, Charles E. "A History and Bibliography of Early American Musical Periodicals, 1782-1852," Ph.D. dissertation, University of Michigan, 1962.

Yerbury, Grace. *Song in America from Early Times to About 1850.* Metuchen, N.J.: The Scarecrow Press, Inc., 1971.

"Young Ladies' Musical Education," *Musical Reporter* (Jan. 1841), 22-26.

Music Collections

The American Harmonicon, or New York Musical Mirror. New York: Firth & Hall, 1835.

The American Musical Miscellany. Northampton, 1798; reprinted New York: Da Capo Press, 1972.

Butler, Charles. *The Silver Bell.* Boston: H. Tolman, 1866.

Cheney, Simeon Pease. *The American Singing Book.* Boston: White, Smith and Co., 1879.

Crown Jewels. A Collection of Living Gems transcribed for the Piano. Boston: Oliver Ditson, 1861.

Dana, Mary S.B. *The Northern Harp.* Boston: Oliver Ditson, 1841.

_____. *The Southern Harp.* Boston: Oliver Ditson, 1842.

Fitz, Asa, ed. *The Parlor Harp or Boston Social Melodist.* Boston, 1848.

Foster, Stephen. *The Social Orchestra.* New York, 1854; reprinted New York: Da Capo Press, 1973.

Franklin Square Song Collection. Favorite songs and hymns for schools, homes, nursery and friends. Selected, J.P. McCaskey. New York: Harper & Bros., 1881-91.

Gems of Sacred Song. Boston: Oliver Ditson & Co., 1866.

Good Old Songs. Boston: Oliver Ditson, 1887 and 1895.

Hauser, William, ed. *The Hesperian Harp.* Philadelphia, 1848.

Heart Songs. New York World Syndicate Co. [1909].

The Home Melodist. A Collection of Songs and Ballads. Boston: Oliver Ditson & Co., 1859.

Howe, Elias, ed. *The Family Circle Glee Book.* Boston: E. Howe, 1857.

Jarvis, Charles. *The Young Folks Glee Book.* New York: S.T. Gordon, 1854.

Johnson, Helen Kendrick. *Our Familiar Songs.* New York: Henry Holt & Co., 1881.

Kingsbury, Howard, ed. *Happy Hours.* A Collection of Songs for Schools and Academies. New York, 1868.

Lloyd, Mrs. M.B., and Miss M.E.Bailey, eds. *Parlour Melodies.* New York: Harper & Bros., 1842.

Marsan, Henry de., ed. *New Comic and Sentimental Singer's Journal.* Containing all the most popular songs of the day. New York, 1868-92.

The Musical Annual. A Choice Collection of Songs and Pieces for the Piano-forte. Philadelphia: Lindsay & Blakeston, 1847.

The Parlor Companion or Boston Musical Library. Boston [1850].

The Parlour Companion [Songster], or Polite Song Book, comprising a choice selection of fashionable and popular songs, Vol. I. Philadelphia; Dickinson; New York: Atwill's, 1836.

Root, George F. *The Academy Vocalist.* New York, 1852.

_____. *The Young Ladies' Choir.* New York, 1846.

Salon and Opera. A Collection of Admired Ballads and Cavatinas by Eminent Authors. St. Louis: Balmer & Weber [1850].

Sentimental Songs for the Lady's Songster. Philadelphia: Fisher & Brother [1848-50].

The Shower of Pearls. A Collection of the Most Beautiful Duets. Boston: Oliver Ditson & Co., 1859.

The Silver Chord: A Companion to the "Home Circle." Boston: Oliver Ditson & Co., 1862.

Sloman, Jane, ed. *The Melodist.* New York: Wm. Hall & Son, 1850.

Smith, Eva Munson, ed. *Women in Sacred Song.* A Library of Hymns, Religious Poems and Sacred Music by Women. Boston: D. Lothrop, 1885.

Sullivan, Marion Dix. *Bible Songs.* Boston: Nathan Richardson, 1856.

_____. *The Juniata Ballads.* Boston: Nathan Richardson, 1855.

Turner, Michael R. *The Parlour Song Book.* London: Michael Joseph Ltd., 1972.

Walker, William, ed. *The Southern Harmony.* New Haven, Conn.: 1835.

Waters, Horace ed. *Day School Bell.* New York: Horace Waters, 1861.

Webb, George J. *The Young Ladies' Vocal Classbook.* Boston: Jenks and Palmer, 1843.

Wienandt, Elwyn A. *The Bicentennial Collection of American Music, Vol. I: 1698-1800.* Carol Stream, Ill.: Hope Publishing Co., 1974.

The Welcome Guest. A Collection of Pianoforte Music. Boston: Henry Tolman & Co. [1830].

The Wreath of Gems. Boston: Oliver Ditson, 1868.

Index

Abrams, Harriet, 9, 58, 59
  composer, 9, 59
  songs, 58, 59
American music, 2-3, 5-6, 13-31, 58-72, 73-192
  development by women, 2-3
  1830-70, 21-31, 95
  feminine vs. masculine compositions, 5-6
  instrumental, 65-72, 126-42
  1770-1830, 13-20
  vocal, 58-65, 73-125

Baker, Sophia, 73
  composer, 73
Beach, Amy, 146, 230, 231-32
  biography, 231-32
  composer, 146, 230, 231
  compositions, 232
  style, 232
Bellchamber, Julliet, 73, 94, 99, 100-03
  composer, 73
  composition, 73, 94, 99, 100-03
Bernard, Caroline, 8
  composer, 8
Browne, Augusta, 9, 142, 146, 150-62, 216
  biography, 150-62
  composer, 9, 142, 146, 150-62, 216
  compositions, 142, 150-62
  style, 152-53
Browne, Harriet, 8, 73, 77-83, 223
  composer, 8, 73, 77, 223
  compositions, 78-83, 223
  style, 77
Burtis, Mrs. S.R., 142
  composer, 142
  compositions, 142

Calder, Hattie, 139
  composer, 139
  compositions, 139
Cavendish, Georgiana Spencer, 58
  composer, 58
  compositions, 58
Clark, Caroline, 65

Commercial music, 3, 4, 57, 74-75, 222
  composer attribution, 74-75, 222
  publishing, 3, 4, 57
Composer attributions, 74-75, 222
Cothbert, Mrs., 223-24
  composer, 223-24
  compositions, 224

Daly, Julia, 73, 95
  composer, 73, 95
  compositions, 95
Dana, Mary S.B., 76, 119
  The Northern Harp, 119
  The Southern Harp, 76
De Lisle, Estelle, 139
  composer, 139
  compositions, 139
Deming, Mrs. L.L., 93
  composer, 93
  compositions, 93
Disbrow, Mrs. William, 93
  composer, 93
  compositions, 93
Durham, Miss M.T., 117, 118
  composer, 117
  compositions, 117, 118
Dwight, John S., 29, 45
  on musical amateurs, 29
  on musical education, 45

Feminization of American music, 5-6, 216,
  224-29
Flower, Eliza, 58-59
  composer, 58-59
  compositions, 58-59
Foster, Stephen, 5-6, 74-75, 201
  and Mrs. E.A. Parkhurst, 201
  composer attributions, 74-75
  masculine vs. feminine music style, 5-6
Fricker, Anne, 223
  composer, 223
  compositions, 223

Gabriel, Virginia, 223
  composer, 223
  compositions, 223
Garrett, Augusta Browne. *See* Browne,
  Augusta
Gerrard, Miss, 139
  composer, 139
  compositions, 139
Godey's Lady's Book, 25, 84, 95
  compositions by women, 84, 95
  musical women, 25

Hancock, Mrs. W.S., 223
Hemans, Felicia, 28-29, 77
  song texts, 28-29, 77
Hewitt, James, 41, 58, 59
  composer, 58, 59
  teacher, 41
Hewitt, Laura, 93
  composer, 93
  compositions, 93
Higgins, Elizabeth, 116
  composer, 93
  compositions, 116
Hodges, Faustina Hasse, 8, 9, 73, 95, 146, 162-
  88, 216
  biography, 162-88
  composer, 8, 9, 73, 95, 146, 162-88, 216
  compositions, 73, 95, 162, 163-88
  style, 162, 171, 188
Hohnstock, Adele, 126, 127-38
  composer, 126
  compositions, 126, 127-38
Horn, Kate, 116
  composer, 116
  compositions, 116
Hopekirk, Helen, 3
Hughes, Rupert, 146, 163, 228-29
  on Faustina Hodges, 163
  music critic, 146, 228-29
Huneker, James, 218
  critic, 218
Hutchinson, Abby, 73, 99-100, 113-15, 116, 223
  composer, 73, 223
  compositions, 99-100, 113-15, 116, 223

Ives, Charles, 5
  masculine vs. feminine styles of, 5

Jordan, Dorothea Bland, 58
  composer, 58
  compositions, 58

Knapp, Phoebe Palmer, 8, 9, 117, 119, 120-21,
  146, 223
  composer, 8, 9, 117, 146, 223
  compositions, 117, 119, 120-21, 223

Ladies magazines, 84, 92, 142, 151
  catalyst for change, 84, 92, 142
  Garrett, Augusta Browne, 151
Lane, Alice, 116
  composer, 116
  compositions, 116
Lang, Margaret Ruthven, 2, 146, 228-29, 230
  and feminine aesthetic, 228-29
  composer, 2, 146, 228-29, 230
  compositions, 230
Luyster, Mrs. A.R., 94
  composer, 94
  compositions, 94

Mather, Cotton, 14
  and music, 14
Moore, Thomas, 66, 75, 99, 153
  influence of, 66, 99, 153
  Irish Melodies, 75
More, Hannah, 19
  writer on etiquette, 19
Music composition, 4, 92-95, 142, 145, 216
  female composers' sphere and their role, 4,
    92-95, 142, 145, 216
Music education, 2, 6, 7-8, 13-20, 23, 26-31, 33-
  56, 216, 217-18, 224-26
  as part of female education, 7-8, 13, 15, 18-20,
    26-31, 33-56, 217-18
  as symbol of a "lady," 2, 6, 13-20, 23, 41
  in seminaries, 33-56, 216
  social meaning, 7, 13-20, 26, 216, 224-26
Music schools, 19, 33-56
  curriculum, 34-40, 42-44
  general, 33-56
  ideal, 19
  instrumental instruction, 40-42
Music traditions, 6, 7, 13-31, 33-56, 73, 74, 77-
  142, 216, 217-19
  feminine accomplishment, 6, 7, 13-20, 21-31,
    33, 55-56, 73, 74, 142, 216, 217
  in transition, 73, 77, 142, 217
  training, 7, 16, 33-56, 217-19

Norton, Caroline, 78, 84, 85-91, 93
  composer, 78, 84, 93
  compositions, 78, 84, 85-91

Parkhurst, Mrs. E.A. (Susan), 2, 8, 9, 60, 116,
  146, 191-215, 216, 223
  and Stephen Foster, 201
  biography, 191-215
  composer, 2, 8, 9, 116, 146, 191-215, 216, 223
  compositions, 8, 60, 191-215, 223
  style, 199, 201, 207
Parlor music, 4, 6, 21-23, 92-143, 153, 216
  and romance, 22-23, 93-94
  as emotional and physical cure-all, 21-22

instrumental, 126-42
sacred songs, 117-25, 142
style, 95-99, 116-42
themes of, 93-94, 116-25, 142-43, 153
women as composers of, 4, 6, 92-142, 216
Pattiani, Eliza, 139
composers, 139
compositions, 139
Peterson, Mrs. Charlotte, 139, 142
composer, 139, 142
compositions, 139, 142
Phelps, Almira, 24-25, 28-29, 77
education, 24-25
view on song texts, 28-29, 77
Phillipps, Adelaide, 171
singer of parlor songs, 171
Pitt, Emma, 223
Pownall, Mary Ann, 2, 8, 9, 58-59, 60-62
biography, 58-59
composer, 2, 8, 9, 58-59
compositions, 60-62

Richards, Grace, 57, 63, 69
composer, 57
compositions, 57, 63, 64
Ritter, Fanny, 221
music critic, 221
Rogers, Clara, 3, 230-31
biography, 230-31
composer, 3, 230-31
compositions, 231
Rowson, Susanna, 20, 63
boarding school, 20
composer, 20, 63
compositions, 63
Runcie, Constance, 230
biography, 230
composer, 230

Sanderson, Mrs. E., 139
composer, 139
compositions, 139
Schindler, Miss M.L., 139
composer, 139
compositions, 139
Scott, Miss M.B., 99, 104-6
composer, 99
compositions, 99, 104-6
Scott, Mrs. Clara H., 223
Sheet music, 3, 8, 63, 95, 126-42, 216
first published by a woman, 3
in magazines, 95
in modern anthologies, 8

instrumental, 126-42
professional songwriters, 63, 216
Shindler, Mary Dana, 9, 119, 121-25, 142
biography, 119
composer, 9, 119, 121, 142
compositions, 119, 122-25
Siegling, Marie, 139
composer, 139
compositions, 139
Sigourney, Lydia, 23-24
writer on etiquette, 23-24
Sloman, Jane, 9, 38, 73, 146, 188-91, 216
biography, 188-91
composer, 9, 38, 73, 146, 188-91, 216
compositions, 189-91
style, 188-91
Smith, Penelope, 73, 99, 107-8
composer, 73
compositions, 73, 99, 107-8
Stith, Mrs. Townshend, 94-98
composer, 94
compositions, 94-98
Sullivan, Marion Dix, 2, 8, 9, 73, 75, 146-50, 216
biography, 146-50
composer, 2, 8, 9, 75, 146-50, 216
compositions, 73, 146-50

Torry, Jane Sloman. *See* Sloman, Jane
Troy Seminary, 40, 226
music education in, 40
teachers, 226

Van Hagen, Elizabeth, 9, 65-66
biography, 66
composer, 9, 65-66

Weir, Margaret, 116
composer, 116
compositions, 116
Willard, Emma, 119
composer, 119
compositions, 119
Women as composers, 58-65, 65-73, 95-99, 116-19, 142, 145, 216, 224-33
Women as musicians, 2-3, 17-18, 19, 23, 25, 27-31, 126, 142, 219-20
as "true woman," 23
conventions, 17-18
etiquette for, 27-31, 220
professionalism, 31, 126, 142, 219-21
public performance, 19, 25
stereotype, 2-3